International Marketing Strategy

Paul Fifield and Keith Lewis

*Published on behalf of
the Chartered Institute of Marketing*

This book is dedicated to our partners, Jan and Jane, without whose support and encouragement not a single page would have been produced.

Butterworth-Heinemann Ltd
Linacre House, Jordan Hill, Oxford OX2 8DP

A member of the Reed Elsevier plc group

OXFORD   LONDON   BOSTON
MUNICH   NEW DELHI   SINGAPORE   SYDNEY
TOKYO   TORONTO   WELLINGTON

First published 1995

British Library Cataloguing in Publication Data
A catalogue record for this book is available from the British Library

ISBN 0 7506 1987 2

Composition by Genesis Typesetting, Laser Quay, Rochester, Kent
Printed and bound in Great Britain

International Marketing Strategy

The Marketing Series is one of the most comprehensive collections of books in marketing and sales available from the UK today.

Published by Butterworth-Heinemann on behalf of the Chartered Institute of Marketing, the series is divided into three distinct groups: *Student* (fulfilling the needs of those taking the Institute's certificate and diploma qualifications); *Professional Development* (for those on formal or self-study vocational training programmes); and *Practitioner* (presented in a more informal, motivating and highly practical manner for the busy marketer).

Formed in 1911, the Chartered Institute of Marketing is now the largest professional marketing management body in Europe with over 24,000 members and 28,000 students located worldwide. Its primary objectives are focused on the development of awareness and understanding of marketing throughout UK industry and commerce and in the raising of standards of professionalism in the education, training and practice of this key business discipline.

The CIM Student Workbook Series: Marketing

Business Communication
Misiura

Effective Management for Marketing
Hatton and Worsam

International Marketing Strategy
Fifield and Lewis

Management Information for Sales and Marketing
Hines

Marketing Communications Strategy
Yeshin

Marketing Fundamentals
Lancaster and Withey

Marketing Operations
Worsam

Promotional Practice
Ace

Sales and Marketing Environment
Oldroyd

Strategic Marketing Management
Fifield and Gilligan

Understanding Customers
Phipps and Simmons

Contents

Preface

The development by the Chartered Institute of Marketing of Syllabus '94 has led to a far greater emphasis at the Diploma level upon the strategic aspects of marketing, a move which is reflected in the refocusing of all four of the Diploma syllabuses – including International Marketing Strategy. In writing this workbook we have paid particular attention both to the strategic aspects of the subject and to an exploration of the strong linkages which exist – and which students are expected to demonstrate – between the International Marketing paper and the other papers in the Diploma examination.

Students will note that International aspects have been known to form a major part of the Analysis and Decision paper in recent years. It must, however, be recognized from the start that candidates for the Diploma are expected to demonstrate a depth and breadth of their understanding of marketing and this workbook is designed as a complement to and not a substitute for a far wider programme of reading, research and individual study. It is for this reason that throughout the text you will find references to four other books that you will be told to read. They are:

International Marketing, S. Paliwoda, Butterworth-Heinemann, 1993.
International Marketing Strategy, C. Phillips, I. Doole and R. Lowe, Routledge, 1994.
Global Marketing Strategies, J.-P. Jeannet and H. D. Hennessey, Houghton Mifflin, 1994.
International Marketing, V. Terpstra and R. Sarathy, The Dryden Press, 1994.

Further, this workbook has concentrated on exploring the major differences in International Marketing Strategy from Domestic Marketing Strategy. Students will need a sound basis of understanding in domestic marketing strategy if they are to gain the full value from this workbook. Four other books that you will do well to read are:

Strategic Marketing Management: planning, implementation and control, R. M. R. Wilson and C. Gilligan with D. Pearson, Butterworth-Heinemann, 1992.
Marketing Strategy, P. Fifield, Butterworth-Heinemann, 1992.
Strategic Marketing Management Workbook, P. Fifield and C. Gilligan, Butterworth-Heinemann, 1995.
Marketing Communication Strategy Woorkbook, T. Yeshin, Butterworth-Heinemann, 1995.

We wish you success in the examinations.

Paul Fifield
Keith Lewis

Acknowledgements

The authors would like to thank Maggie Duncan and Tina Green for word processing the manuscript. Also Jonathan Glasspool and Sandra Benko at Butterworth-Heinemann for constantly moving the deadlines to allow us the time to write this book.

How to use your CIM workbook

The authors have been careful to structure your book with the exams in mind. Each unit, therefore, covers an essential part of the syllabus. You need to work through the complete workbook systematically to ensure that you have covered everything you need to know.

This workbook is divided into 15 units each containing the following standard elements:

Objectives tell you what part of the syllabus you will be covering and what you will be expected to know having read the unit.

Study guides tell you how long the unit is and how long its activities take to do.

Exam questions are designed to give you practice – they will be similar to those that you will be faced with in the examination.

Exam answers give you a suggested format for answering exam questions. *Remember* there is no such thing as a model answer – you should use these examples only as guidelines.

Activities give you the chance to put what you have learned into practice.

Exam hints are tips from the senior examiner or examiner which are designed to help you avoid common mistakes made by previous candidates.

Definitions are useful words you must know to pass the exam.

Extending knowledge sections are designed to help you use your time most effectively. It is not possible for the workbook to cover *everything* you need to know to pass. What you read here needs to be supplemented by your classes, practical experience at work and day-to-day reading.

Summaries cover what you should have picked up from reading the unit.

A quick word from the Chief Examiner

I am delighted to recommend to you the new series of CIM workbooks. All of these have been written by either the Senior Examiner or Examiners responsible for marking and setting the papers.

Preparing for the CIM Exams is hard work. These workbooks are designed to make that work as interesting and illuminating as possible, as well as providing you with the knowledge you need to pass. I wish you success.

Trevor Watkins,
CIM Chief Examiner,
Deputy Vice Chancellor,
South Bank University

Introduction

The International Marketing Strategy component of the Diploma in Marketing has two concise objectives:

1 To enable students to acquire expertise in developing marketing strategies for countries other than their own and thereby to extend their range of marketing understanding, to deal with both international marketing to suit the situations in non-domestic markets and the impact of international competitors on their domestic market.

2 To promote an understanding of the factors determining the extent to which standardization in strategy implementation is appropriate for success in international markets.

This is achieved by focusing on a number of key issues that logically follow each other in the strategic marketing process:

Stage 1: Where are we now and where do we want to be? (Strategic financial and marketing analysis followed by strategic direction and strategy formulation.)

Stage 2: How might we get there? (Strategic choice.)

Stage 3: How do we ensure arrival? (Strategic implementation and control.)

At the same time, the content of the module has been designed to complement the syllabuses for the other three Diploma papers, Marketing Communications Strategy, Strategic Marketing Management – Planning and Control and Strategic Marketing Management – Analysis and Decision (see Figure I.1) and to build upon material at the Certificate and Advanced Certificate levels.

Given its structure, and in particular the nature of the interrelationship between international marketing strategy and the other aspects of marketing strategy, this workbook has been designed to provide you with a clear insight into the analysis, planning and control processes in international marketing and the ways in which these can be best applied within the international business and commercial world as well as, of course, to the CIM's Diploma examination paper.

In doing this we give considerable emphasis to the three elements that underpin all the CIM's syllabuses: knowing, understanding and doing. Thus, in each of the units we outline and discuss the relevant concepts so that your knowledge and understanding is increased. We

Marketing Communications Strategy	International Marketing Strategy	Strategic Marketing Management	
		Planning and Control	Analysis and Decision

Figure I.1 Diploma in Marketing

then address the issue of 'doing' by means of a series of exercises and questions and, of course, through the mini-case study that forms Section 1 of the International Marketing Strategy exam paper. It needs to be recognized from the outset however, that a workbook cannot explore the complexity of concepts in the same way that a textbook can. For this reason, we make reference at various stages to two books that you may well find useful. These are:

International Marketing, S Paliwoda, Butterworth-Heinemann, 1993.
International Marketing Strategy, Phillips, Doole and Lowe, Routledge, 1994.

Both books were written specifically for the CIM's International Marketing Strategy syllabus and with the needs of the prospective students in mind.

International marketing strategy

International marketing strategy has always been a major factor in the success of important trading nations such as Britain. Now that membership of the EU has been secured, international marketing skills are becoming even more important to marketers. In this unit you will:

- Understand the range of tasks involved in international marketing strategy
- Review the strategic process
- Understand the Diploma International Marketing syllabus
- Understand what is meant by international marketing

Having completed this unit you will be able to:

- Explain how to avoid problems in international marketing
- Appreciate the key questions involved in 'going international'
- Advise an organization on whether to go international and the key questions involved in this strategic decision
- Explain the role of international marketing in the overall international business process

This workbook is critical to an overall understanding of the International Marketing Strategy process. The key:

- Development of international marketing strategy
- Implementation of strategy
- Evaluation and control of strategy

come from an understanding of the organization's objectives and ambitions for its international operations.

The organization may treat its international business as an 'add-on' to its domestic operations or as an integral part of its mission. This will influence the importance that international marketing has in the organization, the resources allocated to it and the control systems applied to support implementation.

As you work through this unit, remember that:

- Domestic and international marketing work on the same principles – customers must be satisfied
- Customers in foreign markets may have different needs and may become drivers for different marketing policies
- The biggest problem in international marketing is often not the foreign customer but the international marketer.

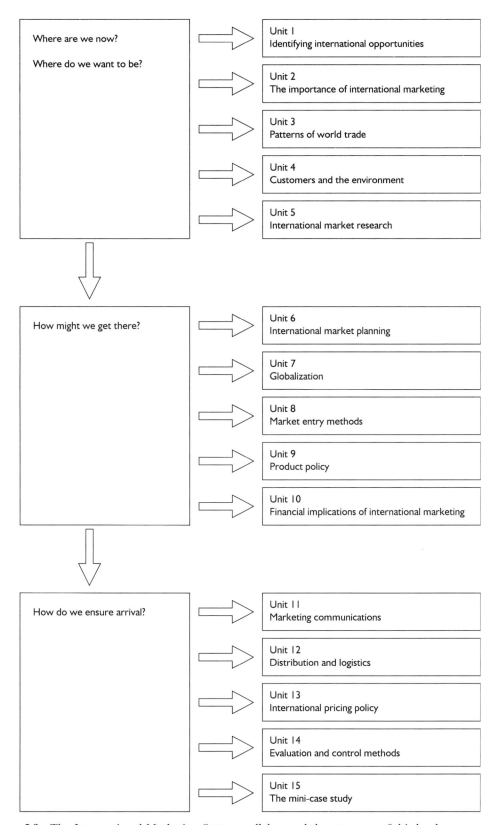

Figure I.2 The International Marketing Strategy syllabus and the structure of this book

We commented earlier that the International Marketing Strategy syllabus focuses upon three key issues: these are illustrated in Figure I.2.

In Units 1–5 we are concerned with the various ways in which managers might identify their organization's current position and assess its true level of international marketing capability. The assessment of the organization's capability and the options open to it in its marketplaces can be seen as one of the principal foundation stones for any strategic planning process – domestic or international – since it determines exactly what the organization is or should be capable of achieving. Marketing capability by itself is, of course, only one part of the planning process and needs to be looked at against the background of the organization as a whole as well as the nature and shape of the international environment in which it is or might choose to operate. Units 3 and 4 concentrate on the nature of the international trading environment and the all-important influences upon customers that may create opportunities for the organization.

Having assessed the current capability of the organization and the opportunities and threats in the international marketplace, in units 6–10 we start to consider practical ways in which the organization can start to turn its international opportunities into profits.

Units 11–14 assess the all-important question of how we manage, evaluate and control our marketing activities in the international environment in order to achieve the pre-set strategic plans.

Approaching the International Marketing Strategy examination

The syllabus for International Marketing Strategy is very detailed in its approach and has a number of clear and distinct learning outcomes that emerge from a successful completion of the programme. This means that at the end of your course you should be able to:

- Understand the changing nature of the international trading environment
- Understand differences in business and social/cultural conventions which affect buying behaviours and marketing approaches in international markets
- Differentiate between marketing strategies appropriate to industrialized, developing and less developed economies
- Identify sources of information, methods of information collection and methods of information analysis suitable for international marketing operations
- Compare and contrast strategies for export, international, multinational and transnational marketing
- Identify the major organizational changes to be made when a company moves from national to international to global marketing
- Evaluate the factors which influence the implementation of a product, price, distribution and marketing communication mix in non-domestic markets
- Understand the financial implications of different international marketing strategies
- Evaluate the suitability of specific international marketing strategies.

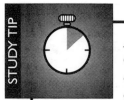

STUDY TIP

After each examination the senior examiners write a report for the Chartered Institute in which they discuss how the students coped with the examination and highlight any particular problems that have been experienced. In looking back at the reports which have been written over the past few years there are several issues which have been referred to on almost every occasion. Obtain a set of examiner's reports for yourself and make sure that you don't forfeit marks needlessly.

What is international marketing?

International marketing may appear, at first glance, to be an impossibly complex subject involving all functional areas of management. In fact, there is surprisingly little extra knowledge or specific management technique required. International marketing differs very little from domestic marketing in that the objective of the marketer is the same – to understand customer and market needs and strive to meet them with the capabilities which the organization has at its disposal. Internationally, the organization must strive to understand its international marketing environment and then be able to adapt familiar techniques to possibly unfamiliar circumstances.

The organization feels the effect of its international environment in a number of ways, not only in its approach to its overseas customers but also in its raw material or component sourcing, in its financing requirements, in its domestic market through international competition and in its general business level which is affected by the world trade cycle.

One of the most important factors in international marketing, and in international business generally, is not the new and different techniques which have to be learned to deal with overseas markets but in the mindset of the managers attempting to satisfy overseas or international market needs. Every manager or marketer is the product of his or her own culture. The end result of centuries of conditioning in what our domestic culture considers to be acceptable and non-acceptable modes of behaviour colours all our perceptions of foreign market and customer behaviour. The single most important problem any organization faces within its international setting often comes not from the environment but from its own reactions to that environment.

> 'The self-reference criterion is the unconscious reference to one's own cultural values, and is the root cause of most business problems abroad.' (James A. Lee)

James Lee refers to the self-reference criterion (SRC) and compares this 'cultural conditioning' to an iceberg: we are not aware of nine-tenths of it. The sequence of comments uttered by many domestic marketers considering international markets for the first time is often as follows:

'That's interesting!'
'That's different (from what we do at home).'
'That's wrong! (it's not what we do at home).'

The third comment is driven directly by the manager's SRC and often results in the application (normally unsuccessful) of domestic marketing policies in overseas market situations. In order to avoid errors in business decisions, the SRC must be recognized and isolated so that its biasing effect is minimized, if not eliminated completely, from international marketing strategy decisions.

The key questions in international marketing
As can be seen from Figure I.3, there are four broad questions which are relevant to the international marketer. These questions can be addressed in a sequential order.

Whether to go international?
There are between 190 and 200 countries in the world with governments which can lay claim to being independent – the number tends to change on a weekly basis! Although they are often classified as being either 'industrialized', 'less developed' or 'advanced' such simplicity is misleading to the international marketer. Organizations operating internationally must analyse the environment in which they will be working; how people think and act – be they customers, agents, employees or governments. It is the organization's international environment which will largely determine the actions that can be taken and the kinds of adaptation that must be made in international operations. In Units 3 and 4 we will look in detail at the ways in which the international environment can be analysed and in Unit 5 we will spend some time considering the mechanical approaches of market research that may be required to uncover the important parameters of the international environment.

Where to operate?
Of all the various markets and the different opportunities that appear to be open to the organization, where should the marketer concentrate his or her efforts? Despite talk of collapsing national boundaries and the global information infrastructure, the world still remains a very big place. Rather than spread the resources of the organization too thinly (the Marmite approach!) it is important that the international marketer is able to focus the

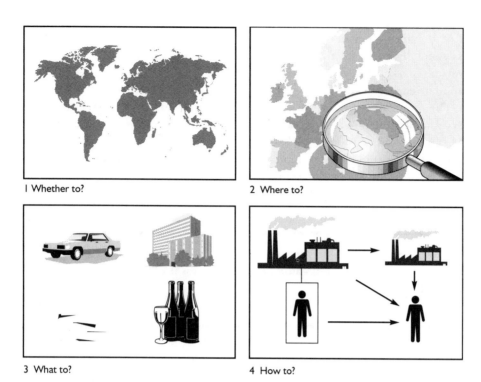

| 1 Whether to? | 2 Where to? |
| 3 What to? | 4 How to? |

Figure I.3   The key questions in international marketing

resources of the organization on the market or markets where it is felt the returns may be the most promising. How can these markets be selected? In Unit 4 specifically we will address the question of target markets selection and the basis upon which an informed choice might be made.

What to market in the overseas environment?

Although most organizations would prefer to market a single product or service to all international markets, the market pressures are such that some adaptation will often have to be made. These adaptations may be caused by differing use conditions, tastes or habit or government regulation. Other areas of product mix may need modification, for example packaging (language or literacy requirements and different transport and distribution systems) or brand and trade marks (may not travel well due to differences in language, idiom or aesthetics). In Unit 9 we will discuss the implications of product policy for overseas markets in more detail.

How should we operate internationally?

Once the organization has decided where it will operate and concentrate its effort, and what the market requires from it, the final decision is how to operate in those overseas markets. Decisions such as method of market entry and whether to use local agents, distributors or develop a wholly owned subsidiary will be considered in greater depth in Units 6, 8 and 12.

EXAM QUESTION

Examine the steps taken by a firm moving from a domestic business to an international business (December 1992).
(**See** Exam answers at the end of this unit.)

Understanding the international marketing strategy process

In order to understand the international process it needs to be viewed schematically from the first decision-making processes through to implementation and control. This entire process is outlined in Figure I.4 which can be explained in more detail as follows.

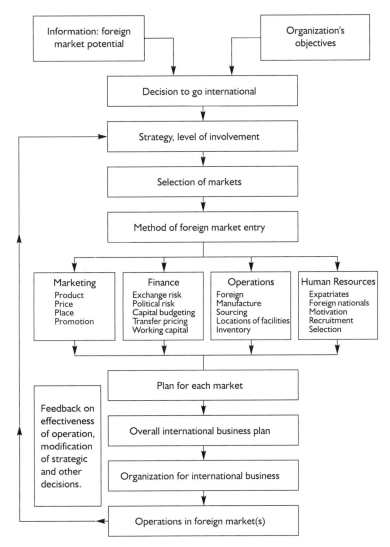

Figure I.4 The international business process

Information: foreign market potential

Any decision to go international must be based on solid and reliable market information on the potential to the organization from the foreign market.

Organization's objectives

A clear understanding of the organization's corporate and marketing objectives will help the marketer to understand whether international marketing and/or the selection of particular key markets is in line with the organization's objectives and ambitions for the future.

Decision to go international

The difference between an organization deciding strategically to take an international role in its business rather than opportunistically following up the odd foreign sales lead has a very different effect on the organization and the way it approaches its international markets. With a corporate decision to take international business as a serious activity, the organization is likely to put the resources required behind the effort and to treat it as a key activity in the future.

Strategy 'level of involvement'

The first strategic decision the organization makes on its route to internationalization, is to decide how deeply involved it wishes to become in the international marketplace. The organization's chosen level of involvement in international business will determine (at least in the short term) the marketing, financial, operation and human resource strategies that can be employed. The different levels of international involvement range from active exporting through joint ventures to marketing subsidiaries overseas as far as foreign production and foreign marketing. These options will be analysed and described in more detail in Units 6 and 12.

Selecting the markets

The organization should resist temptation to attack too many markets thereby spreading effort and resources too thinly to be successful. The most successful international operations often come from making an initial effort into a single market and then extending this to other possibly neighbouring markets as learning in international business increases. Market selection can be based on three criteria: market potential, similarity to home or other foreign markets and market accessibility. These methods of market selection will be considered in more depth in Unit 4.

Method of foreign market entry

Unlike domestic marketing, the organization often has a clear choice of how it proposes to enter overseas markets. How the method of market entry is selected will determine the freedom of action the organization has over the various elements of the marketing mix. As with level of involvement, method of entry may dictate marketing activities in the short term. Alternative methods of market entry will be considered in more detail in Unit 8.

Foreign market planning

Although the international marketing strategy syllabus is primarily concerned with marketing activities in overseas markets, the modern marketer can ill afford to ignore the international aspects and pressures upon other functional areas of the business. Not only must decisions be made on the marketing mix most appropriate to international markets but also the other functional requirements of the organization must be considered if any strategic marketing activity is to be successful. Financial considerations of international operations are considerable and will cover areas such as exchange risk, political risk, capital budgeting, transfer pricing and working capital requirements. These will be considered in more detail in Unit 10. International operations may also represent a major cost centre and questions such as foreign manufacture, working stock and location of facilities will be considered in Unit 12. Human resources are an equally important area and these will be considered in Units 6, 11 and 12.

EXAM QUESTION

Select two contrasting countries and examine how international marketing plans would need to take account of the similarities and differences between those two countries (June 1994).
(**See** Exam answers at the end of this unit.)

Plan for each market

In order to control the marketing and business operations in overseas markets it is important that a plan is developed for each individual market based upon the differing marketing characteristics and customer expectations from that marketplace (see Unit 6).

Overall international business plan

International business planning requires that the individual market plans be coordinated and controlled for international operations. Unlike the domestic situation where there is a single market and easily understood planning parameters, the international environment tends to be much more fragmented and may require differing resources at different stages and levels of allocation. It is important that the organization attempts to remain in control of the situation and the coordination of (often diverse) national or market plans becomes a major strategic activity.

Organization for international business

Structure can be a severe brake on any organization's international ambitions and new organization structures may be required in order to facilitate and promote international business. This will be discussed in more detail in Unit 6.

Operations in foreign markets

As operations and activity 'on the ground' begin to unfold it is important that evaluation and control methods be in place for the organization continually to improve its activity in international markets. Evaluation and control methodology will be considered in more detail in Unit 14.

Summary

In this introductory unit we have considered the format and approach that this book will take in addressing the international marketing strategy syllabus and the importance of using this book in conjunction with the two primary texts recommended for the examination. We have also considered the detailed analysis of the syllabus as well as the all-important learning objectives and outcomes required for a successful attempt at the examination itself. Finally, we considered the overall nature of the international marketing tasks and we concluded that:

- There is little conceptual difference between international marketing and domestic marketing.
- The focus of the international marketer's activity is the customer (as in the domestic situation), but the customer happens to be in a foreign market with all that that entails.
- A primary problem in successful international business is the social/cultural conditioning of the international marketer (remember the SRC).
- International marketing consists of four interrelated questions: whether to, where to, what to, how to.
- The international marketing strategic process can be seen as a logical series of steps which will take the organization from domestic dependence to an international organization.

Questions

As a check on your understanding of what has been covered in this unit, consider the following questions:

- How is the organization affected by international business trends?
- How can the international marketer's own cultural background affect the organization's international market strategy?
- What are the four key questions in international marketing?
- What are the two key drivers which may start off an organization's entry into foreign markets?
- What is meant by 'level of involvement'?
- What tactical effects will the strategic decision on 'how to enter a foreign market' have?
- What are the three criteria for foreign market selection?
- What are the special factors to be taken into account when planning for international marketing strategy?

For a more detailed treatment of what international marketing strategy means, read:

International Marketing, S. Paliwoda, Butterworth-Heinemann, 1993, pp. 1–8.
International Marketing Strategy, C. Phillips, I. Doole and R. Lowe, Routledge, 1994, pp. 5–42.

EXTENDING KNOWLEDGE

December 1992   Your answer should have considered all the steps in the transferation process and the questions that the firm asked itself at every step of the way. To reach a pass level, your answer should have *examined* the steps in the process – simply *identifying* them would not be enough. Good grades in the examination would be obtained by candidates who also considered changes in orientation inside the business and took account of the difficulties in moving from an 'ethnocentric' organization (one based on the culture of the domestic market) and organization structure to a culture and organization more suited to international operations.

June 1994   To have received a pass mark, your answer should have taken two *contrasting countries* to show how *international marketing plans* would take account of similarities/ differences. As you will see as you work through this book, most failures in the exams come from not answering the question posed by the examiner. Your answer should select and name two countries of your choice and have identified similarities and differences in each. Then you should show how international marketing planning needs to allow for these similarities/differences. The main reasons for failure on the day were caused by candidates limiting their answers mainly to environmental difference and similarity.

Identifying international opportunities

In this unit we will consider how the organization might identify opportunities for itself in overseas markets. We will consider the risks inherent in an international marketing operation and how these might be assessed alongside the opportunities to give a balanced view on any likely strategic planning. In this unit you will:

• Understand the reasons why organizations 'go international'
• Review the principal forms of financial risk for the international organization
• Consider the role of the Marketing information system in reducing the risk of international expansion
• Review the range of models that may be of use in assessing foreign market opportunities.

Having completed this unit you will be able to:

• Identify the key drivers behind an organization's international strategy.
• Evaluate the main areas of risk in international operations.
• Establish ways of reducing risk in planning an organization's international marketing strategy.

This unit explains the essential balance that needs to be struck between 'Sales' and 'Profits'. Too many markets still operate at primarily a tactical level, believing that their only responsibility is to bring home maximum sales revenue or market share to their organization. No business lives and grows just by market share but needs a consistent flow of profits.

International opportunities must be assessed by both sales potential and the likely potential for repatriated profits that can be obtained from the activity. Operating just to maximize sales or market share, perhaps at the expense of profitability is not necessarily good marketing.

Some reasons for 'going international'

There are many reasons why an organization might consider going international and the following are some of the most common:

1 *Saturated home market* If the home market for an organization's products or service is saturated or competition is so intense that it can no longer gain any significant market share improvement it might consider extending its market activity to overseas markets. This move might be considered under market extension or even diversification strategies in the Ansoff matrix.

2 *Competition* There are two separate but interrelated reasons why an organization may decide to go international in this instance. The first case is that competition may be less intense in overseas markets than in the domestic market. Competition, as we all know, may have benefits for customers but it is always extremely expensive for the organization. Despite the often increased risk of operating overseas it may be that the organization faces a better potential return by operating in markets where there is less intense competition for its products and services. A second competition related factor in moving internationally may be that an organization is faced by particularly virulent international competition in its domestic marketplace. In some instances it is difficult to compete from a domestic base against international competitors. In such cases the organization may consider moving internationally in order to be able to compete on a more equal footing with the opponent organization.

3 *Excess capacity* Where an organization is operating successfully in its domestic marketplace but is operating at below optimal capacity levels there is excess capacity available for production. In these instances it may be wise to consider international operations where the product or service can be costed at marginal cost, thereby giving a potential price advantage for overseas marketing operations.

4 *Comparative advantage in product, skill or technology* The organization may discover, when analysing overseas market opportunities, that it has a comparative advantage against local competition in the foreign market. This advantage might be in product, skill or technology but, subject to local market demand and tastes, it could be the makings of a profitable venture. Comparative advantage is often the case when organizations are based in advanced countries and consider marketing internationally to lesser developed countries.

EXAM QUESTION

Examine the factors that would influence a multinational enterprise to export (December 1993).

(**See** Exam answers at the end of this unit.)

5 *Product life cycle differences* As you will know from studies in domestic marketing, as a product or service progresses through the life cycle it often changes in style, performance or efficiency. When considering international markets the marketer may discover that foreign markets are at a different point of development in the product or industry life cycle. The marketer may decide to exploit these differences, either by exporting product which is no longer suitable for the domestic market place (the life cycle requirements have moved on) or by entering the foreign market with a more advanced product than the local competition has yet developed.

EXAM HINT

The product life cycle is probably one of the best known but least understood concepts in marketing. Do you know how to apply the product life cycle concept in domestic marketing? Do you know how to extend the product life cycle applications into international marketing?

6 *Geographic diversification* Linked to items above, an organization may discover in its domestic marketing strategy that either its market is saturated or competition is becoming more intense in established markets. To continue to grow and develop it must extend its operations in terms of either products or markets. The classical development of the Ansoff matrix normally considers just domestic operations but international options can be considered too. When considering 'market extension' strategies the organization can include institutional markets as well as other domestic markets for further growth. A number of companies have preferred to focus their attention on a single product or very limited range in a number of markets for growth rather than take on the risk of developing new products.

7 *Organizational reasons* Often an organization may find itself haphazardly involved in international business and marketing operations through the acquisition of random activities during acquisition and merger operations or through the piecemeal exporting activities of its own subsidiaries. Often a point in the organization's development arrives when it is time to put order into the previously piecemeal approach to international operations. This often results in the creation of an international marketing division where the various activities are brought together, rationalized and coordinated. This 'house keeping' often provides areas of significant international potential.

8 *Financial reasons* There are a range of financial reasons why an organization may decide to take the international route to its business and these might include investment incentives in overseas markets and the availability of venture capital as well as the option to maximize profits or minimize losses through international rather than simple domestic operations.

Broadly, international marketing will prove to be a more successful venture for the organization that is exporting a positive advantage than for one exporting to cover a domestic weakness.

Financial risk in international operations

One major difference in operations carried out internationally rather than domestically is that the funds flows occur in a variety of currencies and in a variety of nations. These currency and national differences, in turn, create risks unique to international business which are explored in greater detail in Unit 10.

There are two types of financial risk unique to international marketing operations:

1 *Foreign exchange risk* This arises from the need to operate in more than one currency.

2 *Political risk* This is a term used to cover those risks arising from an array of legal, political, social and cultural differences. Political risk normally produces losses when there is a conflict between the goals of the organization and those of the host government.

Home country (domestic) law is also important in that it defines acceptable behaviour for the organization in all its activities – whether at home or abroad. Figure 1.1 demonstrates the nature of this relationship between the organization, the host government and the home government.

Figure 1.1 The organization and 'political risk'

The international management information system (MIS)

It will be seen from the above that the establishment and maintenance of a high-quality management information system is essential for two primary reasons:

1 Helping the organization to decide whether to follow an international route by quantifying opportunities
2 Helping management to develop and implement suitable marketing strategies and programmes that will allow the organization to exploit the foreign opportunities to the full.

These two key drivers create the need for two different types of data:

1 *Feasibility Data* The decisions which the organization needs to make in terms of whether it should go international and if so which markets it should enter are all to be captured under the title of feasibility data collection. Data in this area will facilitate decisions such as to go international or not, where to go, what to offer.

ACTIVITY 1.1

What information does your company collect for its international markets? What gaps, if any, can you identify?

2 *Operational Data* The second form of data required by the organization is that which will allow it constantly to offer the products and services that the markets require, and according to terms and conditions which the local customers and governments find acceptable. We have already seen that market conditions and governmentally imposed regulations are subject to regular change. Long-term profitability depends upon the organization's ability to anticipate and, if possible, avoid such restrictions. The operational data collection process should highlight the likely imposition of such restrictive measures in time for the organization to take action. The market information and analysis process will be discussed in more depth in Unit 5.

Models to assist in the assessment of risk and opportunity

There are a number of models that have been devised over recent years in order to help organizations assess the opportunity/risk in international markets. From the recommended texts you will be able to identify the various approaches and advantages/disadvantages of each of these models. The models you may come across might include:

• The Sheth–Lutz model
• Business Environment Risk Index (BERI)
• Litvuk and Banting model
• Good, New and Hausz model
• Gilligan & Hird model
• Harrell & Kiefer model

EXAM QUESTION

Examine the problems of using product portfolio analysis in international marketing (June 1994).
     (**See** Exam answers at the end of this unit.)

In your studies you are likely to encounter a number of different models which apply to various areas of international marketing. You should bear in mind when assessing these models that many have been developed not with a larger view of international or global strategy in mind but to meet the specific needs of a particular market or industry or product sector. Greatest success is likely to come if you are able to tap into the models at a conceptual level, understanding what they mean in broad strategic terms rather than treating them as a blueprint for guaranteed success under any circumstances. Often you will find that blending one or two models will give you a greater insight into the existence (or not) of international marketing opportunities for your organization or the case study.

Summary

In this unit we have seen that there are a number of very good reasons why organizations may decide to 'go international'. The opportunities and potential profits for an organization can often be quite sizeable. At the same time, there are some significant risks in such operations, particularly foreign exchange risk and political risk. In any event, some detailed market research and analysis is required in order to uncover likely marketplace opportunities for the organization and a range of models exist to help you in this evaluation process.

One final word of warning is that you should bring some common sense to bear on the market research data when available. The data analysis and scanning may identify gaps in the marketplace – the international marketer has to decide whether there is a market in the gap!

Question

As a check on your understanding of what has been covered in this unit, consider the following questions:

- What are the main reasons that an organization might consider going international?
- How might intense domestic competition encourage an organization to develop markets abroad?
- How can we apply the concept of the product life cycle (PLC) in international business?
- What are the two main forms of financial risk in international business?
- What are the two particular management decisions that research can help support?
- What are the two types of international data that might be collected by an organization?

For a more detailed review of international opportunities, read:
International Marketing S. Paliwoda, Butterworth-Heinemann, 1993, pp. 88–97.
International Marketing Strategy C. Phillips, I. Doole and R. Lowe, Routledge, 1994, pp. 129–42.

December 1993 Has your answer concentrated on the MNE and not just looked at 'standard ways to export' for inexperienced exporters? To pass, your answer should have defined what is meant by MNE. There are many definitions but the important elements are:

- Experience in international business
- Foreign direct investment in at least one other country
- Sales and profits derived from a minimum of one country in addition to the home market.

The reasons an MNE would prefer to export will be different from those of an inexperienced exporter. The MNE might prefer to export rather than to expand its operations through subsidiaries because:

- Need to test market first
- Reduce financial/political risk in foreign markets
- Use subsidiaries as regional producer and develop export satellites.

Can you think of additional reasons?

June 1994   To pass this question you need to:

1   Know about portfolio analysis
2   Be able to apply this knowledge to product planning in international markets

Has your answer properly explained what is meant by product portfolio analysis?

The literature over recent years has contained much criticism about these analyses and about the past misapplication of these models. Are you aware of this debate?

How might portfolio analysis be applied to product planning in international markets? Has your answer considered the benefits and drawbacks of using these markets? Despite the problems, does product portfolio analysis offer any advantage for the international marketer?

The Diploma examination expects candidates to be aware of current debates in marketing and to have the ability to put and justify a point of view based on analysis and reflection. Does your answer demonstrate this level of thinking?

The importance of international marketing

OBJECTIVES

In this unit we highlight the growing importance of international marketing and the changes that are accelerating its importance. Understanding the changes that are underpinning the development of world trade – events that are shaping everyone's life wherever they might live and work. In this unit you will:

• Appreciate the growth and scale of world trade.
• Consider just how 'international' our everyday lives are

• Understand the macro forces at work shaping the business world of today and the future.
• Study the factors that are increasingly important in defining success.

Having completed the unit you will be able to:

• Identify the key drivers in world trade
• Appreciate what is creating convergence in consumer behaviour
• Understand the changes in international business
• Recognize that domestic horizons are increasingly meaningless in the fast-changing 'global village'.

STUDY GUIDE

International marketing does not begin or end with the activities of the firm – it happens within the environment. Whereas companies and individuals have a sound understanding of their domestic or home market, few take sufficient time to consider events worldwide. It is these that are the basic business drivers and will make increasing impact on the domestic firm. The term 'global village' is familiar to many – that it has arrived and what its impact might mean (in terms of opportunities and threats) has been considered in depth by few. From an examination perspective Syllabus '94 requires candidates to have a broad view of the macro/strategic forces in the world marketplace.

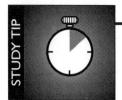

Understanding changes in international business factors underpinning international and global marketing

The year 1990 saw the world trade in goods exceed £2.3 billion – rising by more than 12 per cent over the previous year. A comparison with earlier years shows a clear upward trend and, despite the current recession, there seems no reason to suppose that growth will not continue.

World trade in services – financial services, travel and tourism, banking etc. referred to as 'invisible trade', although lower in value than visible goods at approximately £470 billion in 1990, is set to grow even faster. Even education is an important service export with approximately 50 per cent of CIM Diploma candidates studying overseas and increasingly UK students are studying for part of their degree in foreign countries.

These figures in themselves represent meaningless statistics to most of us. Perhaps a more meaningful perspective of the impact of the international and global market can be taken from an observation of our lives. Look at it this way:

Woken in the morning by Sony alarm radio, usually hurrying through toiletry routine using on the way a Bic razor, Gillette foam, Imperial Leather soap, Head & Shoulders shampoo and Colgate toothpaste. Gulping down a cup of Nescafé and rushing through a bowl of Kelloggs cereal, donning a Hugo Boss suit and setting off for work in a BMW. On arrival, checking the NEC fax machine, switch on the IBM clone and get working.

The description could easily continue with what is a pretty mundane everyday life but the point is that executives are surrounded by international products produced by multinational or global corporations. The products portrayed are the fabric of many people's lives. Furthermore, entertainment and leisure is also similarly inclined, be it a Hollywood movie, a foreign holiday or even a 'foreign meal' (this could include McDonald's and Coca-Cola); usually wearing Levis and Timberland shoes.

What's actually going on here? It's evident that internationalism is all-embracing. The description above is not exclusive to the UK. Any international executive can observe the same broad activity taking place. There are no national boundaries or chauvinistic tendencies at work here. This is the 'global village' in action! Why is this so?

Macro factors in international marketing

The 'global village' – a phrase coined in the 1970s – has arrived and it is here to stay. It's a relatively new phenomenon. After all, Levitt penned his now – classic article on Globalization as recently as 1983 and even today many still challenge his views (rightly). The 1960s saw the massive development of multinational companies but at that stage they were more concerned with acquisition and geographical spread than the internationalization of the marketing of their products/services. International marketing, management and control is a later development for most, i.e. treating large sections (or regions) of the world and addressing consumers' needs on the basis of similarities. The forces underpinning the rapid development of international marketing can be summarized as follows.

Population explosion

The world population is growing faster than at any time. To put it simply, this means more consumers, potentially bigger markets and profits. But this growth is not uniform. Post-industrial countries have stabilized their population while others are growing at an accelerating rate. The British with an average family size of 2 children is effectively 7+ children at a global level. Fast-growing populations are reflected in growing demand which stimulates rapid economic growth. A good example of this is Thailand and Malaysia, where much of the 8–10 per cent annual growth rate is internal and not export driven. So from an international perspective why aren't you considering operating in these fast-growing markets? Tom Peters wrote recently: 'The population of Indonesia is edging close to 200 million – what are you doing about it?' Instead, companies focus their efforts on Hungary and other East European countries, failing completely to capture the main business opportunities.

Increasing affluence

Not simply the rich are getting richer, but everybody's getting richer albeit with some notable exceptions and these, in the main, are in Africa. Global wealth is increasing and this is again reflected in higher demand. Increasing affluence and commercial dynamism has seen new nations such as Singapore overtake the UK in terms of GDP per head. Increasing affluence and demand simply means that consumers will actively seek choice with the result that competition is emerging as companies compete to win the battle for disposable income. Countries or at least large sections of them are moving into a world away from commodity purchase – maize or rice – into consumer goods, i.e. packaged and marketed to their personal needs.

A one-world youth culture

Population and affluence together with other macro forces has helped create a 'one-world youth culture'. In many countries, particularly the newly industrialized countries (NICs) more than half the population is pre-adult, creating one of the world's biggest single market – the youth market. Everywhere adolescents project worldwide cultural icons – Niké, Coke, Marlborough, Benetton, Sony Walkman, Michael Jackson and now Sega, Nintendo, etc. This is new, it is only just beginning in the timescale of new 'market' development. Ten years from now when 'virtual reality' is commonplace the one-world youth culture market will exceed all others as a general category for marketers. Parochial, local and ethnic growth products will, with exceptions, cease to exist. We will have created the global youth village. I recently heard that one US toy manufacturer tested new products on over 1000 children a week to determine their opinions and in the last five years or so Toys 'R' Us have spread across much of the world (or at the very least the key nations).

An additional viewpoint is that one of the international icons of the last 5 or 6 years, the pop star Madonna, has virtually made a market for herself by symbolizing current cultural status – Madonna the Material Girl. An offshoot from this is that women's role and their perception is changing rapidly just about everywhere. Not everyone (governments or religions) approves but the changing role of women is going to be a powerful force for change. It is happening here. I would guess there are more female brand managers than male and the trend is continuing upwards.

Global consumers

As an offshoot from the previous point, older consumers will be increasingly non-national in their identity – not from their personal identity, as I am sure the Scots will remain Scottish and the French will likewise resolve to hang on to their cultural heritage, but from the perspective of the consumable fabric of their lives; driving increasingly international cars, watching international programmes on television, using international hardware and software, one of which may have little or no 'nationality' in terms of corporate ownership. (Does anyone know or care that Reebok sneakers are American-owned, made in South Korea?) This general point has been made earlier, i.e. that our whole lives are taken up with global corporations and that we are global consumers to a greater or lesser degree. International consumption is accelerating and boundaries of product ownership are increasingly blurred.

To reinforce the points made so far, wander around your home and list how many international products or services are part of your everyday life. Give thought as to where they come from ie country of origin. Ask yourself the question 'Could I get by without international products/ services?

Very frequently examiners ask questions demanding that you demonstrate your knowledge via examples. So, at the end of this unit or major activity, write down examples and commit them to memory. This will save you desperately trying to 'think on the spot' in the examination. International Marketing Strategy, on average, requires more examples than, say, Planning and Control.

Multinationals and transnational/global corporations

The message here is again simple. The big are getting bigger. Consider the following. The top 500 world corporations account for

- 30 per cent of gross global product
- 70 per cent of global trade
- 80 per cent of international investment

Stop! Don't just gloss over these figures. five hundred – that's a very small number of firms who dominate the world. Take the figure of 80 per cent of international investment. That leaves practically nothing in terms of global investment for other companies (some of them large). For example, how many UK companies are there in the top 500 world corporations? What hope do small companies have? Plenty, providing they are extraordinarily special. Without being special and occupying a particular niche they have little hope to succeed on a large scale into the next century. That small firms will succeed is stating the obvious – but the leap from small to large will be more difficult.

Here's another powerful fact. Six companies control 63 per cent of all aluminium production, and in general (there are always exceptions) the major primary and secondary markets for products and services are dominated by a handful of multinational or transnational organizations.

A third and final fact for the moment, for we intend to return and discuss multinationals later:

$1 trillion cross national boundaries daily

Money is a commodity, traded 24 hours a day. It has no home and is the fuel of international business.

Write a list of multinational/global corporations. What products/services are they famous for?

Shrinking communications

Nowhere and nobody is far away! Take a walk down your High Street. Check out your local travel agent. Bali, Mexico, Beijing are now as commonplace as Benidorm, Marbella and Blackpool. Check the prices. Even impecunious students frequently return from the summer break having visited India, Thailand, California, etc. Winter holidays in skiing resorts now challenge the traditional summer break. We are international in terms of our travelling. As a guest lecturer, I frequently travel to Singapore for the weekend. Fax, mobile phones and other technology-led creations keep us constantly in touch anywhere in the world. (Incidentally, for the record, the fax machine has been around for 100 years or so – that's how they transmitted the 'Wanted Dead or Alive' posters in the Wild West. It is modern technology that has miniaturized it to a desktop communications tool.)

We do not labour the point that communications are breaking down narrow local thinking in international business. British Airways operates its worldwide 'exceptional request' facility such as wheelchair assistance needed for a passenger from a centre in Bombay. Indian universities are turning out computer-literate graduates by the hundred. They are intelligent, capable and keen and they are inexpensive to hire as is local property to rent. The cost of transmitting data processing from London to Bombay, a distance of some 7000 miles, is no more than sending the same information 7 miles. It is suggested that British Airways plans to run its worldwide ticketing operation from Bombay soon. This has serious implications for the owners of high-rise and expensive tower blocks in the suburbs of London. There is no earthly reason why Barclays Bank, shall we say, shouldn't do much of its data processing in New Delhi. (India, incidentally, is now the No. 2 producer of computer disks.) Dell Computers, by the way, has its European helpline in Ireland. Just use the 0800 number.

Communication companies are taking the lead in global development. It is no accident that Atlanta was chosen to host the 1996 Olympic Games. Atlanta's competitive advantage over other cities bidding for the Games was that it was the home of Ted Turner's organization CNN – a company you'd never heard of 10 years ago. CNN offered global communications and transmisson of events more efficiently than by the alternative route of negotiating with separate countries with their 'local' television networks.

The information revolution

Following on from shrinking communications it is apparent that information is power. At the touch of a button we can access information on the key factors that determine our business. News is a 24-hour a day service. (Each morning my radio informs me of the US, German and Japanese currency rates and world trading fortunes.) Manufacturers wanting to know the price of coffee beans or the relevant position of competitors in terms of their share price or in terms of new product activity have it at their immediate disposal.

Another factor for consideration. Newly emerging countries are abandoning thoughts of investing in land-based technology for communications. The technology of satellite communication has made land cables and telephone lines redundant. The telephone has leapfrogged technology and enabled developing countries to catch up and even be ahead!

Time! The competitive differential

To succeed in tomorrow's even busier crowded world market, success will come from firms that can adapt to change. The past (and present) is full of firms that aren't going to make it. Cantor wrote: 'In the future we will all have to enjoy dancing on the moving carpet.' Note, Cantor does not say dance on the moving carpet but enjoy dancing. *The Economist* recently said something pretty sensational: 'The humbling of big firms has only just begun.' The future lies in the hands of the flexible organization that sees time as its competitive differential. Today's crowded marketplace has little place or sympathy for me-toos. Ever fickle consumers (that's you and me) are demanding new, interesting products. Tom Peters recently spoke of buying his first lap-top computer. He took it home and showed it proudly to his 26-year-old son who replied: 'Dad, you bought one of the old ones (practically an antique), it's been out four months already!' Well, Peters told it as a joke but the thought behind it was deadly serious.

Bill Gates has come from a zero base to being the richest man in the world via the creation of Microsoft. He knows that without huge investment in R&D, and just as importantly in intelligent and imaginative thinking of what the world might be like 10 years hence, his business could be blown away as fast as it arrived.

For those organizations who slavishly follow current marketing theories about focusing on lowest cost, a word of warning. Just think of how the biggest and most cost-effective producer of radio and television valves felt when somebody discovered the transistor.

ACTIVITY 2.3

Select an area where technology is leading product development. Try to identify a company/product that made a breakthrough in the way Sony did 10 years ago with its Walkman. Work out how long it took for competitors to imitate.

Global product standardization

This is really one of the outcomes of the macrofactors underpinning the rapid evolution and development of international marketing. The opening to this chapter aptly demonstrated the recent spread of global products. Levitt in his 1983 article on Globalization describes modernity as the technological driving force towards the world of global products. True enough, but it is the speed of technological advancement that is the initiator of standardization. Microsoft Windows, for example, has universal application. Soon other newly emergent technological standards will make their impact and, being new, will form the single standard(s) for the next century. In service technologies and telecommunications it is inevitable that global standards will prevail. Following on, software and other spin-offs will also adopt a world standard approach from the outset.

Take the position of multinational organizations. They will be the organizations that will dictate the adoption of standardized hardware and software applications so that their information and reporting systems will be standardized from Argentina to Zimbabwe. Most multinationals already have standardized systems in operation.

World brands

Everybody is now familiar with world brands. Examples abound. However, they are, in the main, a new phenomenon. Microsoft, Sega, Nintendo, McDonald's, Niké, etc. did not straddle the world 10 years ago, or even 5 years ago in the case of Sega and Nintendo. The creation of World Brands is a relatively new development. The point is that world brand development is in its infancy, not its maturity. To quote a famous former US president, 'You ain't seen nothing yet!'

It is safe to say that 10 years from now, one quarter of the world brands will be for companies you may never have heard of today. The leaders of this development will come from the world of communications. I've already spoken briefly of CNN and they're just one of dozens of global communication companies that will develop over the next decade (e.g. Viacom).

EXAM HINT

Write down a list of world brands. There is frequently a question on globalization in the examination.

Urbanization

Changing tack for a minute. We've discussed population and affluence. There is another change occurring in this area, the rise of urbanization. With some exceptions in the post-industrial world, populations are migrating from the countryside to the city seeking work and hoped-for prosperity. The world is moving into gigantic conurbations. The population of

Greater Tokyo is soon to be close to 30 million; Mexico, 15 million already. Cities such as Lagos, Buenos Aires and Djakarta will outstrip cities such as Paris, London, Rome if they haven't already done so. This has powerful implications for marketers. Urbanization equates to simplifying the marketing environment. Urban dwellers require similar products (packaged conveniently and easy to carry). Similarly, they demand services (telephones and transportation of all kinds – commercial vehicles, buses, trains, taxis etc.). Additionally, they crave modern visual communications such as television. Obviously I could continue. The second spin-off of urbanization is, of course, that customers are accessible. We know where they are and can communicate with them efficiently via supermarkets and advertising and other marketing communication tools.

ACTIVITY 2.4

Consider, from a marketing perspective, the significance of a nation's population growth to the international marketer. Identify countries with the fastest-growing population (in overall terms and also in percentage growth) and compare them with some of the world's stable populations)

Global capital

The point has essentially been made. Money is sourced from anywhere round the world. To quote Kenichi Ohmae – money is a truly global product. It has no direct home and money lives in a borderless world. For students of globalization, Ohmae's book, *The Borderless World*, is essential reading.

Consider next the flow of international funds. The emergence of China has radically altered world capital flows. US investment in China has progressed thus:

1992	1993
$11 billion	$111 billion

You don't have to calculate the percentage to see the rate of growth over one year alone. The USA is not the only country investing in China. All the major industrial countries are pouring in money. But hold on, money is limited – it's not in an inexhaustible supply so capital flowing into China must mean capital (or potential capital at least) not flowing into other countries. So China's gain might be the UK's loss as US corporations globalize and move to where production is cheap and efficient. There is no doubt that China's gain is hampering the regeneration of Russia and Eastern Europe.

The enormous infusion of capital into China has helped make it the world's third largest economy in 1994 (after purchasing power – parity adjustment) United States and Japan topping the league.

Globalization of marketing skills

Time was when marketing skills were in the hands of a few well-educated individuals in Western countries. How things have changed. Goldstar, Samsung, Daewoo from South Korea and Proton from Malaysia have all captured marketing know-how. The introduction of Proton cars into the UK has proven to be the most successful new car company launch ever. Certainly they needed our help but the strategic thinking was theirs. Marketing skills are becoming universal business tools. Around half of the CIM Diploma candidates are non-UK based.

Development of world technologies

This point has largely been dealt with under the headings, Global product standardization, World brands and with reference to multinationals and the information revolution. But it is worth noting that corporations are simplifying their manufacturing operations to take advantage of convergence of global consumer needs. Ford, for example, in its Project 2000 initiative is concentrating its production into five critical regions each of which is coordinated in its development of a world car. This is not to say that they intend to build one single global vehicle but that the technology underpinning production and operation will have worldwide application.

Strategic and transnational cooperation

Not a week goes by without some announcement in the quality press of a strategic alliance. Although disagreement exists on the precise definition of a strategic alliance (e.g. are they long-term commitments or stop-gap tactics?) it is safe to say that developments in the modern business world will proceed faster if major organizations cooperate rather than seeking breakthroughs on their own.

The sheer cost of creating technological innovation, the development time involved, and the marketing and distribution costs preclude many companies from going it alone. Instead they form partnership agreements often developing value chains (see Porter for value chain structures)) for the purpose of achieving competitive advantages. Toshiba has strategic alliances with Motorola, Olivetti, AT&T, RSI Logic Corporation, General Electric, Siemens, and probably others.

The basis for alliances is not to subvert competition but rather to create additional value to each firm's offering as it finds its own individual position in the marketplace. Why spend billions perfecting flat-screen technology for computers and televisions when you can cooperate with others in its development, which can be exploited by all parties involved in the strategic alliance?

EXAM HINT

It is essential that you identify recent examples of strategic alliances. This area is a high-profile topic in International Marketing and knowing what is going on can gain valuable marks. The source for this information is not the textbooks but the quality newspapers.

Some examples of the basis of alliance include:

- Technology swaps
- R&D development
- Manufacturing (e.g. the development of a common car platform for Saab, Fiat and Lancia)
- Distribution relationships
- Cross-licensing
- Marketing relationships
- Government cooperation

Government cooperation can now be added to strategic alliance in that in the move towards regionalization (e.g. the European Union) has developed several instances of government cooperation. The most celebrated of these is the European Airbus created to challenge the global domination of the passenger aircraft industry by Boeing.

Success factors in strategic alliances are:

- Alliances survive as long as each party regards the other as its best partner. Ideally (though this is seldom achieved) some equity ought to be exchanged. But key factors include
- Mutual need. This is more important than who controls the alliance (or think they control it). Each partner must take whatever steps it can to ensure that the other continues to need mutual benefit.
- Shared objective. Agreement reached on what it is they intend to 'maximize' together.
- Shared risk. No loading of the risks onto one partner.

- Relationship and trust. This is the heart of the alliance, but companies don't invest enough in building trust – which takes years. Honda were particularly upset at British Aerospace's decision to sell Rover cars to BMW after 15 years of close cooperation. Alarmingly, for UK companies, the Japanese as an industrial nation will have taken close note of this behaviour by a major British firm.

EXAM QUESTION

Identify the key changes that have occurred in the international trading environment in the last decade. To what degree have their changes affected the strategies adopted by companies involved in international trade? Illustrate your answer with specific examples (December 1994).

(**See** Exam answers at the end of this unit.)

Summary

Having read this unit you should be in no doubt that international marketing is a driving force in developing world trade. Fewer firms can restrict their thinking to the narrow confines of domestic marketing. International influences are affecting everyone's behaviour. Reliance on a 'home' market can only be sustainable where government protection prevails – and that is in decline. Facing up to international trends in planning for inward competition is an essential prerequisite of every organization.

Questions

To check on your understanding of what has been covered consider the following questions:

- Why is international marketing so important to UK firms?
- Identify five prominent UK companies seriously involved in worldwide marketing. Choose one, preferably one close to your town/city. Study the comments made by the chairman about international marketing – examine its importance to the firm.
- In what way is your life, particularly your business career, related to development on international marketing? Think personally on how events might shape your future career. What will your firm/industry look like 5 or even 10 years from now?
- The big are getting bigger – the paradox is that this leaves more opportunities for small, nimble organizations to prosper. Identify a industry (market). Plot the shapers in terms of macro factors, then see if you can come up with ideas for niche operators.

EXTENDING KNOWLEDGE

For a more detailed study of this unit read:

International Marketing Strategy, C. Phillips, I. Doole and R. Lowe, Routledge 1994, Chapter 2.
Global Marketing Strategies, J.-P. Jeannet and H. D. Hennessey; Houghton Mifflin, 1994, Chapter 1–4.
International Marketing, V. Terpstra and R. Sarathy; The Dryden Press, 1994, Chapters 1, 2, 18.
International Marketing, S. Paliwoda, Butterworth-Heinemann, 1993, Chapter 1.
The quality press; *Financial Times, The Economist, The Guardian, The Times*, etc.

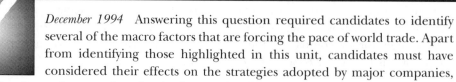

December 1994 Answering this question required candidates to identify several of the macro factors that are forcing the pace of world trade. Apart from identifying those highlighted in this unit, candidates must have considered their effects on the strategies adopted by major companies, e.g. the increasing need to be in international markets, resiting of subsidiaries, internationalization of marketing, product, human resources, the greater need for planning and control, wider sourcing, more research and information, speeding up NPD. The list is extensive. The question demanded the use of examples (see exam hint earlier in the unit).

Patterns of world trade

The preceding unit outlined the major forces that underpin world trade. This unit reviews patterns of world trade and the key institutions that are important in facilitating its development. In doing so the unit:

- Presents a brief overview of world trade – this examines the linkages between nations
- Considers the balance between exports versus imports among the world's leading nations
- Reviews the development towards regionalization and the possible creation of the Triad economies
- Considers the position and growth of China and, briefly, India as they advance towards being key players in the future world economy
- Briefly comment on the impact and relevance of the EU. (Candidates should be well versed and knowledgeable in the development of the EU. Therefore it is proposed not to consider this important item in this text.)
- Reviews the facilitators of world trade.

Upon completion of the unit you will be able to:

- Explain the essential balance of trade between the key trading nations.
- Discuss potential future developments and the impact of the emergence of new giant economies.
- Debate whether regionalism will be a force for good or bad.
- Understand barriers to trade and their impact.
- Initiate discussion on the role of the key facilitating agencies, (e.g. GATT/WTO) and relate their relevance to the nation state and the individual firm.

STUDY GUIDE

Nation trades with nation. They exchange values. It is extremely useful to understand in outline the balance and, indeed, the overall scale of world trade. It has increased faster than the rate of increase of most individual countries. We consider the issues of impediments to its growth – which in effect are impediments to our continual prosperity as a nation. In your study you will realize the importance of the continued interaction of trade between nations.

STUDY TIP

Though the unit contains some data on size and movements, etc. it is important that students read widely around this unit as support to their study. The cutting edge of discussion and decision is in the daily press. All the subjects raised here are intensely topical. Make sure you are abreast of development.

Start today by building a series of files created by cutting articles from the quality press. Create two sorts of files:

1 *Country files* Here it is a good idea to build information on types of countries, e.g. NICs, Third World countries, advanced industrialized nations. For example, frequently the quality press e.g. *The Times*, will have features on South Korea, India, China, Nigeria, Mexico, etc. This information base will be of considerable value if you use it as an example.

2 *Activity files* Create a series of headings relating to this unit. (e.g. The European Union, GATT/WTO. World wage comparisons, International mergers, etc.). Once again this will be a helpful aid in the examination in addition to building your knowledge from a work perspective.

Nations trade with nations

Countries, like individuals, are not completely self-sufficient; they exchange 'values' – goods, services, money, etc. We have already highlighted that foreign goods are indispensable to living standards everywhere. However, there is considerable variation among countries concerning the scale of and their reliance on international trade. Table 3.1 illustrates some of the gaps between imports and exports.

The table makes interesting reading for it shows the internal economy as the real engine of growth for the two major countries which are largely self-reliant. It shatters or seriously dents the myth that Japan is a nation of exporters. Germany is the world No. 1 exporting country. Obviously, smaller nations (e.g. Holland and Belgium) have to export and import in order to survive. They cannot specialize in everything. Similarly, many developing countries have a high export and import ratio in their economy.

Table 3.1 Import and exports as percentage of GDP, 1990 estimate $billion

	GDP	Imports/GDP %	Exports/GDP %
Industrialized countries			
USA	5550	9	7
Japan	2932	8	9
Germany	1617	21	25
Holland	272	47	48
Switzerland	228	32	29
Developing countries			
Korea	235	30	28
Mexico	230	12	11

Source: EIU, January 1991

Table 3.2 Leading Exporters of Commercial Services 1988 (% of Total Exports)

USA	22
France	26
UK	25
West Germany	12
Italy	21
Japan	11
South Korea	13
Mexico	21

Source: *The Economist*, 1990

But services are also an important and rapidly expanding part of world trade, accounting for approximately 20 per cent of total exports. Services account for around 60 per cent of GDP in the UK and the figure for USA exceeds 70 per cent (and over 75 per cent of US employment is in services – (see Table 3.2).

At the recent GATT/WTO round pressure mounted to bring services into the agreement but it failed. But it is anticipated that services will at some stage be incorporated into the set of principles.

Growth in world trade: the Triad economies and regionalism

Growth in world trade has been discussed earlier but the principle of free trade as evolved under GATT/WTO has led to the building of country interdependence. With the world fast becoming a 'global village' current thinking is that the faster-growing and most dynamic trading nations will join together in a series of regional trading areas. This has been under development for the past 25 years. The European Union is the most familiar but others include ASEAN (Singapore, Malaylsia, Indonesia, Thailand, Philippines and Brunei) and NAFTA (the USA, Canada and Mexico – created in 1994). It is believed possible that by the end of the decade three 'super blocs' will emerge. The EU, the Americas, and South-east Asia. These three trading blocs are referred to as the Triad economies. Each bloc will develop its own internal market with varying degrees of political, economic and monetary union between the member states.

Figure 3.1 shows the development of three major trading blocks (with the rest of the world, included to illustrate the power of the Triad). The implication of this diagram is that the Triad economies now account for approximately 85 per cent of world trade growing from 70 per cent a decade ago. A further point for consideration is that around 90 per cent of world trade is accounted for by ten countries.

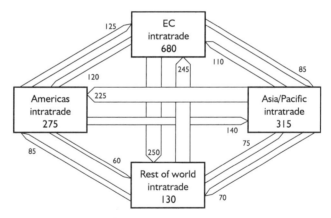

Figure 3.1 World trade flows, 1989 (billions of dollars). (*Source*: 'The world economy', *The Economist*, 5 January 1991, p. 22. © The Economist Newspaper Ltd. Reprinted with permission)

Figure 3.2 shows the distribution of trade (in goods) based on the value of export and imports of the different regions of the world. From this we see that Western Europe alone accounts for nearly 50 per cent of world trade volume with the EU accounting for 46 per cent of world trade. However, this proportion is expected to shift (downwards) as China and the Asian Tigers raise their performance from 12 per cent in 1993 to a likely 20 per cent (or more) a decade hence.

Further examination of the Triad suggests that it is either going to fuel a rapid expansion of world trade or the opposite. The danger is the creation of a fortress mentality with each trading bloc being capable of producing, internally, virtually all its needs; it might well build barriers to prevent competition from eroding the economies and industrial bases of member states. However although this might be speculation, the long-term planning horizons for major industrial corporations needs to take all views into account.

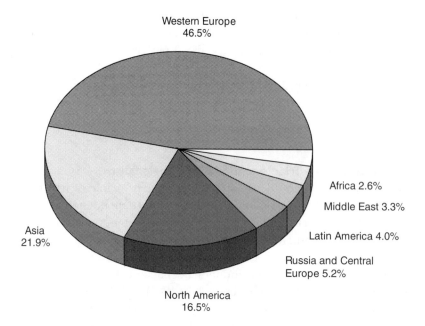

Western Europe
46.5%

Africa 2.6%

Middle East 3.3%

Latin America 4.0%

Russia and Central
Europe 5.2%

Asia
21.9%

North America
16.5%

Figure 3.2 Distribution of international trade in goods, 1993. (*Source:* GATT)

Reread the data in the text so far. Grasp the importance of the scale of world trade.

Of the regions the EU is most familiar. Currently intratrade, i.e. trade between the 15 countries of the EU, accounts for approximately 70 per cent of EU trade and in the North American Free Trade Area (NAFTA) intratrade accounts for 42 per cent of all trade.

Data and information on the EU abound and students are expected to acquire knowledge of the scale and strength of the European economy and the advantages accruing from the establishment of the EU. For those who are unfamiliar, here is a list of the key benefits of the Single European Market:

- The removal of tariff barriers
- The removal of technical barriers
- The opening up of public procurement
- The free movement of labour
- The opening up of the professions
- The harmonization of financial services
- The removal of border transport documentation
- The removal of restrictions on capital flows
- The standardization of company law
- The removal of fiscal barriers
- More consistent environmental protection

To reinforce what has already been said it is imperative you create a file on the EU. The subject is topical and examinable.

Americas to establish largest free trade bloc

Monstrous disparities create a problem for treaty negotiators, **Martin Walker** in Miami reports

STILLING their suspicions of US economic and cultural dominance, its anti-immigration and drug control policies, the 33 other countries of North and South America agreed at the weekend to establish a Free Trade Area of the Americas.

They also decided to maintain its momentum with biennial summits, and to complete negotiations by 2005.

President Clinton, whose strategy is to place the US at the heart of the vast new trading blocs of the global economy, hailed the FTAA yesterday as a historic step that will create the world's largest market.

The US had to overcome its own doubts, and accept vaguely worded assurances on human and worker's rights, and on environmental protection, as the price of dominating the new economic order for the two continents.

But the unity on display among the 34 leaders in Miami disguised a monstrous disparity in size and in economic prospects, far sharper than the fast-track, slow-track divisions in Europe. The North America Free Trade Agreement states – the US, Canada, Mexico and soon Chile – are the dominant and most developed partners, with about 40 per cent of the population of the two continents and more than 80 per cent of their wealth.

The multiplicity of treaties threatens to create a real Tower of Babel

Argentina and Brazil form a secondary weaker grouping, the Mercosur group, with which the EU is to open trade co-operation talks. Then comes the medium-sized economies like Columbia and Venezuela, the little ones like Peru and Ecuador, and finally the small fry of the Caribbean islands.

The 'Caribbean nations raised concerns that free trade not swamp their own industries nor hurt their access to US and Canadian markets', a Canadian official said, 'Many of these economies are very fragile.'

They are particularly at risk from non-tariff barriers, like the legal suits being brought by US agribusiness against the privileged access of Caribbean bananas to Europe. The US trade representative, Mickey Kantor, had to promise an immediate review of the matter to stop the summit stalling.

A series of regional trade groupings like Nafta, Mercosur, the Andrean Pact, the Central American Common Market and Caricom, the Caribbean community, are in place, pursuing their own agendas and their own separate agreements with Japan, the Apec-Asia Pacific group, and the EU.

'This evident multiplicity of treaties, both bilateral and multilateral, threatens to create a real Tower of Babel for trade,' warned Chile's president, Eduardo Frei. The real job of the FTAA would be to integrate these regional groupings, he said, while also opening economies to the rest of the world.

'We have pledged that our FTAA will not raise new barriers to nations outside our region and will be fully consistent with the rules of the World Trade Organization,' President Clinton said yesterday.

Figure 3.3

It may be of interest that the North American Free Trade Area (NAFTA) established as recently as 1994 is planning to expand and become the Free Trade Area of the Americas (FTAA) by the year 2005, embracing 34 countries. In a decade it plans to be the world's largest market. The article shown in Figure 3.3 reinforces the point.

- Identify three different types of trading blocs in the world. Take one specific trading bloc and examine how changes that are taking place will influence marketing opportunities within and outside that trading bloc (June 1994).
- For a trading group of your choice, discuss the likely changes in trading patterns between the trading group of countries and the rest of the world. How might these changes affect a company wishing to trade with some members of the group (December 1992).

China

While on the subject of trading blocs it is worth exploring developments in China. This is probably more fruitful than a discussion on the future expansion of the 'Tiger' economies of South-east Asia (Singapore, Hong Kong, South Korea, etc.). Remember these countries' economies have been growing at an average rate of 8-10 per cent per annum for a decade or more compared with European countries' growth at less than half that rate. But successful though they are, they are all relatively small countries whereas China, the global giant in population, is about to surpass all known growth records. Its potential is awesome. To begin with, far from being a slowly emerging force, China is already the world's third largest economy. The IMF now calculating GDP in terms of a currency's purchasing power at home suggests that China outstrips all European countries. The article shown in Figure 3.4 shows this.

The message is again simple. The Pacific Rim is the region for the new millennium and it begs the question to UK companies. Are you there? If not, you'd better have a good reason

Zooming Up in the Charts

TWO WEEKS AGO, China had the 10th largest economy in the world. This week it junmps to third, behind the US and Japan. India, formerly No. 11, leaps to No. 6. Mexico climbs from No. 12 to No. 10.

What has been going on? A stunning advance in Third World productivity? The sudden arrival of a new Green Revolution in the agricultural sector? No, something more mundane but almost as far-reaching is taking place as the Washington-based International Monetary Fund switches to a different system for estimating the size of each country's economy. Those most affected are rapidly industrializing nations such as Mexico, Brazil, India, Indonesia and Thailand, and their upgraded status is likely to change perceptions of the world's economic balance of power. Says Robert Hormats, vice-chairman of Goldman Sachs International: 'This new accounting underscores in quantitative terms just how powerful China, India and other developing countries are today, both as markets and as competitors.'

The IMF's latest calculations replace an accounting technique that valued in US dollars the output of goods and services in every nation. That system, still widely used by economists as well as by multilateral lenders like the World Bank, produces swings in a country's gross national product, its total output of goods and services, every time the value of its currency

shifts in relation to the US dollar. If the Chilean peso, for example, loses 5 per cent of its value against the greenback, estimates of the country's growth – 10.4 per cent in 1992 – are automatically reduced by the amount of the devaluation, as is the economy's total size. When currencies are kept in an artificial relation to the dollar, as in many of Asia's developing economies, wild distortions can occur. By the dollar-based method, the economic output of Asia, excluding Japan, accounts for only 7.3 per cent of the world total, less than the Asian share of 10 years ago. 'That's absurd given that Asia is the fastest growing region of the world,' a senior IMF official points out. Distortions of that sort argued for a change.

The IMF's new gauge relies on 'purchasing-power parity,' a means of calculating national income that many economists believe should have been put into practice long ago. Rather than GNP being measured in dollars, a national basket of goods and services encompassing the likes of transport, food, clothing and shelter is tallied in local currency and compared with purchasing power of similar goods and services in other parts of the world. This method provides a more accurate assessment of the value of what each person is able to buy, a figure that is multiplied by a country's total population to reach an estimate of national output. Using this standard, the IMF pegs China's output at $1.7

trillion last year, far above the $400 billion used in earlier estimates China's per capita income rises from $370 to $1600. Taken as a whole, the developing world's share of global output expands from 18 per cent to 34 per cent.

While the higher IMF estimates may be better yardsticks of economic progress, they have also aroused Third World concern that some hard-pressed developing nations may suddenly be seen as too well-off to receive needed World Bank loans. Under current rules, only countries with a per capita GDP of less than $765 qualify for 35-year interest-free loans, the most favourable terms available. World Bank officials insist that they have no plans to change their own measuring techniques to match the IMF's revised numbers. So the worries in some countries may be justified.

The IMF's new tallies are still controversial, some economists believe that in a number of cases, the value of goods and services in different countries cannot be meaningfully compared. But a majority of economists seem to applaud the change. Nor is the end in sight, forecasters who use IMF methods in adding the economies of Hong Kong and Taiwan to that of China – envisaging a greater China, so to speak – calculate that that total output will exceed the US's in less than a decade.

–By Adam Zagorin/Washington

Figure 3.4

not to be! For example, Guandung Province alone with tens of millions of consumers already represents Procter & Gamble's second largest market for shampoo, while there are 14,000 Avon ladies in the province selling cosmetics. In Shanghai to the north this growth is being repeated. Here a city of 13 million people has 2 million enter and leave it daily. One retail development estimates it serves 1 million customers daily. Along the Chinese coastal belt alone live 300 million people whose income is set to grow at 11 per cent per year for the next 10 years. Never in human history have so many grown so rich so fast! It will be the biggest economic player in the history of mankind, says Lee Kuan Yew, former Prime Minister of Singapore. China with 1.2 billion people, 25 per cent the world's population and a rapidly expanding economy (10 per cent+ per annum), offers the single greatest opportunity and threat for Western products.

India

India, already Asia's third strongest economy and with a population of over 900 million, is also posing great opportunities and threats. What's significant here is that 150 million Indians fit into the emerging educated and prosperous middle class. Internal domestic growth alone will see India make major advances in the world's economic success league. Just to meet its energy needs India is building ten major power stations each year until 2007.

ACTIVITY 3.3

Stop and think what you have learned so far. Reread the first part of the unit. Be sure you understand what is happening in terms of the patterns of world trade before you go on to discover the facilitators.

The facilitators of international trade

Barriers to trade

One of the difficulties in international trading is that each nation, or rather its government, feels it needs to exercise control over its trade and, through its trade, its economy. This will vary from country to country depending on the percentage of the GDP associated with export/import flows. Traditionally, either to protect mature (moribund) industries from foreign competition or to encourage infant industries that might be still-born under the pressure from foreign competition, governments have resorted to manipulate imports by imposing barriers in the form of tariffs or non-tariff restriction. A tariff is simply a tax levied on volume (e.g. on a 70cl bottle of wine) or alternatively on value (i.e. *ad valorem*). A further reason for imposing restrictions may be to earn revenue and, as mentioned above, to nurture and/or protect domestic industries. The recommended textbooks cover barriers to international trade in considerable depth. However, government additionally enforce what are known as non-tariff or invisible barriers which are far more difficult to detect and lead to a feeling of natural distrust between nation states. Invisible barriers may include:

Technical specifications
- Packaging regulations
- Size and weight regulations
- Health and safety regulations
- Product design specifications
- Manufacturing specifications

Government regulations
- Boycott
- Government procurement
- Granting of credit lines/subsidies for local producers
- Unnecessary and complicated administration
- Complicated local documentation

- Centralization of documentation
- Sample shipments to be sent in advance

More formal restrictions
- Special insurance requirements
- Special transport
- Port taxes and border surcharges and deposits

Quantitative restrictions
- Quotas
- Embargoes
- Licensing regulations
- Restrictive business conditions
- Exchange control

Again the recommended texts elaborate on invisible barriers. However, it is worth noting that protectionist methods taken by one country have traditionally produced retaliation by others. The overall conclusion of this activity is that *it does not work* (although there are exceptions – but even these ultimately are temporary restraints as consumers invariably seek out superior product offerings and are prepared to pay the price for superiority).

EXAM HINT

The subject of protection against foreign competition appears with some regularity in examination papers. Make sure you not only understand the means through which countries endeavour to restrict foreign imports but are fully cognisant with the impact and outcomes of such activities.

GATT (General Agreement on Tariffs and Trade) (now renamed World Trade Organization (1995))

Back in the 1920s and 1930s world trade was practically brought to a halt by protectionist methods with all the major countries imposing barriers to prevent 'foreign' competitors entering their home markets and destroying jobs. The term 'beggar my neighbour' was coined. After the Second World War, GATT (General Agreement on Tariffs and Trade) was formed following the Bretton Woods Economic Conference in 1944. Beginning in 1947/8 with 23 countries it has expanded today to over 100 (including associate members such as Russia). The purpose of GATT was to reduce tariff barriers. Despite undergoing traumas at its regular meetings GATT has been astonishingly successful. Tariffs have been reduced from 47 per cent in 1948 to approximately 5 per cent today with firm proposals following the Uruguay round of talks to reduce this to 2.5 per cent over the decade. The reduction of tariffs and the resulting freeing of the flow of goods has increased world trade by 500 per cent and global output by 200 per cent. Signatories to the GATT agreement today account for 90 per cent of world trade.

The most recent GATT round began in 1987 in Uruguay and concluded late in 1993 and is still being ratified by member countries. GATT's very survival was under threat. Had it failed after 7 years of discussion the prospects for world trade into the next century would have been grim with the world retreating into trading blocs (EU, NAFTA, etc.). As mentioned previously the EU is largely self-sufficient with nearly 70 per cent of its trade as intracountry member trade and hypothetically Europe can provide over 90 per cent of its needs inside the Union – albeit at a cost. The major losers would have been the multinational and transnational corporations which spread their production facilities and supply chains around the world. It is clear that the major winners from the GATT agreement are not just the 100 or so countries but multinational corporations. Incidentally, the stumbling point in the 1993 talks related not to manufactured goods but to agricultural policies (probably of greater psychological concern to nation states than real trading importance). The other area of contention, still unresolved is the establishment of principles of trade applied to services. This is of growing concern as services account for an ever-increasing proportion of world trade.

The USA is particularly anxious to tackle the issue of services for its economy is now dominated by service industries which increasingly look to export as a source of growth. Between 1980 and 1992 US exports of services increased by 115 per cent whilst product exports lagged at 70 per cent. The French, taking a chauvinist view, feel threatened by American cultural imperialism – their film and television industries being vulnerable to Hollywood are resisting liberalization of trade in services.

Longer term the major threat to GATT is the trend towards regionalism and the creation of fortress mentalities among powerful nations or Triad economies. In fact one commentator remarked that it was the creation of NAFTA that spurred on the conclusion of the Uruguay round in 1993.

EXAM HINT

GATT is being renamed as the World Trade Organization (WTO). Being up to date and abreast of current developments, show a keen interest in the subject. This is a specific point but the general one of being on top of the subject matter – through the use of examples – will be rewarded by the examiner, (e.g, NAFTA possibly being FTAA by 2005).

International Monetary Fund (IMF)

Founded at the same time as GATT from the same Bretton Woods conference in 1944, the purpose of the IMF was to give stability to exchange rate fluctuation. Although the notion of pegged currency rates is now largely dead (except in the minds of certain European countries) the IMF remains. Having said that, it is still conceivable that monetary union could happen among some members of the EU, notably Germany, Austria, Belgium, Holland, Luxembourg and France, before the end of the decade.

The IMF's current role is essentially to provide a forum for international monetary cooperation, lessening the chances of nations taking arbitrary action and returning to the financial chaos of the 1930s. Additionally its role is to offer financial support to nations whose economies and currencies are in turmoil, (e.g., Mexico in Spring 1995). In that respect it operates like a bank helping a business over a temporary crisis.

Like any prudent banker, the IMF generally imposes (or threatens) draconian conditions on borrowers which are unpopular to the citizens and politicians of the affected state. This has given the IMF the reputation of the bank of last resort – and the bank one loves to hate.

The World Bank (International Bank for Reconstruction and Development)

The IBRD or the World Bank is yet another Bretton Woods creation. Its impact differs from that of the IMF. Whereas the IMF involves itself with short-term financial crises the World Bank underpins long-term aid via capital loans to further economic development providing, over $10 billion per year. Its 'soft' loans with long-term payback supports many of the world's major developments (e.g. infrastructures, agriculture, tourism and population control initiatives).

Organization for Economic Cooperation and Development (OECD)

This is a United Nations (UN) offshoot comprising 24 leading economies. Its role is basically of providing bi-monthly statistics on the performance of the world's major trading nations and indication of future performance. Its views are respected by governments and multinationals for directional advice.

United Nations Conference on Trade and Development (UNCTAD)

This is a permanent organ of the UN comprising 160 countries. Its aim is to further the development of emerging nations by concentrating on commodities and primary products.

If the commodity-producing nations who are mainly in the Third World could organize themselves into some form of co-operative, then prices would rise to the benefit of their countries. UNCTAD's progress has been modest. Commodity prices (in real terms) have fallen consistently over the past two decades.

Regional Economic Associations

Earlier we spoke of the development of the Triad economies and the implications for international business. We return to the subject under the banner of regionalism to distinguish between the different types of regional cooperation. Regional groupings result from countries agreeing to cooperate in various economic (and sometimes political) matters. Although some political corporation is unavoidable, how else can the region otherwise be created? Our role as marketers is confined to economic benefits. Regionalism is an attempt by nations to achieve goals they could otherwise not achieve by 'going it alone'.

Some principal regional economic associations

- EU: (Economic Union): The UK, France, Denmark, Germany, Italy, Spain, the Netherlands, Portugal, Spain, Ireland, Belgium, Luxembourg and (in 1995) Austria, Finland and Sweden
- ASEAN Association of South-east Asian Nations): Indonesia, Malaysia, Singapore, Philippines, Thailand and Brunei
- NAFTA (North American Free Trade Association): The USA, Canada, Mexico

There are others, of course, embracing West Africa (ECOWAS), Western South America (ANCOM), North Africa (AMU) and Central America (CACM).

Types of regional groupings

Broadly, the different types of regional groupings can be described under the following headings:

- *Free Trade Area* (e.g. NAFTA) The simplest level of corporation in which member countries agree to free movement of goods among themselves. (i.e. no tariffs or quotas). EFTA (now defunct) was a European equivalent.
- *Customs Union* Before 1992 the then European Community (EC) was an example with uniform tariffs as trade with non-members presenting a united front to the rest of the world. Its advantages are in stronger economic interaction accelerating intranations trade. However, it necessitates higher levels of political integration and some loss of sovereignty.
- *Common Market* The current EU aim is such with harmonization of internal tariffs, leading to their abolition in the future and a free flow of all factors of production between members including materials, services and people. In fact the closest example of a Common Market is the USA, but even here the model is not complete. Within Europe there is much debate over the Maastricht agreement which sets out the defined stages towards the Common Market (i.e. United States of Europe) with its development of the single currency and political union (both of which are inextricably linked).
- *Other Groupings* ASEAN, for the record, is different again being in effect a force for collaboration between its member states. It is early days to see if ASEAN will develop into something more positive and effective.

Summary

Trade between nations is the engine that drives the world economy. It needs supporting otherwise the alternative (i.e. a breakdown in international trade) will result in misery for everyone. Yet unfettered trading can also create a perilous scenario. Of crucial importance is balance – equilibrium with openness and liberalization held in perspective by world forces. But this balance is constantly under threat as individual nations protect and encourage home industries. Tensions are forever arising as nations expand or decline on the world scene. World trade is not static, it is forever changing.

Questions

Having completed the unit, check your learning by considering the following questions:

- From an international perspective, what can be learned from an examination of the make-up and patterns of world trade?
- What is GATT (now renamed the World Trade Organization)? What is its role in international marketing – and what factors threaten its future?
- South-east Asia seems the growth market for the twenty-first century. What advice might you give to the UK firm in:
  (a) Entering the region?
  (b) Facing competition at home from it?
- Why might a UK company deeply involved in international marketing feel threatened by the formation of the Triad trading blocs? How might it react?
- Who/what are the major institutions facilitating world trade? What are they there for? do we need them?
- Why is trade in services so difficult to manage? What do you think will be the future reaction of nation states to the accelerating growth of international services? What in your opinion should happen?
- In terms of their impact on your nation's economic well being explain the similarities and differences between tariff and non-tariff barriers.

EXTENDING KNOWLEDGE

There are probably many gaps to fill in your knowledge base in the unit. It is important you read widely as the syllabus is now more strategic.

International Marketing, S. Paliwoda, Butterworth-Heinemann, 1993, Chapter 3.
International Marketing Strategy, C. Phillips, I. Doole and R. Lowe, Routledge, 1994, Chapter 2.
International Marketing, V. Terpstra and R. Sarathy, The Dryden Press, 1994. Chapter 2.
Global Marketing Strategies, J.-P. Jeannet and H. D. Hennessey, Houghton Mifflin, 1994, Chapters 2–4.

EXAM ANSWERS

June 1994 The question demanded that candidates identify three different types of trading blocs. Many misread the question and wrote about three trading blocs. You were required to specify three types (i.e. free trade areas, customs unions, common market and monetary and political unions, obviously giving an example of each. The moral here is read the question carefully. Failure to do so meant many candidates did not gain the marks they thought they might! Part 2 of this question concerned a discussion of the implications for a specific bloc (e.g. the EU). Most selected the EU but instead of discussing implications, spent the entire time describing it. The examiner is seeking evidence of the process of international marketing at work.

December 1992 First, you should briefly nominate and describe your trading group: when it was established, what countries it consists of and what kind of trading group it is. Having done that you should discuss the present and likely future impact of the development between the group and the rest of the world. Finally, taking a company outside the group, what are the implications for its further services (i.e. should it make strenuous efforts to become an 'insider'?) This would appear to be the most sensible approach for a major international company. (Generally the question was not well handled by students, simply because they did not know the subject matter and failed to apply themselves to the three parts of the question.)

Customers and the environment

Customers and an understanding of customer needs and motivations are key to any successful marketing strategy – domestic or international. In international marketing strategy the problem is made more complex for two reasons. First, customers tend to be in different countries and different markets with different environmental effects acting upon them. Second, the self-reference criterion makes it difficult for marketers of a different culture to understand fully how and why a given customer in an overseas market may act differently to the same marketing stimulus. In this unit we will look at the key factors which impinge upon customer behaviour in overseas markets and we will attempt to build a picture of how the international marketer must go about trying to understand the nature and complexities of the foreign market selected.

The best way to understand customers (or to attempt to!) is to analyse and identify those factors of the environment that affect the way that they think and behave. In this unit you will:

- Review the factors that affect buyer behaviour
- Evaluate the key elements of culture
- Consider the main aspects of the legal environment
- Consider the main aspects of the political environment
- Consider the main aspects of the economic environment
- Review the process of market selection

Having completed this unit you will be able to:

- Understand the differences in business and social/cultural conventions which affect buying behaviours in international markets
- Understand how different stages of economic growth affect buying behaviours
- Appreciate how marketing approaches for different foreign markets are driven by local needs and environmental conditions
- Prioritize and select foreign markets

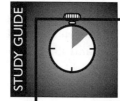

This unit might be considered to be the most important in the whole question of forming international marketing strategy. Good marketing (international as well as domestic) must begin with the customer – not the product.

Success in international operations come not from skilful manipulation of product or promotional strategies but from a good depth of understanding of what our customers want, what drives them and how to read the local environment to understand customers.

The candidate should read this unit more than once. It should be worked in conjunction with all the other units in this book.

Once you have completed this unit, try to apply the data as a key to understanding a foreign market that you know, perhaps one that you have visited on holiday. What can you see from an analysis of the market? Can you place some of the 'different' behaviours in context? What special aspects of the local environment are driving the different behaviours?

Environmental factors

The comparative analysis of world markets is concerned with the environment in which international marketing takes place. The kind of steps that the international marketer can take and the adaptations that organizations must make will be determined largely by this environment. In this unit we will be primarily concerned with the international marketer's sphere of operation, dwelling particularly on the uncontrollable variables and how they affect the international marketing task.

There are a number of ways of categorizing the environment and in international marketing strategy the SLEPT method is preferred (i.e. social, legal, economic, political and technology factors).

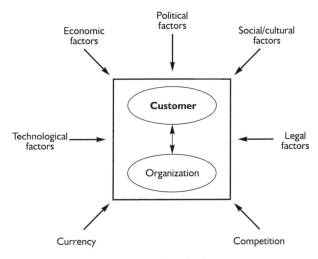

Figure 4.1   Environmental factors in international marketing

Figure 4.1 identifies these various factors which are the most important variables that affect the relationship between the organization and its customer in the foreign market operation. The rest of this unit will consider these factors separately and intends to identify how they impinge upon the international marketers task.

Culture is notoriously difficult to define and many people have tried. Kluckhohn in fact published a book with 257 different definitions. His best composite of all these definitions is:

> Patterned ways of thinking, feeling and reacting, acquired and transmitted mainly by symbols, constituting the distinctive achievements of human groups, including their embodiments in artifacts; the essential case of culture consists of traditional ideas and especially their attached values.

More usefully (perhaps) culture has been described as 'the way we do things around here.'

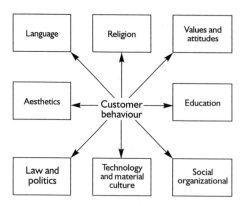

Figure 4.2 The components of cultures (adapted from Terpstra)

The social/cultural environment

It is only in relatively recent years that socio-cultural influences have been identified as critical determinants of marketing behaviour. In other words, marketing is a cultural as well as an economic phenomenon. Culture is so pervasive yet so complex that it is difficult to define in short, simple terms. The easiest way to grasp the complexity of culture is to examine these varied aspects. Up to 73 'cultural universals' have been identified, but we have reduced these to eight for our purposes (see Figure 4.2). While this brief survey is not sufficient to convey any expertise in the area, its main purpose is to alert the prospective marketer to the kind of cultural parameters that can affect international marketing programmes.

The key components of culture in the international marketing environment are as follows.

Language

Foreign markets differ from the domestic in terms of the language which the people speak and the language which is written. In some markets the official language differs from the actual one used, in other markets there is more than one language to deal with in the same population. Countries with more than one official language are relatively easy to spot (Switzerland has four), other countries with widely differing dialects are sometimes more difficult (India = 500, Papua New Guinea = plus or minus 750). In other markets there are differences in the language spoken by the males and the females of the population (Japan).

Your chairman is making his first sales visit to Japan. Write a brief to advise him on the cultural adjustments he might consider making to improve the chances of success (December 1990).

(**See** Exam answers at the end of this unit.)

Religion

Religion is a major cultural variant and has significant if not always apparent effects on marketing strategy. For example, the identification of sacred objects and philosophical systems, beliefs and norms as well as taboos, holidays and rituals are critical for an understanding of marketing interest in a given product or service. Religion will affect the food which a people eat and when they eat it as well as people's attitudes to a whole range of products from deodorants to alcoholic drink.

Values and attitudes

The values that a market has towards things such as time, achievement, work, wealth, change and risk taking will seriously affect not only the products offered but also the packaging and communication activities. 'Old' and 'New' have quite different meanings in the East and in the West. Motivation of the organization's personnel is also strongly influenced by the local culture and practice. Encouraging local sales forces to sell more by offering cars and more money, for example, may not work in all cultures. The SRC is a major obstacle in this area.

Education

The level of formal primary and secondary education in a foreign market will have direct impact upon the 'sophistication' of the target customers. A simple example will be the degree of literacy. The labelling of products, especially those with possibly hazardous side-effects, needs to be taken seriously for a market that has a very low literacy rate.

Social organization

This relates to the way in which a society organizes itself. It should consider kinship, social institutions, interest groups and status systems. The role of women and caste systems are easily identifiable examples. If your organization has a history of successfully marketing to 'the housewife/homemaker' life becomes more difficult where women have no social status at all. An example close to home would include Switzerland, where the majority of people rent rather than own their houses and expect to rent property with domestic appliances installed – in this case the banks are the largest single purchasers of washing machines!

In case you are asked to quote an example, it can be useful to try to understand, in reasonable depth, one or two international markets (culture/technology, etc.) and how things really work. One advanced and one less advanced market is usually enough. Depth knowledge used in one question could make all the difference.

Technology and material culture

This aspect relates not to 'materialism' but to the local market's ability to handle and deal with modern technology. Some cultures find leaving freezers plugged in overnight and servicing cars and trucks that have not yet broken down difficult concepts to manage. In instances such as these the organization is often faced with the choice of either educating the population (expensive) or de-engineering the product or service (often unpalatable to domestic engineers).

Law and politics

The legal and political environments in a foreign market are often and rightly seen as results of the culture of that market. Legal and political systems are often a simple codification of the norms of behaviour deemed acceptable by the local culture. These two aspects will be dealt with in more depth below.

Aesthetics

This area covers the local culture's perception of things such as beauty, good taste and design and dictates what is acceptable or 'appealing' to the local eye. An organization's decision as to aspects of the product or service involving colour, music, architecture or brand names needs to be sympathetic and acceptable to the local culture if purchase is to take place. For the unwary there are many, many traps in this area. Colour means completely different things in different cultures and brand names do not travel well!

Explain how an understanding of cultural factors would enable a salesperson to be more effective in international markets (June 1994). (**See** Exam answers at the end of this unit.)

The political environment

The political environment of international marketing includes any national or international political factor that can affect the organization's operations or its decision making. Politics has come to be recognized as the major factor in many international business decisions. It is a major factor in whether to invest and how to continue marketing. The best way to deal with this problem is for management to become fully informed of the situation and the firm must go beyond traditional market research to include the political environment.

There are a number of aspects to the political environment that should serve to guide you through this area and they are as follows.

The role of the government in the economy

What is the role of the government in the targeted local marketplace? Is it primarily undertaking a 'participation' role (strongly involved in the day-to-day activities of the economy) or is it primarily a 'regulator' (fixes the rules and regulations but tries to leave the market open to local competition and market forces)?

Ideologies and marketing

The ideological background of the government can give good insights into how it is likely to act/react with a foreign company operating in its marketplace. Ideologies such as capitalism, socialism and nationalism will clearly affect the way the government deals with overseas organizations and its likely approach to your marketing programmes when they are implemented.

Political stability

How stable is the government? Here much depends upon the organization's level of involvement and the amount of risk that the organization is prepared to take. Pure exporting is a very low-risk scenario and the political stability is of minor concern. If the organization is planning longer-term involvement and higher investment in the market, longer planning horizons may require a more rigorous analysis of government stability and governmental policy.

International relations

Two forms of international relations are important here: first, the relationship between the home government and the various host government or governments and second, the ongoing relationship between different host governments in those markets in which the organization wishes to operate. In the 1980s owning a subsidiary which operated in apartheid South Africa was a major liability for many international organizations.

If you work in an organization, find out how well your managers know the cultural aspects of their target markets. How well is this knowledge used in international marketing planning? Alternatively, analyse a well-known company and assess how well they do it.

The political threats

The primary consequences of wrongly assessing the political environment can prove extremely costly for the international organization. In the event of a serious 'falling out' between the organization and host government, local officials may have the power to confiscate company assets, expropriate them or simply increase governmental controls over the company assets located in their country. There are a number of instances where these actions have been taken and, despite loud voices and sabre rattling on the part of the home government, the costs to the international organization have been significant.

The legal environment

The legal environment is generated from the political climate and the prevalent attitudes towards business enterprise, that is, the nation's laws and regulations pertaining to business. It is important for the firm to know the legal environment in each of its markets because these laws constitute the 'rules of the game' for business activity. The legal environment in international marketing is more complicated than domestic since it has three dimensions: (1) domestic law, (2) international law and (3), domestic laws in the firm's home base.

There are a number of key aspects to the international legal environment:

- *Local domestic laws* These are all different! The only way to find a route through the legal maze in overseas markets is to use experts on the separate legal systems and laws pertaining in each market targeted.
- *International law* There are a number of 'international laws' that can affect the organization's activity. Some are international laws covering piracy and hijacking, others are more international conventions and agreements and cover items such as IMF and GATT treaties, patents and trademarks legislation (some differences by markets) and harmonization of legal systems within regional economic groupings.
- *Domestic laws* The organization's domestic (home market) legal system is important for two reasons. First, there are often export controls which limit the free export of certain goods and services to particular marketplaces and second, there is the duty of the organization to act and abide by its national laws in all its activities whether domestic or international.
- *Laws and the international marketing activity* It will be readily understandable how domestic international and local legal systems can have a major impact upon the organization's ability to market into particular overseas countries. Laws will affect the marketing mix in terms of products, price, distribution and promotional activities quite dramatically. 'Ignorance is no defence' tends to be a universal in all markets.

Should an international marketing manager concentrate upon customers or quality or competition when developing strategic plans? Justify your answer (December 1993).
(**See** Exam answers at the end of this unit).

The economic environment

The economic environment has long been recognized as an uncontrollable factor in the task of marketing management generally. The economic environment of international marketing is peculiar in two ways. First, it contains an international economic structure that affects marketing between nations, and second, it includes the domestic economy of every nation in which the firm is attempting to market. Thus the international marketer faces the traditional task of economic analysis but in a context that may include a hundred countries or more. This investigation will be directed towards two broad questions: (1) how big is the market and (2) what is the market like?

The first issue confronting the international marketer is to identify the likely size of the target market or markets. We can assess this in a number of ways:

- *Population size and growth* How big is the population and how fast is it growing? This will give an indication of likely current and future demand.
- *Population density and concentration* Where is the population located? How dense is the population and is the population concentrated in specific areas? Population concentration is important for two reasons. First, there are obvious questions of distribution and logistics. Second, when population becomes concentrated it often tends to take on a separate character. 'Urbanization' produces the need for different products and services.
- *Population age and distribution* How old is the average population and what is the distribution among the various age levels? The advanced economies of the West have rapidly ageing populations and offer certain market opportunities for particular products. Some African countries, on the other hand, have 50 per cent of their populations below the age of 15. This offers a completely different market opportunity for the international organization.
- *Disposable income and distribution* What is the available income in the population? Can enough people afford the proposed products or services that the organization can provide? Equally important, is the income concentrated into particular groups of people or is it widely distributed through the population? Remember that even in the poorest markets there are often pockets of extreme wealth that can afford and demand certain high quality luxury goods.

As well as the market size the international marketer should also try to understand the nature of the economy in which he or she proposes operating. There are a number of dimensions to this question:

- *Natural resources* What resources are available in the local marketplace that the organization may wish to use for its production? This may include natural resources (raw materials) as well as local management ability.

ACTIVITY 4.2

Spend some time with an atlas. Look at the world and at the natural topography. Even today these features can affect marketing plans and implementation. Can you see how?

- *Topography* This relates to the physical nature of the marketplace, rivers, mountains, lakes and the like. Natural features such as mountain ranges and rivers can provide serious barriers to communication, both physical and electronic in even the most advanced markets.
- *Climate* The climatic situations prevalent in a marketplace may require adaptations to product or to services from the domestic standard. Climate can affect both the delivery and the operation of the product and service. Consider water-cooled engines in drier climates and the management siesta in the Mediterranean!
- *Economic activity* What is the primary economic activity of the marketplace? Is it basically agricultural or is it industrial? Such indicators will give a good key as to the likely demand, lifestyles and product/service requirements.
- *Energy and communications* Energy sources and communications infrastructures that we take for granted in the advanced Western economies tend to be less readily available or less reliable in underdeveloped or less-developed markets. If the organization's business relies strongly upon speedier reliable communications then overseas markets need to be assessed carefully before entry is made.
- *Urbanisation* To what extent is the local market urbanized or rural? The level of urbanization will affect not only the types of products and services that are demanded but also the way in which these are delivered.

- *Differential inflation* What is the level of inflation relative to that of your domestic market or another market with which the target will be linked? If the organization is used to operating in areas and markets of low inflation, annual inflation rates of 500 or 1000 per cent may be beyond the realm of management expertise.

A number of models exist to classify various markets around the world according to different stages of economic growth and development. Examples of these would be:

1(a) Less developed countries (LDCs)
 (b) Newly industrialized countries (NICs)
 (c) Advanced economies
2(a) Self-sufficiency
 (b) Emergence
 (c) Industrialization
 (d) Mass consumption
 (e) Post-industrial society

(See Figure 4.3). Many of these classifications are useful shorthand and give an instant view of the classification of various economic marketplaces throughout the world. However, it is difficult to capture the special characteristics of individual markets in this way and oversimplification of this sort can be dangerous in any depth analysis. For example, the second model above (Figure 4.3) is based strongly on the natural evolution of economies through a regular industrialization process. It has difficulty in dealing with economies which are either artificially distorted by, for instance, sudden oil revenues or even those markets that are artificially controlled by Communist governments. The moral here is to treat such models as useful guidance but to temper this approach with some degree of commonsense.

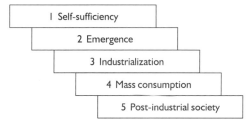

Figure 4.3 Stages of economic development

The technological environment

Technology is no longer subject to country boundaries although it is, to some extent, still subject to economics – not every company can afford to purchase the very latest technology. Technology can be very expensive for a number of organizations and countries, certainly if they wish to acquire state-of-the-art technology which is often necessary just to keep in the race as products and services become more and more developed. On the other hand, technology is currently reducing the barriers to entry to many industries by reducing the necessary scale of operations required to reach economically competitive cost levels.

Therefore we are seeing smaller markets and smaller countries becoming more feasible for the installation of local operations.

The final important aspect of technology, as it increases its worldwide reach, is a tendency on a global scale for production and services to increase. As a result, pressures on price and margins at a global level increase apace.

The competitive environment

Competition worldwide is increasing at both a global and a local level. Local markets are increasing by subject to international and global competition and, in addition, technology is facilitating competition from previously unexpected quarters. No longer are LDCs satisfied merely by exporting raw materials, they also want the additional margin that comes from manufacturing.

ACTIVITY 4.4

For a company and a market of your choice, can you identify:
- All the different forms of competition they face?
- Exactly how competition affects the development of international marketing plans?

At an international level advanced markets are seeing significant competition from both LDCs and NICs who are using modern technology and lower labour prices to compete in hitherto 'protected' marketplaces.

EXAM HINT

Competition is critical to the development of any form of marketing strategy – including international. Are you confident that you can apply Porter's competitive forces model to international marketing? You need to know how.

The complexity of international competition has been heightened by the strategic use of international sourcing of components to achieve competitive advantage. (Reference the Japanese electronics industry.)

The currency environment

The world currency environment, stimulated by worldwide trading and foreign exchange dealing, is an additional complication in the international environment. On top of all the normal vagaries of markets, customer demands, competitive actions and economic infrastructures, foreign exchange parities are likely to change on a regular if unpredictable basis. Such changes can be stimulated by a number of different factors, most of which are completely out of the control of the international marketing organization.

Difficult as it may be, foreign exchange movements need to be understood and, to some extent, predicted where possible. With increasing levels of competition and the consequent reduction in international margins, unpredicted exchange movements can, at a stroke, turn a brilliant strategy into a shambles – and profit into loss.

Foreign market selection

In too many instances the selection of foreign markets, often for considerable investment, would appear to be an informal process. Since a firm's resources are limited it is essential that enough resource is concentrated in a small enough number of markets to have an effect. Resources spread too thinly will not only fall short of 'critical mass' but will also serve to inform competitors of your intentions. Foreign market selection should be a prioritizing activity based on the three rules of 'potential', 'similarity' and 'accessibility'.

An organization should resist the temptation to attack too many markets at one time thereby spreading effort and resources too thinly to be successful. The initial effort should be directed at a single market and extended to other, possibly neighbouring markets later (see Figure 4.4).

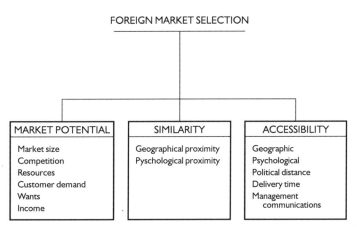

Figure 4.4 Foreign market selection

Market potential

The first critical measure of foreign market attractiveness is to try to assess the potential of the foreign market for profitable operations. There are a number of aspects to this question:

- *Market size*   How big is the market for our intended product or service? Remember that a straight reading of population may not be enough. We are interested in identifying the size of the market which could be potential purchasers for the product or service in question.
- *Competition*   How strong is the competition in the proposed marketplace? What is the picture of domestic and international competition either operating or contemplating entry into the marketplace? Will there be enough competition to stimulate growth but not too much competition to restrict profits to a possibly untenable level?
- *Resources*   What resources are available within the marketplace to support our entry and operations there? What resources ideally do we need? If the resources are not there at the moment can they be brought in from neighbouring markets at reasonable cost?
- *Customer demand, wants, income, etc.*   What do customers actually want? What is the level of demand? To what extent are current needs and wants being met by local or international competition? Is there available income to create profitable demand that the organization can meet? Remember, prospective customers who can't afford to pay is business we can find anywhere in the world!

For your company/a company of your choice what criteria did management actually use to select target foreign markets? How would you suggest improving the selection process?

Similarity (to home or other foreign markets)

In addition to the financial parameters of the marketplace it is important to understand whether the target market is close enough to either our home market (which we ought to understand) or to another foreign market which we understand because we are successfully operating there already:

- *Geographic proximity* Is the intended market geographically close for us to access it with our products or service and with the management expertise needed to satisfy customer needs?
- *Psychological proximity* Do we understand how the people in the marketplace think? Do we have a degree of rapport with the local culture? Will we understand management attitudes and activities in the local marketplace? Will they be able to interact with our organization's established culture and norms of behaviour?

Accessibility

Can we get to the marketplace? Accessibility can be judged on a number of different parameters, all of which are equally important to the development of a successful international marketing strategy:

In what ways would the marketing plans developed for mature products for lesser developed countries (LDCs) differ from plans relating to markets in more industrially advanced countries? Use examples to illustrate your answer, (December 1990).

(**See** Exam answers at the end of this unit.)

- *Geographic accessibility* Can we physically reach the marketplace and the separate segments or parts of the market within the local marketplace? Can we meet the lead times and delivery times required by the local customers to at least match, if not improve upon, competitive performances? Are there any physical or communication barriers which will stop us achieving these needs?
- *Psychological access* Do we understand the local culture and buyer requirements and needs sufficiently to be able to position the products or service to be relevant to local market conditions? Are we able to meet local buyers at an emotional as well as a rational level? (Remember, the majority of purchase decisions are taken on an emotional basis and not rationally – much as we might like them to be so.)
- *Political distance* How far away is the political system and government ideology and activity from what we are used to dealing with? Do we understand the political motivations and are we able to predict activities in the future? Is there a solid rapport between the home government and the host government and between the host government and other markets in which we operate?
- *Management communications* Any international marketing operation will require a level of local management in order to implement its plans. This may be carried out by local agents and/or distributors or local or expatriate staff employed by the company. In any event, the local management will have to be part of the local culture in order to implement any marketing strategy properly. Management attitudes, behaviours and

motivations tend to differ quite markedly among different cultures and it is important that the organization be able to communicate effectively with people on the ground. No international marketing strategy can be successfully implemented without this level of communication.

Summary

In this unit we have considered the various environmental factors which act upon the customer in a given or prospective foreign marketplace. We have seen the heavy impact of culture on buyer behaviour and perceptions as well as the infrastructure constraints delivered by legal, economic and political systems.

Technology, competition and currency are all moving to global stages and are having serious effects on international business worldwide. Although often difficult to predict, these effects cannot be ignored or international profitability will suffer badly.

Finally we considered how to select target markets on the basis of this analysis and the broad parameters required for successful marketing strategy implementation which follows.

Questions

As a check on your understanding of what has been covered in this unit, consider the following questions:

- What are the key aspects of the 'environment' which affect the foreign customer?
- What are the eight key aspects of culture?
- What effects can 'language' have on our international marketing strategy?
- What effects can 'religion' have on our international marketing strategy?
- What effects can 'values and attitudes' have on our international marketing strategy?
- What effects can 'education' have on our international marketing strategy?
- What effects can 'social organization' have on our international marketing strategy?
- What effects can 'technology' have on our international marketing strategy?
- What effects can 'aesthetics' have on our international marketing strategy?
- What are the two main roles of government in the economy? How will our international operations be affected by foreign governments?
- What are the main aspects of the international legal environment? How will our international operations be affected by these?
- What are the key aspects of the international economic environment that the organization should consider? How will these affect our international operations?
- What role can models of economic growth and development play in the formulation of international marketing strategy?
- What are the main aspects of the international technological environment? How will these affect our international operations?
- What are the main aspects of the international competitive environment? How will these affect our international operations?
- What are the three parameters by which we can prioritise and select foreign markets?

For a more detailed analysis and explanation of customers and their environments, read:

International Marketing, S. Paliwoda, Butterworth-Heinemann, 1993, pp. 53–71.
International Marketing Strategy, C. Phillips, I. Doole and R. Lowe, Routledge, 1994, pp. 83–122.

EXTENDING KNOWLEDGE

39

December 1990   To achieve best results your answer should have provided a balanced approach to the question. Too wide an answer just on the importance of culture is not sufficient, neither is a detailed analysis of the importance of colours in Japan! A good answer needs to be realistic. The chairman should try to learn some Japanese but it is unrealistic to expect fluency. The general structure of the answer should have been built around the nature of culture and the impact of the SRC. You might have considered the problems between a meeting of 'low-context' and 'high-context' cultures. The answer should concentrate on the specific requirements of an initial sales visit – the need for good preparation, literature, business cards and the need to understand the decision-making process and to be prepared for the length of time needed before a decision is reached.

June 1994   The main reason for candidates failing this question in 1994 was not understanding what was asked. If your answer is just a jumble of bits and pieces about culture – ignoring selling and the selling process it will not be acceptable. Your answer needs to demonstrate a good understanding of:

- What is selling
- The selling process
- Relationship between selling and the buying process.

Selling requires high-level negotiation skills. Empathy – an important means of understanding buyers – will be considerably impaired without an understanding of cultural factors.

December 1993   This question does not use the word 'culture' in the text but is dominated by cultural implications. Your answer should have covered 'customers', 'quality' and 'competition' – all in an 'international context'.

After defining the terms, a good answer would explain how the company copes with the considerable variations in customer requirements, the customer's ability to pay for high-quality products and great differences in the type and intensity of competition in different parts of the world. Culture is a key factor in understanding both customer needs and perceptions of 'quality'.

December 1991   If your answer is long on culture but short on the industrial buying process it is unlikely to achieve a pass mark. To pass, the candidate must demonstrate an understanding of industrial buying:

- the group process of decision making (DMU)
- different types of buying
- interaction between buyer and seller.

The engineering company needs to apply its knowledge of industrial buyer behaviour to other markets in other countries. This knowledge must be modified by different cultural influences. The SRC must be avoided and the company needs to consider how elements of the culture influence the buying process.

Good answers would develop a conclusion which demonstrated that both a knowledge of the industrial buying process and its application in different cultures is essential for business success. Also important are the appropriate selection of markets and method of market entry.

December 1990   This question asks for much more than just an explanation of how products may need to be modified for international markets. The marketing plans require a review of all elements of the marketing mix.

Good answers to this question need to know how the local environment drives changes in the marketing plan. The LDC environment will differ from that of an advanced country in a number of ways: culture, politics, legal, economics, technology and competition will all be different and will likely require changes to be made in all areas of the marketing mix.

Using examples (these are obligatory, not optional!) show how a range of adaptations are likely to be necessary in a poorer country.

International market research

Knowledge is power. In this unit you will study the key issues relating to gathering information on the international front. The scale of the task is wider and the problems in collecting data multiply as markets and customers differ. The major thrust of the unit is not concerned with the specifics and technical details of gathering information but discusses the management perspective. You will:

- Understand issues relating to scanning international markets to decide initially where we should go in the broadest terms
- Examine models of how to approach the broad tasks of identifying market/product combinations and on to prioritize opportunities
- Study the sources of international data and have to deal with such issues as researching within numerous markets
- Understand the difficulties involved in comparing data across countries/markets – both primary and secondary data
- Know the basic principles of appointing an international market research agency

Having completed the unit you will be able to:

- Explain the difference between gathering data from an international market(s) and that of a domestic one
- Apply the process of narrowing down broad-scale international opportunities and identify specific countries for further more detailed examination
- Match sources of data to specific problems
- Identify the resource implications of international market research.

International market research needs to be considered stage by stage. It is unfeasible for even the major global players to be totally global in their research. Time and the scale of the task dictates a measured approach. Costs are equally important. The unit takes the approach that information searches begin on the broad scale and subsequently narrow down. Initially the question is 'Where should we go?' With as many as 200 countries to select how does one go about prioritizing? Think about the implication of planning and control against this background. Remember as you work through this unit that the biggest problem is not so much obtaining data but being selective about what data is essential rather than 'Let's collect everything we can'. Again, consider the issues surrounding the comparability of data, e.g. specific words are culturally loaded. What is a 'small business'? What does 'healthy' mean or 'leisure', 'home owner' etc.? These words in common use nonetheless mean different things in different countries.

International market research

As international marketing has developed rapidly in recent years so has the need for information and knowledge. For example, international marketing research, (i.e. research into the application of the 4/7 Ps to a market) is taking an increasingly important role in strategic planning. It is estimated that the 1990s have seen its growth exceed 30 per cent per annum – twice the rate of UK domestic research growth.

When discussing the changes taking place in world trading in an earlier chapter it was apparent that information, knowledge gathering and transference attains critical importance in decision making. Peter Bartram, of Applied Research and Communications, identified three key areas of development:

1 Development of improved techniques, data availability and research supplier networks in developing countries. (e.g. India and the Pacific Rim.)
2 In more developed countries where market research is more established the key competence will be:
   - Development of pan-regional or global surveys allowing a comparison of data
   - The identification of niche markets across national boundaries creating clusters of customers with similar motivations and needs
   - The specialization of research organizations on a regional/worldwide basis. The more detailed your knowledge search, the greater will be the need for appropriate expertise
   - Rapid defusion of new products internationally will dictate faster research delivery.
3 In mature markets the forefront of research may move into the development of database market research via electronic transfers and the deeper involvement of research into 'value' discriminators in identifying segments within markets.

This unit adopts the outlook that the decision has been taken to 'go international' and, furthermore, our view is to concentrate on the information gathering that relates to marketing issues (strategic and tactical).

The scale of the task: personnel and money

With around 200 countries to aim at even the Coca-Cola's and McDonald's of this world would find it a challenge to undertake research everywhere. For those medium to large UK companies who in the normal course of events conduct, shall we say, ten pieces of research per annum in the UK the task of replicating that in Europe alone would require a budget way in excess of most companies' resources to say nothing of the organizational and operational ramifications. Clearly there has to be a systematic approach at conducting international marketing research.

What information?

1 *Where to go?* Having decided to internationalize, the first critical consideration is the need to rank countries in order of priority or attractiveness.
2 *How to get there?* Having decided where to go, the next decision area is how to access the market(s), i.e. exporting, licensing or local production, etc.
3 *What shall we market?* Should we modify our product or service, in what way and to what degree, i.e. the start of the application of the marketing mix, the product P.
4 *How to we persuade them to buy it?* The development of the mix via the necessary Ps (place, price, etc.) and incorporating all four or seven depending on the nature of our offer (product or service).

The information stream

What information should market research provide? The following list sets out the least intelligence needed.

1   *Where to go*
    - Assessment of global demand
    - Ranking of potential by country/region
    - Local competition
    - Political risk
2   *How to get there*
    - Size of market/segments
    - Barriers to entry
    - Transport and distribution costs
    - Local competition
    - Government requirements
    - Political risk
3   *What shall we market?*
    - Government regulations
    - Customer sophistication
    - Competitive stance
4   *How do we persuade them to buy it?*
    - Buyer behaviour
    - Competitive practice
    - Distribution channels
    - Media and other promotional channels
    - Company expertise

Table 5.1 augments this abbreviated list and embraces the point that in today's challenging environment the successful domestic firm cannot ignore international market research for

Table 5.1   The task of global marketing research: what should it determine?

	Differences across countries and regions of interest			
The marketing environment	*The competition*	*The product*	*Marketing mix*	*Firm-specific historical data*
Political context: leaders, national goals, ideology, key institutions	Relative market shares	Analysis of users	Channels of distribution: evolution and performance	Sales trends by product and product-line, salesforce and customer
Economic growth prospects, business cycle stage	New product moves Pricing and cost structure	Who are the end-user industries? Industrial and consumer buyers	Relative pricing, elasticities and tactics	Trends by country and region
Per capita income levels, purchasing power	Image and brand reputation Quality: its attributes and positioning relative to competitors	Characteristics: size, age, sex, segment growth rates Purchasing power and intentions	Advertising and promotion: choices and impacts on customers	Contribution margins
End-user industry growth trends		Customer response to new products, price, promotion	Service quality: perceptions and relative positioning	Marketing mix used, marketing response functions across countries and regions
Government: legislation, regulation, standards, barriers to trade	Competitor's strengths: favourite tactics and strategies	Switching behaviour Role of credit and purchasing Future needs Impact of cultural differences	Logistics networks, configuration and change	

Source: Terpstra and Sarathy (1994)

inbound competition is accelerating. This is particularly true within the EU, which should be viewed increasingly as a domestic market.

Research methodology

Scanning international markets/countries

In the initial stage countries are scanned for attraction and prioritization. The search may be extremely wide covering many countries, and three criteria lend themselves to this exercise:

1   *Accessibility*   Can we get there? What's preventing us? Trade barriers, government regulations, etc.?
2   *Profitability*   Can 'they' (i.e. potential customers) afford our product? Is competition too entrenched? Is the market ready? What is the likely payback? Timescale? Will we get paid? Remember, unprofitable business we can get anywhere!
3   *Market size*   Present and future trends.

Gilligan and Hird (1985) identified three types of market opportunities:

1   *Existing markets*   Markets already covered by existing products/suppliers making market entry difficult without a superior offering
2   *Latent markets*   Evidence of potential demand but with no product yet offered, making entry easier. No direct competition
3   *Incipient markets*   No current demand exists but condition and trends suggest future emergent demand.

Figure 5.1 allies the three types of market opportunities to three types of products:

1   *Competitive product*   A 'me too' offering with no significant advantages
2   *Improved product*   While not unique has a discernable advantage over present offerings.
3   *Breakthrough product*   An innovation with significant differentiation.

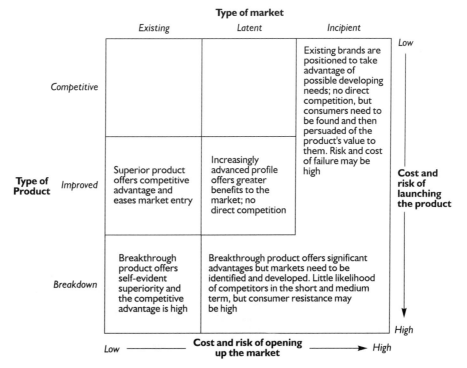

Figure 5.1   Product/market combinations and the scope for competitive advantage on market entry. (*Source*: Gilligan and Hird, 1985)

Figure 5.1 provides an insight into the nature of the marketing task needed. It forms the basis for further detailed investigation (e.g. the degree of competitive advantage and other dynamics).

Method of scanning in underdeveloped countries

Frequently in international marketing it is not easy to obtain relevant information directly, or without resort to expensive research methodologies. When a broad overview only is required/sufficient at this stage and concern is mainly to eliminate non-starters other methods of scanning markets, particularly in developing countries, include the following.

Analogy estimation

Given the absence of significant hard data researchers might rely on analogous countries by either a 'cross-section comparison' of economic indicators, disposable income or a 'time series approach' estimating that country B is developing or following a similar pattern of development (and therefore product usage) as country A. The limitations of analogy estimation is to assume linear patterns of development and should be used as a first stage and inexpensive screening.

Regression analysis

A more sophisticated development of the analogous method involves studying, for example, the relationship between economic growth indicators and demand for specific products in countries with both kinds of data (country A), then transferring it to countries with similar economic growth data, but no product data (country B). For example, if £100 equivalent in per capital GNP in country A resulted in an increase of 10 cars, 20 fridges, 8 TV sets, etc. per 1000 population, the same might well occur in country B. The limitations of this approach are also obvious as no two countries are totally alike.

Cluster analysis

Using macro economic and consumption data is a popular technique of identifying similar markets, for example:

- *Infrastructure dynamics*   energy consumption, urbanization, motorway and other transport facilities such as airports, containerization etc.
- *Consumption variation*   numbers of cars, telephones, educational level
- *Trade data*   import and export figures
- *Health and education*   life expectancy, number of doctors.

Improvisation

This is literally extrapolating data between broadly similar countries and in a way 'second guessing' the potential product need and demand in those countries (Table 5.2).

Finally, there are other methods that may warrant your attention. For example, risk evaluation is obviously important (see political risk).

Table 5.2

Level of institution	Potential markets
1. Market Square	Cloth material (not made up), a village economy
2. Church, elementary school	Small forms economy, packaged goods, radios, bikes, garage, petrol, etc.
3. Secondary school, police, government building	Urbanization (first steps), social dresses, fridges, plumbing, etc.
4. Higher education, sewage system	Factories, office supplies and service industries

Source: Terpstra 2nd edn

International market segmentation: prioritization

The scanning method represents phase 1 in international marketing research. The next stage is to evaluate markets/countries in order to prioritize them for still further investigation. The key issue here is not simply to list countries in terms of priorities, but to group them in clusters or segments. We are searching for *similarities* more than differences. Similarities provide:

1   Economies of scale
2   Optimization in marketing
3   Easier diffusion of products
4   Ease of operation, management and control
5   Greater profitability

Unfortunately marketers spend too much time highlighting differences between markets/ countries and forget to identify the areas of similarity and convergence. It is similarities that determine whether a pan-regional or global approach is possible. This is becoming increasingly critical for companies particularly in the EU, where harmonization is under way.

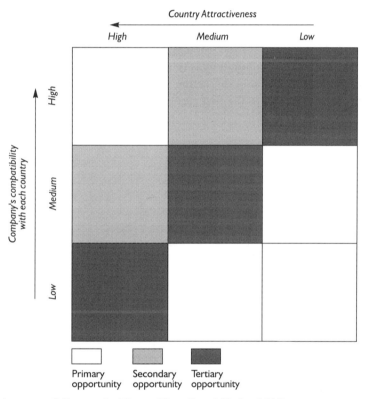

Figure 5.2 Business portfolio matrix (*Source*: Harrell and Kiefer, 1993)

The major methodology is to classify countries into categories as illustrated in Figure 5.2. Broadly, countries fall into three groups:

1   *Primary markets* where high attractiveness coincides with a high degree of company strengths. This might lead to the company investing heavily within the country(ies)
2   *Secondary markets* riskier but where there is still significant business to be gained albeit through a lower level of strategic investment
3   *Tertiary markets* business gained via short-term, *ad hoc* and opportunist activity with no serious commitment in an operational sense. However, good profit may be earned here and it is no reason not to do business providing the level of financial investment and risk to exposure is low.

Once key markets/countries have been identified and prioritized further market research is necessary to identify customer segments within the chosen countries using the recognized and standard quantitative and qualitative research techniques – demographics, buyer behaviour, consumer motivation, lifestyle, etc. This further research is critical for although the international segmentation model described above identifies clusters of countries, the key to successful international marketing is discovering clusters or segments of customers. Country segmentation is therefore often oversimplistic, for it pays insufficient attention to customer similarities across national boundaries.

Kole and Sudharshan (1987) speak of firms needing to achieve strategically equivalent segments (SES) that transcend national boundaries. They contend that to achieve SES companies need to:

1 Identify countries with sufficient infrastructure to support its product and that are lucrative to the company
2 Screen those countries to arrive at a realistic short-list (e.g. those countries with a sufficiently large segment)
3 Develop micro-segments within those countries identified by product characteristics required
4 Identify the key characteristics of the demand of each micro-segment searching for similarities in terms of behaviourial pattern
5 Through cluster analysis identify meaningful cross-national segments which would respond similarly to a consistent marketing mix strategy.

The search is under way to unravel customer behaviour and response similarities across Europe. The major European multinationals (e.g. Nestlé) are fast acquiring and developing Euro brands. To achieve synergies in marketing they are seeking Euro consumers. It is early days but Euro Mosaic is claimed as the first pan-European consumer segmentation system to classify consumers on the basis of neighbourhood having identified ten Euro neighbourhood classifications:

1 Elite suburbs
2 Average areas
3 Luxury flats
4 Low-income city
5 High-rise social housing
6 Industrial communities
7 Dynamic families
8 Low-income families
9 Rural/agricultural
10 Vacation/retirement

As can be seen, the segmentation is broad – and, frankly, is at an early development stage. However, in the absence of more sophisticated approach it is a start.

Nielsen has introduced Quartz, its first pan-European research service, which provides simulated market tests based on consumer reaction in five European countries. Procter & Gamble, Nestlé and in total 25 multinationals subscribe to the service. Europanel, a pan-European panel consortium, checks 55 000 households monitoring the movement and consumptions of consumer goods. Ipsos, a French company, evaluates consumers' viewing and reading habits in major EU countries. The demand for quality multi-country research is still in its infancy and we can anticipate rapid growth in, for example, pan-European quantitative and qualititative comparative research across national boundaries.

The international marketing information system
Phillips, Doole and Lowe (1994) refer to the 12C analysis model for creating an information system:

Country
- General country information
- Basic SLEPT data
- Impact of environmental dimensions.

Choices
- Analysis of supply
- International and external competition
- Characteristics of competitors
- Import analysis
- Competitive strengths and weaknesses.

Concentration
- Structure of the market segments
- Geographical spread.

Culture/consumer behaviour
- Characteristics of the country
- Diversity of cultural grouping
- Nature of decision-making
- Major influences of purchasing behaviour.

Consumption
- Demand and end-use analysis of economic sectors that use the product
- Market share by demand sector
- Growth patterns of sectors
- Evaluation of the threat of substitute products.

Capacity to pay
- Pricing
- Extrapolation of pricing to examine trends
- Culture of pricing
- Conditions of payment
- Insurance terms.

Currency
- Stability
- Restrictions
- Exchange controls.

Channels
- Purchasing behaviour
- Capabilities of intermediaries
- Coverage of distribution costs
- Physical distribution infrastructure.

Commitment
- Access to market
- Trade incentives and barriers
- Custom tariffs
- Government regulations
- Regulations on market entry.

Communication
- Promotion
- Media infrastructure and availability
- Which marketing approaches are effective
- Cost of promotion
- Common selling practices
- Media information.

Contractual obligations
- Business practices
- Insurance
- Legal obligations.

Caveats
- Factors to be aware of.

Without doubt, collection of this information is a formidable task – well beyond the resources of all but the largest firms. Even these will find difficulties in drawing the comparison and making the necessary links between countries to assist in the creation of potentially profitable segments. Having made this point a list is useful as a consistent point of reference.

Identify and justify the marketing researach approach you would recommend to a company that wishes to assess global market potential (December 1994, Question 6).

(**See** Exam answers at the end of this unit.)

Sourcing international market research

Where and how do we find international information – and the problems involved? Terpstra and Sarathy state that because of its complexity international market research generates more and different problems than domestic research. Because countries are different, each poses its own set of problems. Furthermore, how does one deal with gathering information from dozens or up to a hundred countries?

The breadth of the task

International market research covers macro economic, micro economic, cultural, political and a host of other variables. Also, because of the drive towards internationalization, markets can no longer be studied individually – they must be screened for similarities to develop pan-regional or even global markets. It follows that the international market researcher (or the division) has a far wider remit than any domestic research organization making the creation of an MIS system even more important.

The problem of numerous markets

Besides such important considerations as cost and because countries are different the international researchers must take into consideration various problems in designing and interpreting multi-country research. Mayer identifies some basic considerations:

- *Definition error*   countries often define markets and categories differently e.g. the term 'small business' varies across Europe
- *Instrument error*   arising from the detail written on questionnaires
- *Frame error*   sampling frames vary by country
- *Selection error*   problems arising from the way the actual sample is selected from the frame
- *Non-response error*   the cultural variance.

Returning to the issue of costs, how much research can we afford? A sense of realism must prevail, we can't research everything and the organization must refer to its resources and the timescales involved.

Secondary data – acquiring them and problems with them

With so many markets to consider it is essential that companies begin their international market research by seeking and utilizing secondary data, i.e. data that already exist and are generally available at low cost. For those who are unclear in terminology secondary research is frequently referred to as desk research.

Many countries are awash with secondary data but, in general, there is a correlation between the stage of economic development and the availability, depth and accuracy of information. Where it is available it is generally plentiful, cheap and accurate; where it is not its quality is variable, its relevance dubious and its accuracy flawed. As a preliminary stage of investigation secondary research can quickly unearth general background information to eliminate many countries from the scope of enquiries. Such information might include:

- Population, language(s), ethnic differences
- Type of government, political stability and that of neighbouring countries, risk of war, etc., social policies
- Location, geography, topography, climate
- Basic economic data, income and its distribution, employment, industry versus agriculture, policy towards businesses, tax structure, private versus government sector split
- Legal information, regulations, barriers to entry and exit (of profits), member of GATT, etc.
- Overseas trade patterns, with UK, other nations, importance of exports and imports to the economy.

All this material forms a good solid basis for initial screening purposes but falls some way short of providing marketing information to help pinpoint real customer needs and wants. Most of the above information can be unearthed on the majority of countries but it is only in the more sophisticated countries that you might discover the following:

- Size of market (as defined locally), its make-up and structures
- Who are main customers, who buys what (what are the available products) and, very importantly, why they buy (motivations for purchase)
- Competition, scope and practices (marketing mix)
- Promotional practices – availability, sophistication, legal restrictions
- Distribution patterns – where customers buy (supermarkets or market squares), intermediaries (choice and number of stages)
- Pricing, how much customers pay, what the trade structure is in terms of mark-up margins
- Service element; after-sales guarantees, who fixes the product if/when it breaks

Note: The list is not complete, it is indicative of the broad range of data services available in the UK.

Problems with secondary data are as follows:

1. The non-availability of data. Westernized countries apart, the rest of the world varies considerably in its statistical output. The weaker economies have weaker statistical services – many do not carry out a population census. In some countries there is only an estimate of the population.
2. The reliability of the data. Data may have been massaged by governments to prove a particular point or to gain funds from world bodies. Again the data may be time-lagged or even old and therefore may have limited bearing on the status quo.
3. The source of the data will inevitably reflect local/national conditions and may be meaningless to outsiders.
4. Comparability across markets is difficult. The terms 'car owner', 'small business', 'householder', 'youth', 'health', 'engineer' mean different things in each country.
5. Availability of sources either private or public varies enormously. The international major corporation such as A. C. Nielsen (the world's No. 1 researcher) is operating only in 28 countries. It and others are totally absent in more than half the countries in the

world. Trade associations, chambers of commerce, all are equally variable in their existence and indeed in their output for they too mean different things country by country. In France, chambers of commerce are very powerful organizations, but what information might you expect from Bowkino Faso?

Primary research – acquiring it and problems with it

In dealing with primary research we are discussing the everyday research technique utilized in our domestic market to unearth usage and attitude information concerning our company's customers, their choices and preferences, the stimuli that motivates them to behave positively to our products, prices, promotional practices, etc. By the time primary research is to be employed the organization will have narrowed down its choice of potential markets to a few. The complexity and cost of generating new, first-hand information is formidable. For example, a national usage and attitude survey in the UK might cost upwards of £80 000. Imagine replicating this across Europe.

We are not going to discuss the techniques of primary research, which should be familiar to readers. Instead we highlight the problems involved in carrying it out overseas.

Problems with primary research

Countries are different, people are different and respond differently. This makes uniformity of information a potential and often real nightmare from a research standpoint as SRC are imposed. Let us examine some of the more obvious ones:

1   *Costs*   Conducting primary research varies. The UK is one of the least expensive, Japan one of the most expensive.
2   *Language*   In which language should the survey be conducted? Singapore with a population of about 3 million has four official languages requiring four translations and four different ethnic interviewers:
    • Interpretation of languages (translation) is frequently misleading and even back-translation into the author's language can be flawed. What is required is not translation but transposition of the questionnaire into the respondent's cultural framework. This is very sophisticated and difficult.
    • Literacy: pictorials are not easy to understand or interpret. Technical literacy is also a frequent problem, i.e. the non-comprehension of things abstract, etc., time or concepts such as health, leisure, etc.
3   *Sample*   in a non-urban or low urbanized country where will you find AB respondents? They may be scattered far and wide. In Muslim countries who do you interview, buyer (male) or the user (female)? Interviewing the latter is rare.
4   *Geography*   Where do you conduct the survey? For example, in Nigeria, the north is desert, the south Equatorial. Responses in one area may have no relevance in another. Similarly, tribal differences in a country will elicit different responses.
5   *Non Response*   The Japanese always like to please and invariably say 'Yes'. Then they really mean they don't like your product. 'I will consider it very carefully' is Japanese for *no*. In other societies being interviewed has connotations of 'agents of the state' or, worse, tax inspectors.
6   *Social Organization*   In some societies even business-to-business and industrial markets are affected. Unlike the West, companies are often family owned where openness is frowned upon and secrecy is important. Furthermore, Western terminology may have little direct relevance (e.g. cash flow, stock turnover are not everyday terminologies).
7   *Terminology*   The point has already been made concerning the interpretation of language as it is bounded by SRC. What do we mean by holidays, well off, health food, live alone, family, youth, middle aged? In the USA researchers have divided the country into 62 separate classes according to wealth, education, mobility, location, ethnic background etc. Among the new classes are Urban Gold Coasters, Young Literati and Scrubbed Piners (Figure 5.3). Consider also the article in Figure 5.4 which appeared in connection with a survey about attitudes to drink-driving and attempt to explain the categories of offenders to anyone other than to a UK citizen. Come to think of it, explain the concept of drink-driving itself . . . .

A member of the Scrubber class

MARKETING experts have divided the country into 62 separate classes according to wealth and education, mobility, location and ethnic and racial background. Among the new classes are Urban Gold Coasters, Young Literati and Scrubbed Piners.
Washington Post

Yuck, it must be health food

OVERHEARD in a Manhattan health food store as a mother coaxed her son into trying fruit-candy: 'It doesn't taste good,' he complained. 'Of course not,' she replied. 'It's health food.'
New York Times

Figure 5.3 (*Source: The Guardian*, 21 December 1994)

The culprits

Persistent middle-aged offender image 'a myth'

THE IMAGE of the persistent drink-drive offender as middle-class, middle-aged and likely to drink twice the legal limit is dismissed as a myth by a new study, *writes Rebecca Smithers*.

The study, carried out by the Portman Group (a drinks industry initiative against alcohol misuse) in association with the Department of Transport, identified five main types of drink-drive offender; from the 'persisters' likely to have previous convictions and often unemployed, through to the 'young irresponsibles' who new their driving was impaired by drinking but who still took the risk.

The Portman Group says the problem of drinking and driving extends downwards into the teenage years and upwards into the mid-30s. High risk offenders tend to be slightly older – their peak age is 29 compared to 24 for all offenders. But it concludes there is 'little evidence of a significant problem among drivers in the 40s in the higher socio-economic groups'.

The problem of drink driving is still largely a male one; in 1992, only 7 per cent of drink-related fatal accidents involved a woman driver over the legal limit. Last year, only around 12 per cent of those who failed a breath test after an injury accident were women.

Altogether, drink-drive fatalities have fallen from 1550 in 1982 to 550 last year.

The five main types of drink-drive offender are:

☐ Persisters: 23 per cent of sample, aged 25 to 44, typically drinking beer (81 per cent) or strong beer (16 per cent) in pubs or at home before offending. Often unemployed, C2DE men with previous convictions for drink-driving and other crimes.

☐ Refuters: 22 per cent of sample, aged 25 to 54, typically drinking beer (80 per cent) or strong beer (13 per cent) in pubs before offending. They are C2DEs, deny drink-driving is wrong, and feel chances of being stopped are remote. Think they are good drivers, unaffected by drinking.

☐ Devastated professionals: 19 per cent of sample, aged 25 to 44, 72 per cent drinking beer, 16 per cent wine, 16 per cent spirits either in pubs or at home before offending. Predominantly middle-aged, ABs of C1s. Shocked at being treated as criminals. Felt they were able to drive after drinking.

☐ Young irresponsibles: 17 per cent of sample, aged 20 to 35, typically drinking strong beer at home or at friends' homes before offending. C1s and C2s with a carefree attitude to life, easily influenced in a group, and inexperienced drivers. Knew their driving was impaired but still took the risk.

☐ One-offs: 7 per cent of sample, aged 35 to 54, C1C2DEs, typically drinking beer at friends' or relatives' homes before offending. Unusual circumstances such as celebration, argument or depression led to offence. Severely affected by conviction, claimed to be reformed as a result.

Figure 5.4 (*Source: The Guardian*, 21 December 1994)

In conclusion, it is certain that some cultural bias will exist in all primary research activities as SRC are applied. It is also evident that SRC will exist between the client company and the organization(s) conducting the research if they are from different cultures.

Attempts are being made to make order out of cross-country research by using structured questionnaires, telephone interviews and postal surveys, but again infrastructure variables and cultural differences interfere. For example, some countries have a less than perfect postal service and telephone ownership is restricted to the elite. Furthermore such techniques are applicable only to certain areas.

Finally, the key to minimizing the variable response in primary research is superior research design, transposition of words and concepts in its cultural reference, an understanding (by the researcher) of the problem involved and the skill in interpretation of data into information and knowledge. With close to 50 per cent of the world's primary research being conducted in Europe there is clearly a long way to go.

Planning and organizing for international market research

We are going to focus on the medium to large firm as it is apparent that small firms will have too many restrictions to engage in multi-country primary research and will rely on gathering secondary data. Additionally, they will rely on channel intermediaries for their information.

The extent to which medium to large firms will engage in international market research will similarly be guided by the nature of the market and its customers, company resources, its marketing expertise and the scale of the task. A major consideration is whether to conduct the research in-house or to appoint external agencies. An industrial scenario might be handled in-house (there being few customers and each being identifiable) whereas a consumer goods scenario lends itself to the use of external research agencies.

In choosing an agency Phillips, Doole and Lowe suggest six options:

- An agency local to the chosen market
- A domestic agency with overseas subsidiaries
- A domestic agency with overseas associates
- A domestic agency with subcontracted fieldwork
- A domestic agency with competent foreign staff
- A global agency

The choice will depend on the variables in the market(s), the desired strategic level of marketing involvement on the part of the client company and the scale of the marketing task to be undertaken eventually. Further consideration includes:

- Language issues
- The level of 'specialist knowledge of the market'
- The budget
- The level of interpretation post-research

This suggests that there is no one solution and that companies select agencies appropriate to the task. It is vital to brief the agency(ies) carefully and to maintain a close relationship throughout. Piloting the research may be essential if comparative data are required. Care in analysis and interpretation of the data is equally important. The management role in organizing and coordinating international marketing research is not to be underestimated, especially if the findings are to be disseminated from one country to another in assisting marketing planning decisions.

EXAM QUESTIONS

- Identify the factors that would influence the choice of a market research agency the carry out a multi-country survey. Examine the rationale for carrying out research in the countries surrounding the Mediterranean from a base in Cyprus (June 1994, Question 7).
- Explain the process and problems of commissioning a marketing research survey in several different countries in which the comparability of results is a key issue (June 1993, Question 10).

(**See** Exam answers at the end of this unit.)

Summary

All too frequently organizations fall back on one of two strategies when dealing with information issues on the international front. Self-reference criteria i.e. foreigners are just like us and if we licked the problem 'here' we can do it overseas or, alternatively, use guesswork. Both approaches invariably result in grief. It is clear that if information = knowledge = power then it is even more important that we have the facts in dealing with environments beyond our normal range of experience. Knowing where to start and how to go about gathering information on overseas nations and customers must be the fundamental benchwork that underpins all our thinking.

Questions

- As the international marketing for Coca-Cola how would you monitor reactions around the world to a major competitor such as Pepsi?
- Identify the advantages and disadvantages of both secondary and primary data in international marketing.
- Why is it so difficult to assess demand for a product in multi-country research?
- Explain how screening can be used to prioritize international markets. Illustrate your answer by the use of models.
- Select a product category (e.g. Shampoo). What criteria might you apply to evaluate information internationally?
- Identify a major international firm in your locality. Establish what kinds of help in terms of marketing information assistance are available in the UK.
- Contact the DTI (or the equivalent bureau in your country) with a view to obtaining marketing information for a specific country.

For additional supporting information read:
International Marketing, V. Terpstra and R. Sarathy, The Dryden Press, 1944, Chapter 7.
International Marketing Strategy, C. Phillips, I. Doole and R. Lowe, Routledge, 1994, Chapter 4.
International Marketing, S. Paliwoda, Butterworth-Heinemann, 1993, Chapter 4.
Global Marketing Strategies, J.-P. Jeannet and H. D. Hennessey, Houghton Mifflin, 1994, Chapter 6

EXTENDING KNOWLEDGE

December 1994, Question 6 The approach to take is to recognize that the question is discussing global issues. The likely model to apply is possibly OPAR (Objectives, Planning Action and Review) in the broadest sense. The question does not ask you to deal with micro or tactical issues but to show how market research might be used to identify opportunities in broad strategic terms. Here some of the screening models referred to in the first part of the unit would be your point of reference. Clearly the methodology would rest with secondary research – the use of regression analysis and the Gilligan and Hird model, etc. A final yet fundamental point to consider are elements of costs, personnel and, of course, control. See Phillips, Doole and Lowe (1994).

June 1994, Question 7 The question revolves around management issues in international market research. It is essentially a straightforward question and is not complicated (most candidates wrote overcomplicated answers dealing with tactics). In the first place, the agency must have experience and proven competence in carrying out multi-country surveys. They must have an understanding of both the markets and countries concerned, and they must be cost efficient. The agency must have the

EXAM ANSWERS

resources to both carry out (or at least supervise) the field work. The agency must be adaptable and flexible and must ensure comparability and compatibility of results – via translation and transposition of questions in the required languages.

The choice of Cyprus: essentially a neutral country in a multi-ethnic Mediterranean environment in that it is non-aligned politically (ignoring, if one dare, north Cyprus). You may wish to expand on the cultural suitability of Cyprus – relatively sophisticated, good communication within the region, educated workforce – used for interfacing across cultures, etc.

June 1993, Question 10   Again a management of research question. The initial step is the process, i.e. to consider who will do the research (e.g. local agencies versus a UK coordinator using associates). It is likely that the second is the preferred route. The second step raises problems relating to the comparability of results and candidates would be expected to demonstrate knowledge of the problems associated with compatibility, language, translations, frames samples, etc. Be certain your answer deals mainly with primary research and not secondary data, as the question asked you to deal with a multi-country research survey.

International market planning

This unit is concerned with the ways in which the firm can exploit defined marketing opportunities in international markets and how best it can organize itself. In studying the unit you will:

- Understand the concepts of international marketing strategy
- Come to terms with the importance of planning
- Review the key planning models and match marketing variables to strategic international decisions
- Understand the basics of an international marketing plan
- Recognize that control systems are even more important internationally than domestically
- Identify the key organizational issues that concern international development.

Having completed the unit you will be able to:

- Cross-reference planning with strategic issues
- Evaluate the suitability of specific marketing strategies
- Identify the elements of an international marketing plan
- List the stages of the control process and establish key principles of a control system
- Explain the different methods a firm might employ in creating and developing its international organization
- Explain the variables that affect organizational structure
- Evaluate the roles and conflicts of HQ versus local management structures.

This unit is concerned with planning in an international environment. Students must familiarize themselves with the planning process before addressing this unit. Therefore you must first have read one of the recognized texts (e.g. *The Strategic Marketing Management* workbook in this series) which will inform you on additional reading. Most students are unfamiliar with international planning and therefore it is especially important you read the texts in the Extending knowledge section at the end of the unit.

Strategic planning and control

It is not the intention to cover Planning and Control issues in depth as the benefits of Planning and the models we employed in the planning process are dealt with fully in the *Strategic Marketing Management* workbook in this series, authored by Fifield and Gilligan. The models of strategies planned are equally applicable internationally as they are in the domestic marketplace. However, it is important to recognize that planning and control are inescapably linked. The former is a structuree (or series of structures) devised to develop a strategy and utilizing the capabilities of the organization against the background of the environment. Control is the process of monitoring and evaluating the implementation of the chosen strategy so that it can be developed to meet changes in the environment.

Issues in international planning

In marketing domestically the marketeer can readily apply his or her SRC, confident in meeting customer desires. Internationally this is rarely possible as customers, their culture and the environment changes by degree. Table 6.1 shows the issues involved in domestic versus international planning.

The difficulties of planning internationally are further identified by Brandt, Hulbert and Richers and are shown in Table 6.2.

The international planning process

Despite difficulties, planning remains an essential activity if the organization is to succeed. Moreover, planning demands structure and this becomes even more important unless one is dealing with a variety of markets/countries. As stated previously, we are not reviewing the

Table 6.1 Domestic versus international planning factors

Domestic planning		International planning	
1	Single language and nationality	1	Multilingual/multinational/multicultural factors
2	Relatively homogeneous market	2	Fragmented and diverse markets
3	Data available, usually accurate, and collection easy	3	Data collection a formidable task, requiring significantly higher budgets and personnel allocation
4	Political factors relatively unimportant	4	Political factors frequently vital
5	Relative freedom from government interference	5	Involvement in national economic plans; government influences affect business decisions
6	Individual corporation has little effect on environment	6	'Gravitational' distortion by large companies
7	Chauvinism helps	7	Chauvinism hinders
8	Relatively stable business environment	8	Multiple environments, many of which are highly unstable (but may be highly profitable)
9	Uniform financial climate	9	Variety of financial climates ranging from overconservative to wildly inflationary
10	Single currency	10	Currencies differing in stability and real value
11	Business 'rules of the game' mature and understood	11	Rules diverse, changeable, and unclear
12	Management generally accustomed to sharing resonsibilities and using financial controls	12	Management frequently autonomous and unfamiliar with budgets and controls

Source: William W. Cain, 'International planning: mission impossible?' *Columbia Journal of World Business,* July–August 1970, p. 58. Reprinted by permission

Table 6.2 International planning problems

Headquarters	Overseas subsidiary
Management	*Management*
Unclear allocation of responsibilities and authority	Resistance to planning
Lack of multinational orientation	Lack of qualified personnel
Unrealistic expectations	Inadequate abilities
Lack of awareness of foreign markets	Misinterpretation of information
Unclear guidelines	Misunderstanding requirements and objectives
Insensitivity to local decisions	Resentment of HQ involvement
Insufficient provision of useful information	Lack of strategic thinking
	Lack of marketing expertise
Processes	*Processes*
Lack of standardized bases for evaluation	Lack of control by HQ
Poor IT systems and support	Incomplete or outdated internal and market information
Poor feedback and control systems	Poorly developed procedures
Excessive bureaucratic control procedures	Too little communication with HQ
Excessive marketing and financial constraints	Inaccurate data returns
Insufficient participation of subsidiaries in process	Insufficient use of multinational marketing expertise
	Excessive financial and marketing constraints

Source: Brandt, Hulbert and Richers (1980)

models of portfolio analysis but we remind students that the most widely applied methods are:

1 Boston Consulting Group (BCCG)
2 General Electric/McKinsey (GE)
3 Profit Impact of Market Strategy (PIMS)
4 Arthur D. Little
5 Scenario Planning

Students are expected to be knowledgeable in the constructs of the models, their application, relevance and shortcomings. Once again, cross reference can be made with the *Strategic Marketing Management* workbook.

Examine the problems of using product portfolio analysis in international marketing (June 1994, Question 8).
(**See** Exam answers at the end of this unit.)

At the strategic level the organization has six key corporate decisions to take when moving into the international arena, beginning with the question 'Should we go?' and ending with 'What organization structure should we adopt?' Against these six key decisions they need to apply the marketing planning variables. Table 6.3 shows the interface between marketing planning and the key corporate decision to form the basis for strategic market planning.

Table 6.3 Strategic options and marketing planning: marketing planning variables

Key International Decisions	Marketing Environment and Scale of Marketing	Competitors	Objectives	Marketing Mix Variables	Marketing Budgets	Expected Outcomes
Should we go international?						
Where should we go?						
How should we get there?						
What should we sell?						
How should we market it?						
How do we organize?						

ACTIVITY 6.1

Go through Table 6.3 in depth. Select some product categories and then apply what you might consider to be the planning variables. In other words, get some simulated experience of marketing planning in action.

EXAM HINT

The matrix in Table 6.3 could be invaluable in examination terms. It allows you to get to the heart of planning immediately, saving you several pages of writing which means saving time. The marketing plan for any situation will follow the basic principles underpinning all marketing planning:

1 Who are we?
2 Where are we now?
3 Where do we want to be?
4 How might we get there?
5 How do we ensure we get there?

Following on from this the individual country plan should consider the following stages:

1 An evaluation of shareholder/stockholder expectations, together with ambition and resolve of key implementers
2 An audit of the firm's capabilities
3 An assessment of the environment – present and future
4 A statement of vision, mission, corporate objectives
5 An evaluation of strategic alternatives/options
6 An assessment of market/competitor responses
7 The selection and justification of a strategy
8 Effective implementation
9 Monitoring and control procedures
10 Development of organizational systems to ensure effective international co-ordination.

Select two contrasting countries and examine how international marketing plans would need to take account of the similarities and differences between those two countries (June 1994, Question 4).

(**See** Exam answers at the end of this unit.)

Control

The wider the range of international penetration, the greater will be the need and requirement for control. The establishment of an effective control system is interrelated to the organizational systems (people and procedures). The purpose of control is so that the business (not just marketing) activities can be measured. Measurement can only be achieved and proper assessment made if the plan contains clear objecives. No plan goes totally smoothly and deviations from expectations always occur, but without effective monitoring corrective action cannot be implemented. Control is the basic building block of management – not an afterthought. Future plans depend on control, for control is information and information is power. The issues that affect control are:

1　The scale of the task, the size of the firm
2　The diversity of markets, the number and range of markets/countries
3　The method of entry – which may vary by country
4　The availability and accuracy of data and information
5　The distance from the home market and the sophistication of communication, qualitative and quantitative.

Key factors in controlling international markets

The starting point is the marketing plan itself and the objectives it sets out to achieve. In basic terms the key control mechanisms are:

1　Establishing standards
2　Measuring performance against the standards
3　Correcting deviation.

Many methods apply in addressing the first of these two points, not least the establishment of common benchmarks and values across multi-markets. The task is extremely complicated and it is only the largest and most sophisticated organization that can consider a complex intermarket comparison of standards. But all firms can determine standards for individual markets and take the necessary action (see also Unit 14).

Organizing for international and global marketing

Managers are the company's scarcest resource and therefore their most valuable. It seems odd therefore that practically all the accepted textbooks on international marketing place the chapter on organizing for success at the end. People are very much a key resource and the model in Figure 6.1 places Company Objectives and Resources at the top of the linear sequence. Furthermore, planning for international expansion cannot take place in a vacuum, it needs the full consideration of the management of the company.

How an organization can structure itself to exploit overseas opportunities is a matter of considerable debate. As in the case of a 'plan' there is no one correct way. If there is a balance to be struck it should be as follows:

1　The organization should be structured in a way that best meets the task of servicing the customers' needs.
2　The structure must take full account of the environment, domestic and international, and the skills and resources of the organization.

For companies to be successful it is necessary to arrive at the appropriate balance.

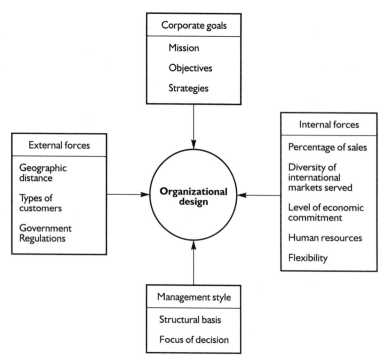

Figure 6.1 Factors affecting organizational design. (*Source:* Jeannet and Hennessey, 1994)

It is not easy, for tensions exist simultaneously between the need for diversity and decentralization in terms of servicing customers in different markets and the corporate requirement of evaluation and control. The ideal organization structure should incorporate both – a goal rarely realized.

We must also recognize that as customers, markets and environments are dynamic, ever changing and never static so the organization and its structural interface with the customer/market must also change. Some companies are already anticipating the shape and nature of global competition and planning for it. Most are reactive to the changing situation.

ACTIVITY 6.2

Review past editions of the quality press, (e.g. *The Economist* or the *Financial Times*). See what information you can discover on firms reorganizing themselves to adapt to changing times. Are they reactive or proactive?

At all times the focus of the organization should be to develop a structure that provides the framework to 'optimize' the relationship between planning, strategy and control. Terpstra and Sarathy (1994) identify some of the variables in this process:

- Size of the business
- Number of markets
- Level of strategic involvement in the markets
- Corporate objectives
- The level of international experience
- The nature of the product category(ies)
- The scale of the marketing task

Types of international organizations

Domestic-led companies

In Unit 9 we see that it is possible for domestically orientated companies to operate in overseas markets receiving enquiries from overseas buyers. Domestic staff will respond as if they were home-based customers – which some may well be. Such companies will have few or no additional costs but they will gain relatively little from the exercise – lacking expertise or scale to profit greatly.

Domestic company with an export department

As the overseas opportunity grows companies begin to employ international specialists and create an export department. This brings advantages in expertise, faster response and the beginnings of a proactive international policy with the export department exploring new country opportunities. But the scale of search for overseas services will be relatively low-key and restricted largely to pockets of opportunity. Furthermore, the tendency will be to market unmodified products thus failing to optimize the potential even where the product is sold. Generally, sales per country will be modest.

Developing the international division

Jeannet and Hennessey suggest that companies should move to this phase when international business represents 15 per cent or so of the company's total. At this scale it is necessary to increase the level of involvement in overseas markets – paying close attention to consumer needs attacking competition, modifying product and the marketing mix to create business proactively. This requires the development of an international division reporting at a senior level and capable of coordinating the business functions across country boundaries.

Stop at this point and see if you can think of any examples of how organizations simulate themselves internationally.

Worldwide organizational structure

Companies recognize the need to coordinate the operation spread geographically to cover large areas of the world. There are five recognized approaches:

1. *Country and regional centres*   This structure allows companies to delve even deeper into the dynamics of consumer behaviour and the environment within a country or region. The difference is essentially a matter of size. On reaching a certain size a market (country or region) will require management – staff located within it to maximize the business opportunity and creating a physical presence in the market, possibly for political as well as business reasons. It is very likely that production may be based within the market. Apart from the limits of economies of scale it allows greater sensitivity in building consumer relationships and understanding the culture, responding faster, being more flexible than operations centralized around HQs. Presently, many organizations are creating European centres to coordinate business functions such as R&D, production, distribution, marketing and finance. This regionalization in attitude is being rewarded with the creation of Eurobrands. For example, Unilever have created a European organization, Lever Europe, eliminating diverse brand names such as Cif, Viss and calling them Jif. Likewise, we have seen the demise of Marathon chocolate bars – renamed Snickers!

2. *Functional operation*   This structure is best suited to companies with a narrow product base with relatively homogenous customers around the world. Thus organizing worldwide on a functional basis is an option open only to a few companies. The structure itself is simple with senior executives having worldwide responsibility for their specialized function be it finance, R&D, marketing, production. etc.

3. *Product structuring*   This is most common among companies with a portfolio of seemingly unrelated product lines where each product group may have its own

international division. A difficulty with this structure is that conflicts will emerge between product groupings and therefore management problems arise with clashes of culture usually at the source. Similarly, a lack of coordination or of cross-fertilization of ideas often occurs. In an attempt to minimize the conflict, companies may provide functional coordination for customer-related activities such as marketing communication and after-sales service.

4 *Matrix structuring* Very popular in the late 1970s but less so nowadays, this organizational structure appeared to offer solutions to the one-dimensional approach of the three previous methods. Matrices are created by combining two (or more) dimensions of equal importance in the decision-making process. Thus an organization has a dual chain of command. The two most popular dimensions are product and market (country/region). Despite appearing to resolve conflicts and giving greater control and flexibility (responsiveness), the matrix system has largely fallen by the wayside – a victim of its complexity as each axis of the matrix attempts to consolidate or indeed optimize its position within the organizational hierarchy. Sadly, matrix structures show up the weakness and fallibilities of human relationships creating power struggles. Matrices can and will work only when organizations can admit to conflict and are capable of resolving conflict positively by adopting an influence system rather than an authoritarian system of management. Phillips was in the vanguard of introducing a matrix structure in the mid-1970s but has abandoned it in favour of global product divisions.

5 *Strategic Business Units* (SBUs) These are currently in vogue and consist of dividing the global organization into defined businesses, each addressing an identified customer base either by country/region or even on a worldwide basis. The advantages are corporate flexibility in disposing of an SBU or, alternatively, the company can refocus the overall business more easily. The integration of new acquisitions is easier and from a financial and operational control perspective SBUs make for good sense. However, the downside is that the company is not optimizing its economies of scale in world markets and it makes acquisition of the company itself by predators easier, so the unwanted SBUs can be disposed of more readily.

Majaro (1991) developed the scenario in Figure 6.2 identifying three basic formats for large international/worldwide organizations calling them macropyramid, umbrella and inter-glomerate structures:

• *Macropyramid* Power is concentrated at the centre – taking strategic decisions concerning marketing along with the standardization of production and R&D. The weakness is self-evident; lack of motivation in the subsidiary, little or no local creativity

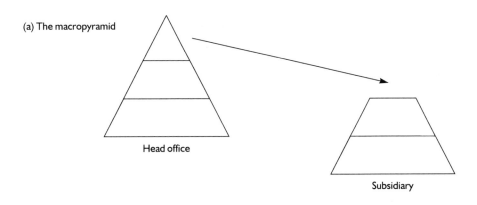

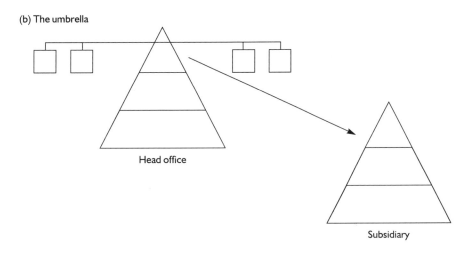

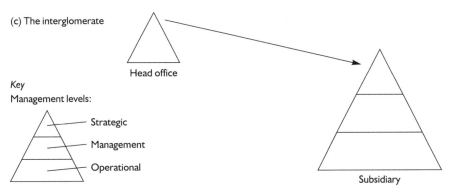

Figure 6.2 Organizational structures and the head office – subsidiary relationship (Majaro, 1991)

or flexibility, with communication being largely one-way and the subsidiary being measured usually on monthly financial performance.

- *Umbrella* This is the opposite approach, with the company creating a clone of itself in each market, decentralizing decision making to the local level and allowing flexibility in product and market mix variables. Although having advantages at the local level there is little global benefit as a plethora of products/brand names erupt with overduplication and little coordination, resulting in the erosion of potential economies of scale. Procter & Gamble and Unilever pioneered this structure though both have moved away from it in recent years.
- *Interglomerate* The centre is run on strict financial criteria allowing the SBUs total autonomy. Such companies are driven by acquisition and break-ups. Hanson is a typical interglomerate.

- Briefly explain the different forms of organizational structure used in international marketing. For each organization's type, indicate the roles of management at different levels and in different locations in the determination of an international marketing plan (December 1994, Question 7).
- Identify and critically comment upon the probable marketing differences between organizations that divide markets between the 'domestic' market and the 'rest of the world' and organizations that take a more geographically neutral approach (December 1993, Question 8).

(**See** Exam answers at the end of this unit.)

Trends in global organizations

Its is abundantly clear that the management issues surrounding international organizations are extremely complex. There are a number of trends to add to the already lengthy discussion:

1 Organizational structures are becoming 'flatter' with individual managers having wider responsibility and more subordinates.
2 Correspondingly, responsibility and authority are being pushed closer to the relevant point of contact with the customer.
3 The trend will therefore be towards the macropyramid format with the centre deciding the global corporate decisions relating to the direction the company should take but the marketing decisions will be made increasingly with the subsidiaries.
4 Transnational organizations – the latest thinking in international management is that being global is not enough. Kenichi Ohmae, a disciple of globalization curiously argues against rigidity, believing that as the world increasingly develops around the Triad economies the global company must be equidistant from each of the three major trading blocs yet simultaneously position itself as an insider within each. This renaissance corporation should exploit whatever economies of scale, technology or branding it has within the Triad. Ohmae's argument is that while tastes may vary, the broad motivations among consumers are similar.

How would a transnational company differ in its marketing approach to a multi-national enterprise (MNE) (June 1993, Question 4).
(**See** Exam answers at the end of this unit.)

Bartlett and Ghoshal (1992) broadly confirm the view that renaissance companies must be composed of specialist managers who network across countries/regions. They explain the management implications as:

- Global managers need to be multi-disciplined providing leadership and innovation.
- The country manager is a pivotal character, being closest to the customer and understanding the finesse required in building customer relationships.
- Global product group managers have the responsibility for quality control and efficiency and driving down costs. Additionally, they will be the architects for worldwide resourcing.

Return to Unit 3 briefly and see how the points made here match the challenges outlined. There should be a direct correlation. No aspect of international planning/organization acts independently of its environment.

5 Shared vision. The task of moulding an organization to the needs of an ever-changing world marketplace involves building a shared vision and developing human resources. For example, Coca-Cola's vision is simple – 'To put Coca-Cola within arms' reach of everyone in the world'.

   To succeed, the company must employ all its talents and avoid the pitfalls of adopting the narrow vision of ethnocentric management employing both a polycentric style yet recognizing the importance of the regiocentric and geocentric contributions.

EXAM QUESTION

In the role of the director responsible for international marketing of a blue-chip company, explain how you would identify and justify the resource requirements for a global marketing plan (June 1993, Question 9).

   (**See** Exam answers at the end of this unit.)

Summary

This unit has covered two strategic aspects of international marketing: first, the line of marketing planning and second the organizational implications. Both involved a high degree of personnel issues. The unit discussed briefly the importance of models in developing strategy and also considered the marketing planning variables set against the key international decision areas. This particular matrix is of considerable help in defining quickly your options (from the perspective of the examination) and the issues revolving around control.

   Likewise, the manner in which the company organizes itself to best deal with its international development establishes the level of involvement and the intensity of its competitive impact. There is a wide variety of choice. Finally, the unit discussed developments that will shape the competitive challenges in the future.

Questions

- In creating an international plan what basic elements might you consider important?
- What are the difficulties in adapting headquarters' broad plan to local countries?
- What impact should competition play in affecting international marketing planning?
- What are the benefits of choosing region, product or function as the basis for organizing the firm on an international basis?
- Headquarters hinder local market development. Discuss.
- What control elements do you consider appropriate in multi-country marketing planning?
- What is the purpose of control systems? What distinguishes a good one?
- What is a marketing audit and what are its strengths and weaknesses in developing international markets?
- What is the relevance of the BCG model in planning for international markets?
- What decisions are best left to local managers?
- Is a transnational approach to strategy the best way forward for a global cooperation? Indicate circumstance where it might or might not be appropriate.

- Itemize and justify six characteristics you consider necessary for an organization to compete successfully in a global market.

International Marketing Strategy, C. Phillips, I. Doole and R. Lowe, Routledge, 1994, Chapters 5 and 6.

International Marketing, S. Paliwoda, Butterworth-Heinemann, 1994, Chapters 13 and 14.

Global Marketing Strategies, J.-P. Jeannet and H. D. Hennessey, Houghton Mifflin, 1994, Chapter 16 and 17.

International Marketing, V. Terpstra and R. Sarathy, The Dryden Press, 1994, Chapter 17.

- *June 1994, Question 8*   Product portfolio analysis is generally used to position products or strategic business units on a comparative basis. In general, such models utilize a matrix. Candidates should begin by exhibiting knowledge of some of the models used in portfolio analysis (for details refer to the *Strategic Marketing Management* workbook). One popular model is BCG.

  In terms of the problems particular attention should be paid to international issues such as:

- The appropriate measures of performance should be similar given all the markets involved
- The performance should be comparable like for like – this is virtually impossible as markets differ
- Decision making following the analysis (e.g. divesting, building or penetration strategies) may not be straightforward. Political, social and infrastructure factors may complicate the decision.

Finally you should conclude that while portfolio analysis is a widely used tool of business strategy the results are rarely crystal-clear and need careful interpretation.

June 1994, Question 4   The heart of this question is to select two contrasting countries. Candidates who have paid attention and created country files containing basic business information on different types of countries (e.g. different stages of economic development) should find this question easy to answer.   So first choose two contrasting markets you know. Issues such as size of market, political factors, competitors, marketing mix variables, etc. are all key elements in the strategic decision of how one might enter a market(s). In terms of implementation the appropriate answer should take the view of demonstrating how the four or seven Ps of the mix might have to be modified. Good candidates would discuss management issues and, of course, the important aspect of control.

December 1993, Question 4   Making the switch from a modest exporter to an aggresssive international operator is a large step. Very few (if any) organizations will tackle it in one step. Sensible answers should recognize this and show how it might be achieved through a series of carefully planned stages. The impact of such a change has many ramifications – management, financial and organizational. Perhaps stage 1 would be the creation of an international division based in the domestic market with specialist international management responsibilities and skills. This would mean moving international issues upwards to board level. Following an appropriate time-lapse to learn and consolidate, another step might be taken to develop an area, function or product structure outside the domestic market with the development of responsibilities into the international sphere. What is certain is that the process is a long-term strategy and requires great commitment at the highest level.

December 1994, Question 7 This question should be tackled in three separate parts, using distinct headings/sub-headings. First, you should describe and explain (briefly) the various organizational structures – area, product, function etc. – and/or consider Majaro's models of macropyramid, umbrella and interglomerate. In this first part you might also consider the influence of company size, e.g. a medium-sized organization versus a multinational and the impact in terms of level of involvement.

The second part of the question is more concerned with the roles of management, i.e. the issues of centralization versus decentralization. Where might the key decisions be taken? Finally, the third part might consider briefly the impact of this in terms of location. In other words, the debate between local versus headquarters on a key issue of power. The approach might be that headquarters takes strategic business decisions but that marketing is largely a local activity.

December 1993, Question 8 The majority of international companies develop their marketing around their experience in the domestic market – modifying as necessary to meet different customer requirements. As a stage 2, dealing with greater internationalization, firms tend to create a 'clone' of their domestic operation in their various overseas markets. In managing the clone they differ mainly in their human resource approach, adopting either ethnocentric or polyethnic stances. Your answer would develop this point.

In contrast, a company setting out to create a geographically central approach (typified by a transnational organization) would try to position itself as an 'insider' in its various markets and in doing so adopt a geocentric approach. But the important thing here is that the company must develop a global mindset – something that very few can ever achieve. For students of the subject Kenichi Ohmae's writings are a valuable source of information.

June 1993, Question 4 Define a transnational company and show how it differs from a multinational. The difference is strategic in its orientation with the transnational adopting a geocentric view of the world. (In a way this question is a continuation of the previous one.) Transnational companies are 'insiders' operating as though the world was one market and the strategies involved are applied unilaterally. The company can switch its resources to wherever the need arises. The multinational tends to operate on a portfolio basis by either country or region measuring performance accordingly – frequently operating via a series of clone structures and clone management. Again Kenichi Ohmae's *The Borderless World* is the seminal text for students who wish to expand their knowledge. Really good candidates should refer to the macro factors underpinning developments in world trade (Unit 2).

June 1993, Question 9 No global plan can be attempted without proper information. The starting point in terms of resources should refer to this point and qualify it in terms of the cost, time and resources in establishing a global MIS. It is only via the MIS that global opportunities can be identified.

In addressing resource requirements your answer would cover such issues as manpower, capital of all kinds, marketing budgets and operational requirements. Naturally, the main thrust of your answer would be on the marketing aspects and include external agencies for country research and advertising. Other relevant factors include marketing costs together with sales force and organizational issues. Really good answers would include: comment on cross-cultural concerns and the development of multi-cultural management teams. One final important point is that of control. Controls have a cost/resource implication and every marketing plan should have in-built monitoring and control.

Globalization

Globalization as a strategic option open to the international organization has been a major topic of discussion since Theodore Levitt wrote his mould-breaking article in 1983 (*Harvard Business Review*). Globalization, in essence, is about treating the world as one market both for marketing and for production purposes. In this unit you will:

- Understand what globalization means
- Consider the factors which drive an organization towards a globalized strategy
- Understand the factors which may affect or inhibit a drive towards globalization
- Be aware of when a globalized strategy is appropriate for an organization and when it is not.

Having completed this unit you will be able to:

- Consider the viability or otherwise of globalization as a strategy for the international organization
- Understand the implications of a globalization strategy upon the organization, its marketing, its production and organizational structure
- Understand the effects of a globalization strategy upon the international marketing mix.

This unit is important to an overall understanding of international marketing strategy. Although globalization represents only a very small part of the syllabus, the effects of following a globalization strategy will be felt throughout the entire operation and implementation of the international marketing mix. Decisions taken at this level will affect both implementation and how activities are evaluated and controlled in the international marketplace.

Globalization as a strategy offers significant potential savings through economies of scale but is also a clearly inappropriate strategy in certain situations. The key to understanding globalization is being able to differentiate the times and occasions when it is a suitable strategy for the organization and when it should be avoided in favour of other, more local, approaches to markets.

As you work through this unit remember that good strategy must be thought out carefully. The international market, as always, must be the inspiration for good marketing and when local needs are so divergent in their nature as to make a standardized (globalized) approach inappropriate the international marketer needs to be able to direct strategy accordingly.

What is globalization?

Globalization as an issue came to the fore in 1983 with the publication of Theodore Levitt's article in the *Harvard Business Review*. Levitt's initial article on globalization put forward the view that there was simply no such thing as local markets, that all markets tended towards a universal standard and that organizations indulging themselves in producing many variants in overseas markets were simply wasting resources on a grand scale. He suggested that organizations would be much more efficient and effective if they were to standardize their marketing approaches to overseas markets. They should not only market themselves and their products on a global basis but also consider production and service on a globalized basis. Since Levitt's first article a number of articles have appeared by various authors both for and against this basic premise. Indeed, Levitt himself joined the fray a few years later, saying that wasn't exactly what he meant and that in some instances 'think global, act local' was the right and proper policy for international markets.

Global marketing can be defined as 'the process of focusing an organization's resources on the selection and exploitation of global market opportunities consistent with and supportive of its short- and long-term strategic objectives and goals' (Source: Toyne and Walters, 1989).

It is relatively easy to see Levitt's original inspiration for the globalization concept. If we consider the North American market, although it is called 'domestic' by US companies, it is far less homogeneous than most other domestic/national markets with which the organization has to deal. While in the domestic marketing situation most US companies will look for similarities among quite often varied market needs, as soon as these same organizations consider overseas markets they start by looking at differences rather than similarities. While there is obviously much fluency in the globalization argument it is equally difficult to understand that it will be universally applicable to all organizations in all situations.

EXAM QUESTION

Your company wishes to develop a 'global brand' of perfume. What implications would this have for the advertising element of the marketing mix (December 1990)?
   (**See** Exam answers at the end of this unit.)

The best way to understand globalization and its applicability for any given organization is to understand the factors which drive globalization and those which may inhibit its implementation in an organization's marketing strategy.

Factors driving to globalization

There are a number of factors in today's modern world which may drive an organization toward a global marketing strategy. Some of the most important are:

1 *The international flow of information* Predictions of the 'global village' were being made 10 and 15 years ago and they are now starting to come true. The flow of information across national boundaries is becoming both faster and greater in quantity. People also are much more able and willing to travel than a decade ago.

This increased flow of international information and customer awareness means that consumers and suppliers are nowadays much more aware of products and services that are available in often very distant markets. With this increased flow of information and awareness comes demand, and markets for products and services grow on a global scale.

2   *The international spread of technology*   As with information, technology is now flowing much more freely across national boundaries and frontiers. With the international spread of technology the ability to design, develop, manufacture and market products and services of all descriptions is available on a much more global scale than 10 or 20 years ago.

3   *Size of investment required*   Driven by the spread of international information and technology, the minimum production batch size is starting to decrease as enabling technology spreads. Consequently, the size of financial and human investment required in developing new products or services has grown. In a number of markets, for example motor cars, military hardware and pharmaceuticals, the absolute size of the investment required to develop the next generation of new products has outstripped the ability of any one single market or company to pay back on the investment. In these industries (among others) investment has to be based on the likely future demand in more than one market, if possible for global application, in order to make such investments financially viable. So we see that developments such as the Ford world car (Mondeo) and the European fighter aircraft are now developed by and for more than one marketplace.

4   *Reduction of trade barriers*   As the world develops into a smaller number of larger economic and political regions (EU, LAFTA, NAFTA) so the number of small, independent markets with their own regulations and legislations requiring adapted or specialized products reduces. As trade barriers and restrictions fall away so the marketplace opens up for much more standardized products and services and makes a globalized international marketing strategy more viable for many organizations.

EXAM QUESTION

Examine the similarities and differences between global branding and global marketing. Are they the same? Under what conditions would each be likely to succeed (December 1993)?

(**See** Exam answers at the end of this unit.)

Factors inhibiting globalization

As well as the easily identifiable factors which encourage organizations to take a more globalized international marketing strategy, there are a number of factors which can be identified that may make such a strategy inappropriate or impractical. Some of the more common factors are as follows:

1   *Customer tastes*   The key concept upon which globalization is based is that of a broadly standardized approach to international markets. Before any form of standardization can be applied it requires that customers' tastes in various markets are also standardized. In many cases this is simply not the case. If customers actually want or need or require different products or services from a neighbouring or other foreign market and if competition is such that their needs can be met, they will not buy the standardized (globalized) products or service. Even where tastes converge, many organizations have found that other elements of the product or marketing mix may need to be varied on a local basis in order to gain acceptability. For example, many American adverts on TV might be visually acceptable but may be have to be dubbed in to the local language – including English!

The debate between total globalization and adaptation to local market needs continues to be waged in the pages of marketing journals. You should be aware of the arguments on both sides. You should have an opinion and be prepared to justify it.

2   *Culture*   As we have already seen from Unit 4, culture is a major force in determining customer and buyer behaviour. In the same way, culture can be a major barrier to globalization strategies. Culture is a major factor in everybody's life and people (and organizations) will seek out products and services which enable them to reinforce their sense of belonging to a given culture and will avoid those products and services that are seen as transgressing particular cultural rules. Certain products and services are evidently the product of an identifiable culture. For example, McDonald's, Coca-Cola and Harley-Davidson are seen as products of US culture. In these cases, they will still be purchased as people wish to sample that culture. In other cases such as Phileas Fogg snacks, the organization may find that while the concept behind the snacks is valid on a worldwide basis the actual products required to deliver the company's promise differ from culture to culture and need to be modified accordingly.

Select a company that is generally thought of as being a global operator. (McDonald's, Coca-Cola, Pepsi, Ford, International Harvester, Compaq, etc.). What degree of standardization are they actually able to achieve? What adaptation in the marketing mix can you identify?

2   *Local market conditions*   As well as the strictly cultural variables at play when considering globalization strategy, there are a number of other variables that also need to be taken into account. These will vary from organization to organization and from product to product but may include issues such as the local market's need for particular national or regional identity, the role of individualism in the target market and the degree of nationalism inherent in local purchase behaviour. In these instances a degree of globalization may be possible but also some degree of adaptation to local requirements may be required.

The Diploma examinations are strategic. Examiners are looking for evidence of candidates' ability to think for themselves about issues that really matter. Globalization, too, has its critics. One, Sir James Goldsmith, is decidedly anti-free trade. He says:

'The doctrine of free trade, if applied globally, will be a disaster.'
'Economies should not be self-serving structures, but directed at promoting the stability and contentment of the societies within which they operate.'
'Europe faces a future of unemployment, poverty and social instability.'
'Britain will become the Mexico of Europe.'
'A reason for this is our quasi-religious belief in free trade. A moral dogma which was born when Britain was the manufacturing centre of the world.'

He suggests the future should be based on:

'Country preference.'
'A world of fenced-off regions with economies that reflect local conditions, cultures and needs.'

You can read more – and make up your own mind – *The Trap*, J. Goldsmith, Macmillan, 1994

EXAM QUESTION

Explain the differences between a standardized global brand approach and an approach based upon identifying and exploiting global marketing opportunities (June 1992).
   (**See** Exam answers at the end of this unit.)

Conclusions

Any discussion on globalization cannot take place in a vacuum. As you consider this concept of a standardized international approach to marketing and production you need also to bear in mind the customers (Unit 3), the infrastructure within which international trade is carried out (Unit 2) as well as the implications for product policy (Unit 9). It is probably fair to say that, given their choice, most organizations would prefer that they provided a completely standardized global product and marketing programme and would ideally have only one major worldwide centre for production. The financial and human resource economies that such an approach would produce are undeniable. However, the international marketer needs to realize that the world simply is not like this. Apart from a few companies who have truly global products, most organizations have to come to grips with the fact that the world is still not homogeneous and needs to be catered for on a local basis. Obviously, it is a question of balance. To what extent can we standardize our approaches to overseas markets and to what extent do we have to make modifications in order to achieve acceptable sales levels in overseas markets? Significant economies can come from standardization but if the standardized product or service is too far from local requirements, sales volumes and revenues may suffer as a result.

In any event, the importance of conducting careful market research (see Unit 4) into the needs and requirements of overseas markets cannot be overemphasized.

Summary

In this unit we have seen that globalization is a major force in international marketing strategy. The benefits from a globalized international marketing approach are significant and offer major economies from a standardized approach to foreign markets.

There are a number of reasons globalization is coming to the fore and many international marketing variables are stimulating interest in this area. There are also a number of factors which may stand in the way of an organization successfully globalizing its marketplaces, and most of these are concerned with local tastes, requirements and perceptions.

In any event, the organization considering globalization should:

1 Not to be dazzled by the rare instances of successful pure globalization
2 Carefully research and understand overseas markets before moving to globalization
3 Look for similarities as well as differences in overseas markets before planning
4 Carefully evaluate the savings to be made from a globalized/standardized approach against the likely loss of sales from not fully meeting local market requirements.

Questions

As a check on your understanding of what has been covered in this unit, consider the following questions:

- What is meant by 'globalization'?
- How practical is a strategy of pure globalization?
- What factors actively promote globalization?
- What factors will inhibit a globalization strategy?
- How close to a true global strategy can an organization plan?

For a more detailed analysis and explanation of globalization, read:

International Marketing, S. Paliwoda, Butterworth-Heinemann, 1993, pp. 210–223, 489–493.
International Marketing Strategy, C. Phillips, I. Doole and R. Lowe, Routledge, 1994, pp 228–32.

December 1990 Has your answer tackled the question specifically as posed? A general discussion of standardization/adaptation will not be sufficient to pass. You are dealing here with a product with a large intangible element. How can standardization be achieved in these circumstances? Perfume will rely upon image very strongly and possibly country of origin. Standardization needs to be explored for both the media and the message components of the advertising.

December 1993 Global marketing can be viewed as a strategic blend of standardization and adaptation to be developed as the company takes a global view of world opportunities. To be global implies considering the world market and maximizing profits from an as-standardized approach as possible for maximum profits. Global branding, on the other hand, requires standardization, especially of the brand name, trade mark, registration and packaging. Visual standardization is the key to global branding. To obtain good marks your answer might mention that incidences of a totally standardized global brand are exceedingly rare.

June 1992 This question comes in two parts and needs to be answered in two parts. Your answer needs to explain what you understand by a standardized global brand approach (see answer above). The second part of the question is looking for a balance between standardization and adaptation, while at the same time taking a global perspective on the strategic planning process.

Market entry methods

The purpose of this unit is to consider the alternative routes through which the firm might enter foreign markets. Having already taken the decision to market overseas, i.e. where we should go, the key decision becomes what the best way is of entering the chosen markets. We review the major routes and markets and criteria for selecting them. In this unit you will:

- Understand the range of options available.
- See that size (or lack of) is no barrier to exporting or foreign production.
- Discuss the criteria for chosing each entry strategy.
- Understand the importance of the level of involvement and the management issues that accompany it.

Having completed the unit you will be able to:

- Grasp the importance of choosing the right method of entry and realize that decisions must be taken with the utmost care
- Understand the implications of your choice from a marketing perspective
- Recognize that each entry method has management implications
- See that there is no one right route. Markets vary, and so we must choose the appropriate route to customers. Flexibility, learning and gaining experience are necessary stages of developing entry strategies.

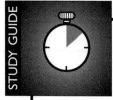

Step by step you will discover the different methods of proceeding into overseas markets. The stages increase in complexity and have management implications. From the crucial and often hesitant initial stage the picture builds to a conclusion that is concerned not so much with entry methods but with how to exploit opportunities within the context of a multi-country scenario.

No ideal strategy exists – one firm may choose a variety of methods, appropriate to each country/market situation. In the same way, entry methods change over time. But underpinning the decision is the firms objectives, attitudes and commitment to successful exploitation of overseas opportunities. The level of involvement referred to in the text (and also in the introduction to the Workbook) is the key factor in determining the correct strategy.

International market entry strategies

Having previously identified where we wish to go in developing overseas business and having addressed our basic marketing strategies, the next step is deciding how we might get there – the market entry strategy. This is of critical importance for it sets the agenda for future battles. It signals to competitors the scale of our intention and, with it, our commitment.

There is no one ideal way of entering an overseas market. There are options to suit all sizes of firms and all situations. There are no barriers preventing the smallest firm from taking the first tentative steps overseas, for international marketing is not the exclusive preserve of large companies. Indeed, large companies do not pursue a rigid policy in exploiting opportunities but often seek to take the most appropriate route for each market judged as an entity. Du Pont operates with wholly owned or joint-venture operations in 40 countries, with marketing subsidiaries in 20 and with distributors in 60. McDonald's has a mixture of wholly owned or franchised operations. No route is the correct one.

However, the chosen entry method requires the greatest of care. Once selected and resourced, it may not be easy to change or withdraw from the market. (Exit strategies are also important, especially in high-risk markets.) Similarly, the extent to which the company's marketing strategy can be employed is also dependent upon the decision. So the alternatives must be weighed most carefully and should be viewed by the international marketer over the longer- rather than the shorter-term horizons. A straightforward exports orientated company can take a short-term tactical approach but international marketing involves dialogue with consumers, understanding their needs and wants, creating appropriate satisfactions and managing the relationship between the company, its intermediaries and its consumers.

Entry strategy alternatives

- If international marketing is about relationships with overseas customers/consumers then the starting point in considering market entry alternatives is a strategic not a tactical one and revolves around the question of 'level of involvement', or, putting it simpler 'how close do I need to be to the consumer in order to succeed?' As in all markets, closeness to the consumer is the discriminator of success. Refer here to the International Business Process model in the section 'What is international marketing?' for guidance and reinforcement of the point.

Level of involvement

This is dictated by the following:

- Corporate objectives/ambition/resources. These will shape the market entry strategy in terms of narrowing the options but will not necessarily constrain the organization to a single-entry choice.
- Nature of the markets/product category/competition. The scale of the market, the number of markets, the nature of the product category and the level of competition will influence market entry strategy.
- Nature of consumer culture. What customers buy, where they buy, why they buy and how often will certainly focus thinking.
- Coverage of the market – breadth, depth and quality. Again, this is largely dictated by consumer needs. The product has to be available where the customer expects to find it. The basic choice of market entry strategy is influenced by the required penetration demands.
- Speed of entry. The nature of the product, where it is on the product life cycle, the rate of new product innovation diffusion and the pace of market development will have a profound bearing on our choice.
- Level of control. What feedback is required? What research information do we need on customer purchasing to assist future planning and to effect current and future controls?
- Marketing costs and commitment. Consumer demands and competitive pressure will influence this. Clearly, the greater the marketing cost, the higher will be the level of involvement.
- Profit payback. This is related to corporate aims and objectives but varying by company and by country. The general rule is that paybacks are longer overseas. Sony, when

entering the UK market, took a corporate decision not to take profit for the first 10 years, but to invest it in the development of its market share. At the other extreme, a leading question might be 'Can I get my money out?'. This, too, will colour the approach to market entry.

- Investment costs. The deeper the involvement, the higher the costs; inventory, finance, credit, management, etc.
- Administrative requirements. Documentation, detailed knowledge of legal requirements, foreign taxation.
- Personnel. This obviously increases with greater involvement; management, training, language, cultural assimilation are all factors to consider.
- Flexibility. Learning from doing; testing the situation before heavy involvement, political risk, multi-market entry are just some of the factors to take into account in planning the entry strategy.

ACTIVITY 8.1

What does level of involvement mean? Take a small firm and compare it with a major multinational. See how this equates with cost.

EXAM HINT

Practically every examination paper has questions on entry methods either in the mini case or in the Section B part of the examination. It is extremely rare that the subject is not included in the paper. Therefore it is essential you have a very thorough grasp of the subject.

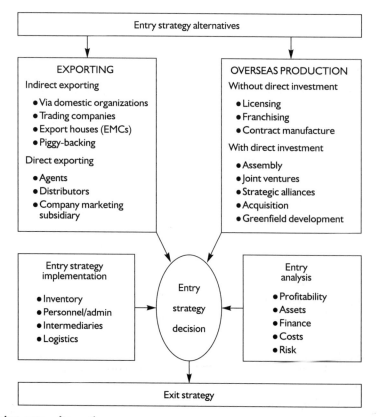

Figure 8.1   Market entry alternatives

With entry strategy alternatives two basic routes present themselves:

1 Exporting – defined as 'Making it here, selling it there'.
2 Overseas Production – 'Making it there and selling it there' (not necessarily the same country)

Figure 8.1 sets out the strategic alternatives under both headings. The choice is extensive and we propose to comment briefly on all of them. But before doing so it is important to recognize that the level of involvement increases in descending order and that overseas production requires greater involvement than exporting.

Exporting

Indirect exporting
This deals with exports as if they were domestic sales. No specific overseas knowledge is required as the work is done by others. New opportunities can be opened up but control is limited and profitability generally low (others are taking the risk, doing the work). Various methods exist:

- *Overseas organizations with buyers in domestic markets*   Major retailers have UK buyers (e.g. Macy's in New York has buying offices in 30 countries). The Body Shop procures products from obscure sources (e.g. the Kayapo Indians deep within the Brazilian rainforest).
- *Multinationals' procurement offices*   The major multinationals source widely.

Study some trade magazines in more than one industry (e.g. fashion, electrical equipment, etc.). What avenues and approaches are there for small firms to export?

ACTIVITY 8.2

- *International trading companies*   With their roots in the colonial era and consequently of fading importance, nevertheless ITCs are important in gaining access to many Third World countries. United Africa Company, a Unilever subsidiary, is the largest trader in Africa. The Japanese Sogo Shosha, as their ITCs are known, are major international players embracing Mitsui and Mitsubishi. The Sogo Shosha handle the majority of Japanese imports today. Their advantages are wide market coverage and fast, easy access to markets. However, they will carry a wide portfolio of products, often competitors, and therefore there will be a dilution of effort. Additionally, a feeling of resentment may persist in some countries due to the historical legacy of colonialism. Burma and Egypt have nationalized ITCs to rid themselves of foreign influence. In summary, sales are less stable but there is little company control.
- *Export houses (Export Management Companies – EMCs in American textbooks)*   This is by far the most important method of exporting (numerically) with around 800 operating in the UK. Ranging from generalist to specialist (by industry and country), they provide the performance of an export department without direct involvement and generally allow the company some (if small) degree of cooperation and control. Most suitable for the small to medium firm. The *CIM Quarterly Review* (Autumn 1987) suggested that 63 per cent of small/medium firms involved in exporting used export houses.

Further advantages include: instant market contact and knowledge (particularly local purchasing practices and government regulations). They are paid on commission and therefore are motivated to develop the business (ensuring that the product is attractive to sell). Additionally they offer freight savings by consolidating shipments and, if selling complementary products, can enhance the representation. Disadvantages include: the country coverage by the export house may not coincide with the company's objectives, and they may carry too many products (including competitive ones) thus diluting the effort.

Therefore care must be taken in choosing the appropriate export house. The company's trade association is often a helpful source of advice.

- *Piggy-backing* This is essentially a form of cooperation in exporting where one company uses its facilities to sell another's product. It is more common between US multinationals and exporters than in Europe. Generally, piggy-backing involves longer-term involvement and it is certain that partner choice requires great care. The advantages are introductions to new markets via an organization established and respected in the country together with savings in infrastructure costs covering warehousing marketing and sales. *Note:* Piggy-backing is often included under direct exporting as this utilizes the resources of an intermediary based in overseas countries.

Direct exporting

This is exporting using intermediaries located in foreign markets. In doing so the exporter is becoming more involved and committed to the new marketplace, adding investment, time and management expertise. The benefits of greater involvement are more influence, greater strategic leverage (variable) control (also variable) and, of course, profit. The step from indirect to direct exporting should not be taken lightly as the costs and expertise levels rise sharply and therefore the company must be sure it has the capabilities of managing this significantly higher workload and knowledge requirement. Mahon and Vachini (1992) suggest that a 'beach-head' strategy be employed initially, thereby testing overseas markets (small countries or niche markets) prior to a full-scale abandonment of indirect exporting.

Factors for success

- Top management commitment
- Confidence
- International marketing skills
- Detailed planning
- Commitment to quality
- Research and development
- Reliability/relationship building

Factors for failure

- Failure to research the market
- Inadequate funds/financial backing
- Failure of commitment/perseverance
- Under representation in the market
- Failure to understand cultural reference
- Inexperienced management and personnel

Once individual countries have been selected the first decision is how the company will be represented. The size of the market, the nature of the product category, the level of involvement and contact with the consumer pre- and post-purchase will influence the degree of contact between the company and the market (e.g. a full-time staff in residence at one end of the spectrum to a home-based export sales manager liaising with intermediaries or, alternatively, simply communicating by telephone and fax at the other end).

Agents

These represent the lowest level of direct involvement in exporting. Their distinguishing feature is that they are country/territory bound (be sure your contact states this to avoid parallel exporting/importing). Paid on commission for orders obtained they, as a norm, represent non-competing manufacturers with sole rights. The critical fact to keep in mind is that agents do not take title to the goods (although there are exceptions). Their advantage lies in that they are paid by results, there is limited risk involved, they can tap into existing contacts, they have a cultural and linguistic affinity. Furthermore start-up costs are low. Their disadvantages stem from quality of service, coverage of the market, conflict of interest (dilution factor), lack of control over them. They are difficult to fire due to legal complexities, stretched resources, communication (both inward and outward), motivation, distribution and their financial competence, i.e. you getting paid! Great care needs to be taken in drafting the agreement and agents are usually chosen when high-price, low-volume goods are ordered – business-to-business or industrial products.

Distributors

These differ considerably from agents in both the level of involvement and the relationship. Distributors represent the major (most popular) form of international distribution numerically. They are used by small and large firms alike for entering markets where a marketing as well as a sales presence is required. This marketing input accounts largely for the deeper level of involvement. Distributors differ from agents also by buying the goods themselves and selling them on – usually at their own determined price (although company considerations and cooperation in pricing the product is important). In other words, distributors 'take title to the goods'.

It is apparent that success in the market is largely dependent on the performance of the chosen distributor (the selection process is critical). The challenge then becomes 'how to motivate the distributor'. The key is through building intercompany relationships; by continually rewarding the distributor to do as well, treating them as if they were in your own organization. Recognizing such perfection is unlikely, the company should take all necessary steps to create distributor loyalty, e.g. ensuring an adequate payment structure, developing training programmes, determining agreed targets and other performance standards; and evaluating those performance levels regularly at the same time as maintaining an efficient communication system.

The distributor is not your employee but your business partner and your sole representation in a country. Treat the arrangement on a mutually (equally) beneficial one, for an unhappy or disgruntled distributor can inflict great damage. Gaining success breeds confidence and greater cooperation. Finally, the advantages and disadvantage of distribution broadly coincide with those for agents.

ACTIVITY 8.4

Examine the question 'When exporting, you are only as good as your distributor'. Draw up a plan for forging a positive relationship.

Examine the conflicts between improving customer service levels and controlling costs in export marketing (December 1992).

Examine the factors that would influence a multinational enterprise to export (December 1993).

(**See** Exam answers at the end of this unit.)

Other direct export methods

These include management contracts and usually relate to large-scale undertakings, e.g. the running of international hotels, turnkey projects, etc. Also included is the growing field of direct marketing via 0800 numbers and/or direct mail brought about by advances in information technology and converges in consumer lifestyles.

Operating through an overseas sales/marketing subsidiary

This subject is examined in Unit 11 dealing with international promotion. However, it is often the case that companies set up overseas sales/marketing subsidiaries either to operate within the market via expatriates or to manage a local sales force. Additionally, an overseas subsidiary might provide technical back-up in terms of after-sales service to distributors contract manufacturers or licensees.

The advantages of an overseas presence are closer contact, specialized know-how and faster/more efficient control. The disadvantages include higher initial costs and a time-lag in becoming estabished, no initial local contacts, cultural disharmony and a risk to company reputation if failure is the result. Re-establishing the company's presence in the marketplace may not be straightforward re-entry.

ACTIVITY 8.5

Do some digging. Identify firms, by example, who are involved in each of the identified methods of entry. This will serve you well in examination terms.

EXAM HINT

Questions occur frequently on indirect and direct market entry. Look back at some past question papers. Be absolutely certain you understand the differences between, for example, agents and distributors. Often candidates mix these two alternatives in terms of description using such phrases as 'appointing agents or distributors'. This is a fatal error – they are patently not similar.

Overseas productions

This is the starting point for serious involvement – making the product overseas. For most companies the determining factor in manufacturing overseas is the size of the market and the profit potential. The greater the opportunity, the more is the likelihood of production overseas. However, before discussing the alternatives it is important to point out that overseeing production in foreign markets is a vast step upwards in terms of company commitment and involvement from the previous entry strategies. Although labour and buildings may be cheaper, the additional costs involved in transferring technological know-how, quality control and the management of the operation together with the finance involved should not be underestimated. Usually the additional 'pressure' is placed on the domestic production and operational staff who are transferred overseas to supervise the new start-up, often with regressive performance on domestic quality and supply. Reasons for producing overseas include:

- Size of market and profitability
- Tariff barriers reduce competitiveness in the chosen market
- Government regulations (e.g. India, Egypt) demand production be located there
- A major client company moves into overseas production. Japanese sub-contractors moved into the USA when Honda set up production
- Government contacts and support to inward investment
- Regionalization – being an 'insider' within the EU is important and, as a result, Toyota and Nissan have opened plants in the UK
- Speed of response, delivery, feedback and after-sales service.

Having decided to become involved in overseas production it is possible to hedge the limit of that involvement from licensing at one extreme to building a manufacturing plant on a greenfield site at the other.

Examine the steps taken by a firm moving from a domestic business to an international business (December 1992).
(**See** Exam answers at the end of this unit.)

Foreign manufacture without direct investment

Licensing
This requires a low level of direct investment. It confers the right to utilize a company-specific patent, trademark, copyright, product or process for an agreed fee, in a given country, over a prescribed timespan. The benefits to the licensor i.e. the company giving the licence are:

- No capital outlay, considerable cost savings
- Attractive to small and large firms alike
- Multi-market penetration quickly, especially important when dealing with 'products' with a short life-cycle (e.g. *Jurassic Park* merchandising, Power Rangers, Ninja Turtles, computer games. etc.)
- Access to local distribution
- Payment by results

It is easy to see how licensing has emerged as one of the frontrunners in penetrating global markets speedily. Furthermore, licensing is attractive where markets are politically sensitive, the risk is high, the tariff barriers are prohibitive or government regulations forbid company control in the market. The disadvantages are:

- Limitations on control of licensee
- May be establishing competition at end of the agreement
- Limited returns – the licensee is doing the work and will seek the major reward. Licensing fees can vary from 2–3 per cent for industrial products to 30 per cent for faster-moving short life-span products.
- Quality control and assurance. Given these circumstances, it is hardly surprising that the company's home standards or quality levels may have limited relevance.

Managing the licensing agreements
With these pitfalls in mind:

- Careful selection of the licensee is essential, especially in the area of quality control.
- Careful drafting of the agreement is necessary (domestic language and legal systems whenever possible).

- Retain control of key component/formulation. Coca-Cola is a licensing operation worldwide. The essence is produced in Atlanta, shipped everywhere to which 99 per cent local product is added (i.e. water!).
- Don't license latest state-of-the-art technology – license yesterday's technology (dependent, of course, on the market).
- Limit the geographic area of the licence.
- Register all trademarks, patents, copyrights, etc. in licensor's name.
- Finally, make the agreement attractive to retain.

Franchising

This has similarities with licensing but is more complex and involves greater management commitment and expertise as the franchiser makes a total production, operational and marketing programme available. Usually the franchise includes the full process of overseas operations and all the factors involved are prescribed.

Generally, franchises involve a service element and well-known international franchises include The Body Shop and McDonald's. Franchising, too, is expanding rapidly. It is a fast track to internationalization for many organizations. As the franchisee pays into the franchise the capital outlay is reduced and the financial risk lies mainly with the franchisee. McDonald's has recently announced that it is opening 1200 new outlets every year until the end of the century. It already has 14 000 outlets in 70 countries and is planning to expand this to 20 000 by opening up more outlets in Eastern Europe and launching in India. The vast majority of McDonald's outlets are franchises – although it is customary for the company initially to enter a country with its wholly owned outlets to establish standards of service and to train franchisees. For the record, in the UK McDonald's can open a restaurant for around £400 000 in 30 days. Most of this outlay (i.e. £250 000+) will be put up by the franchisee.

For the franchisee the benefits enable the small, independent, entrepreneurial individual(s) to enjoy the benefits of belonging to a large organization with all its power of economies of scale and marketing expertise.

Franchising is very fast-growing but not without its problems which centre on standards of efficiency and service levels and reflect cultural expectations. Even McDonald's has bowed to cultural values, and Kentucky Fried Chicken (KFC) in Japan has succeeded (after initial failure) by adapting to Japanese cultural values and expectation of what a US product should feel like. Similarly, The Body Shop sets its overriding corporate standards but the management and the delivery of the 'product offer' are left to locally determined values.

Contract manufacture

This is manufacturing by proxy, with a third party producing the product under contract. Besides obviating the need for investment and therefore entailing less risk, it avoids labour problems but enables the company to advertise 'local made'. Differing from licensing in that the end product is usually turned over to the company for distribution, sales, marketing, etc., contract manufacture is usually undertaken where political risk is high, the country is economically unstable, sales volumes are relatively low or tariffs are high.

In seeking contract manufacturers the company should give consideration to quality control issues and not produce where there is only one manufacturer, seeking to offset alternative producers. Finally, proxy manufacturing should take place where the marketing effort is of crucial importance to the success.

EXAM HINT

In the same way as candidates mix up agents and distributors, they do the same when considering licensing and franchising. Make sure you know the differences. Return to the text and check this point now.

Foreign manufacture with direct investment

In moving toward direct investment the company is again increasing its level of involvement.

Assembly

This typically involves the last stages of manufacture and usually depends on the ready supply of components shipped from another overseas country(ies). The key figures in this practice are the world's major car manufacturers who have created integrated component supply and assembly from CKD (Completely Knocked Down) operations, often referred to as 'screwdriver plants' to extensive deconstruction arrangements with specialized components, gearboxes, engines, etc. being made in highly automated plants and then shipped to a common assembly point – usually within a region (e.g. the EU).

Often local governments force manufacturers into assembly operations by banning the import of fully made-up vehicles. BMW, Mercedes and others are assembled in Thailand and Malaysia. The success of Proton cars, the indigenous Malaysian producer, partly reflects barriers and taxes on imported vehicles.

Other reasons for establishing foreign production include:

- *To defend existing business* Fearing US government intervention against Japanese imported vehicles, Honda started the move to produce within the USA. Other Japanese vehicle producers have followed this trend.
- *Moving with established customer* Once Honda moved to producing cars in the USA its Japanese suppliers soon followed to maintain the relationship and partnership bonding at the same time preventing US suppliers from cutting in on 'their market'. Suppliers here include banking and financial services and not just vehicle component suppliers.
- *To cut costs* With total quality management (TQM) becoming increasingly global manufacturers no longer feel so insecure about moving production overseas to benefit from lower labour costs, fewer restrictions or less taxes. The massive inward investment in China, India and Indonesia reflects this move and it will further accelerate.

Joint ventures

In joint ventures two companies decide to get together and form a third company that is co-owned (not necessarily equally). The third company then is an entity in itself and the proceeds (and pitfalls) are jointly shared according to the proportion of ownership. Generally, the two parties contribute complementary expertise of resources to the joint company. Joint ventures differ from licensing in that an equity stake exists in the newly formed company.

Increasingly, joint ventures are an attractive option for international companies. Factors accounting for this include:

- Technological development is prohibitively expensive but necessary to achieve break-throughs. Companies increasingly compete on this front.
- Rapid internationalization of many markets is beyond the resources of many major companies. Cooperation on production, distribution and marketing have brought benefits.
- Complementary management or skills and especially finance deals have led to new companies being jointly formed.
- Many countries restrict foreign ownership. China, India and South Korea are among those who insist on a form of joint venture.

Many hi-tech companies are now forging joint venture links to cut the costs of development and speed up market development. Those companies moving into Russia or Eastern Europe are nearly all doing so via this route. In 1990 Russia saw 150 joint venture deals signed, McDonald's and Pepsi among them. Obviously, partner choice is important. McDonald's and Pepsi chose the city of Moscow as its partner; Procter & Gamble's chosen partner in Russia is the University of St Petersburg. All three partners are preferred to the normal commercial arrangement partly because none of any substance or reputation exists.

On a negative note there is always the possibility of joint venture divorce. Some points for consideration before entering into the arrangement are:

- The venture must develop its own culture
- Venture partners must be prepared to share the problems, not try to blame the other party
- The venture managers must have access to top management of both parties
- The venture should receive sufficient capital and finance to develop
- The venture should not be overcontrolled by central bureaucracy

Strategic alliances

A strategic alliance has no precise definition but is different from a joint venture in that there is often no equity involvement, no separate organization is created. Loosely described, a strategic alliance is a 'swap shop' between two or more organizations who agree to cooperate strategically to the mutual benefit of both or all parties to the arrangement.

The development of strategic alliances is continuing apace. Hardly a month elapses without one or more being announced. The forces underpinning the creation of strategic alliances include:

- High R&D costs
- Pace of innovation and market diffusion
- Concentration of firms in mature industries
- Insufficient resources to exploit new technological breakthroughs
- Government cooperation
- Regionalization
- The fast-developing global consumer – the fundamental and most important reason
- Self-protection against predators
- Access to otherwise difficult markets.

Like joint ventures, strategic alliances need to be considered carefully before entering into the agreement. They should either be seen as a short-term, stop-gap arrangement or as a long-term partnership. Divorce is always messy and reneging on strategic alliances often brings repercussions at a later date. British Aerospace's cavalier abandonment of a 15-year partnership with Honda will hardly have gone unnoticed in Japan Inc. with a potentially long-term impact on future development of this kind between UK and Japanese firms.

ACTIVITY 8.6

Read the quality press, cut out examples/articles of joint ventures and strategic alliances – they are happening weekly. Create a file. Build your knowledge. It could be vital in the examination.

Wholly owned overseas production

One hundred per cent ownership representing the maximum level of commitment, complete management control and maximum profitability optimizes international integration – but is exposed to foreign problems and could face higher risk. Two main routes present themselves:

1 Acquisition
2 Development of facilities from a 'greenfield' situation

Acquisition is the quick way in, direct in approach with a clear picture of what is being bought – trained labour, management, sales, market share, distribution and an immediate return on the investment. However, many come to grief due to existing management leaving and clashes in cultural approach with management. Firms buy in haste but repent at leisure for, in buying an overseas firm, the company may be taking on board everything that is culturally at odds with the home way of doing things. Selecting the right company to acquire is difficult. It is easy to buy up a weak or 'poor firm' but turning it into a high-performance competitor is difficult. Volkswagen has struggled for years to come to terms with Seat (its Spanish subsidiary)s' inability to match Volkswagen standards of output and quality. Good-quality firms are not always available for purchase and are difficult to acquire – often requiring paying 'over the odds'. When Nestlé acquired Rowntrees in 1984 for £1.4 billion (at the time this was 30 per cent of the projected cost for constructing the Channel Tunnel) *The Economist* remarked: 'What price for 2 ft, (60 cm), of Supermarket Shelfspace – £1.4 billion!'. Nestlé were not just buying technology, factories, management – they were paying £1.4 billion for Brands, primarily Kit Kat, the UK brand leader in chocolate snack bars, and in doing so were eliminating uncertainty and risk in their market growth and search for pan-European brands.

With greenfield development, of course Nestlé could have chosen the option of building its own factories, developing its own brand over time. But time is a premium in today's marketplace and success in new product introduction is often ephemeral – few achieve it. Cadbury's spent years and a fortune in creating and developing Wispa (a chocolate bar) – a success but nowhere near on the scale of Kit-Kat.

Having said that the benefits of greenfield developments are also significant. Nissan and Toyota deliberately located their new plants in locations away from exposure and experience in motor car construction so as to inculcate new employees with modern Japanese work patterns. (Acquiring firms means that you acquire their bad habits as well as their good ones.)

In summary, the pendulum has swung towards acquisition, particularly in the world of modern developments such as information, technology, multimedia and other communications (e.g. satellite stations and entertainment industries). In 1994 Viacom (ever heard of them?) acquired Paramount Communications for $8.4 billion and it is rumoured that CBS will shortly be the subject of a bid.

ACTIVITY 8.7

Who's merging or taking over whom? Again study the quality press – something big is happening regularly. Create a file of examples. Additionally, consider the benefits accruing from each example you discover.

EXAM QUESTION

Why is there such a variation in market entry approaches? Using specific examples, show how a company uses different market entry methods in different country markets (December 1994).

(**See** Exam answers at the end of this unit.)

Entry strategy implementation

This aspect of the model has been covered comprehensively in the section dealing with channel distribution and logistics.

Entry analysis

A simple method of examining the options can be found in Terpstra and Sarathy; and also in Cateora. It is brief but does give the reader insight into some of the variables of choice (Table 8.1).

Jeannet and Hennessey have assembled a more complex model analysing the data required to assist the company in selecting its entry mode (Figure 8.2). It is complex for the variables are many. Getting it right is important. There must be a clear relationship between the benefits accruing from the method chosen and the implication for the firm.

Table 8.1 Matrix for comparing alternative methods of market entry

Evaluation criteria	Entry methods						
	Indirect export	Direct export	Marketing subsidiary	Marketing subsidiary– local assembly	Licensing	Joint venture	Wholly owned operation
1 Number of markets							
2 Market penentration							
3 Market feedback							
4 International Marketing Learning							
5 Control							
6 Marketing costs							
7 Profits							
8 Investment							
9 Administration							
10 Foreign problems							
11 Flexibility							
12 Risk							

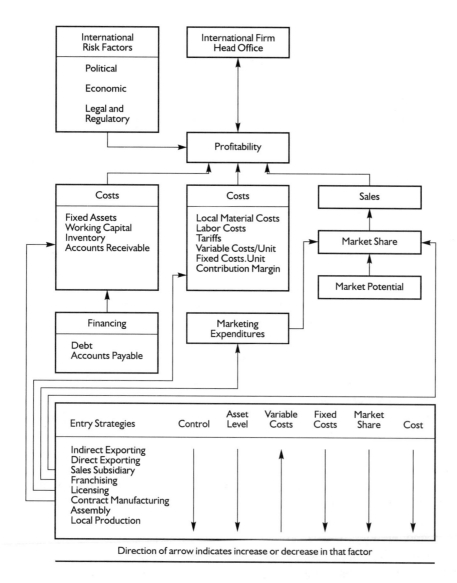

Figure 8.2 Considerations for market entry decisions (*source:* Jeannett and Hennessey)

Exit strategy

Painful as it may be, companies are sometimes forced to leave a market(s). The conclusion is that with foresight firms may dispose of their assets profitably (occasionally) and consideration should always be given to evacuating a lost-cause position 'before' taking the plunge and entering a market.

Political reasons

Changing political situations sometimes force companies to exit markets. Expropriation is often a risk in some countries and companies are advised to plan their entry strategies accordingly. Coca-Cola departed the Indian market rather than sell its controlling interest to local investors as required by local laws. Now it is re-entering the market after an absence of almost a decade.

Business failure

Before entering any market, consideration should be given to the cost of failure. Peugeot, Renault and others have left the US market with their fingers burned. Volvo similarly pulled out (at the last minute) of a strategic alliance with Renault. Lancia have withdrawn from the UK car market. Abandonment of a market, especially a major one such as the US is very expensive and can be damaging to the reputation of the organization.

Summary

Choosing the appropriate entry strategy is probably the most perplexing decision that companies have to make. A survey among CEOs of American companies suggested that they spent more time deliberating this question than any other in international business. Once the decision is taken it determines the rest of your strategy – financial, managerial as well as marketing. Moreover, it establishes the terms of engagement on the war for sales in a chosen marketplace. Such decisions are not taken lightly. But success in the future is not for the slow or the timid. Companies are going to have to become more ambitious and radical in their approach to the question – joint ventures, strategic alliances, complex partnerships between firms and governments are becoming the order of the day. The pace of advancement, customer demand and technology are forcing developments. Yet exit strategies are also important considerations. So the final thought is that flexibility will prevail over rigidity in the future.

Questions

- Identify the ways in which a domestic organization might obtain foreign sales without having any knowledge of overseas markets.
- Outline what might be some of the goals that a company might set itself in individual country markets.
- Consider for each of the market entry options the control elements the firm might wish to apply.
- What is meant by control? What are the difficulties in implementing control in international marketing?
- What procedures should a firm consider in appointing an agent, distributor, licensee?
- When might contract manufacturing be the 'right' method of entry?
- What criteria would you attach to appointing a franchisee?
- Acquisition, the easy route: greenfield development, the tough one. Discuss the pros and cons of each.
- Strategic alliances often fail. Can you explain why?

International Marketing, S. Paliwoda Butterworth-Heinemann, 1994, Chapter 6.
International Marketing Strategy, C. Phillips, I. Doole and R. Lowe, Routledge, 1994, Chapter 7.
International Marketing, V. Terpstra and R. Sarathy, The Dryden Press, 1994, Chapter 10.
Global Marketing Strategies, J.-P. Jeannet and H. D. Hennessey, Houghton Mifflin, 1994, Chapter 9.

December 1993 Textbook theories often state that companies succeed through satisfying customers' needs and wants. They are correct in this statement although successful marketing achieves a balance of exchange of values – usually accepted in benefits versus price. Always recognize that unprofitable business can be got anywhere! In the markets, domestic or international, the marketeer needs to determine what the balance is in terms of improving customer service levels (benefits) and the control costs in delivering the 'offer'. Increasingly, the cutting edge of competitive advantage in the majority of markets is customer service levels. But whereas in domestic markets improvements in service levels may be relatively easy to achieve (e.g. speed of delivery, consistency of delivery, ability to deal with special orders, small order delivery, flexibility of delivery, etc.), providing the same response overseas presents a formidable task. If it can be done, the cost impact may be enormous and totally outweigh the benefits. You should be capable of enlarging your answer along these lines. For example, The Body Shop UK demands weekly deliveries to each of its 150-plus shops within a 2-hour 'window' on a specified day. Could you do this in, say, Mexico?

December 1993 The answer should begin with a clear definition of a multinational enterprise (MNE), i.e. an organization producing and marketing in multi-country environments – with direct investment, etc. A description of one or more (by example) further supports your answer. As to why it should choose to export rather than produce in a given market, your response should be wide ranging. Issues are raised such as cost, logistics, the scale/size of the market, benefits from concentrated production in large factories, political risk, economic uncertainty, management topics embracing culture, tax efficiencies, government regulations (unlisting on joint ventures etc.). This is an easy question providing you know your subject. Of course, really high marks are awarded to those candidates who can support their answer by examples.

December 1922 Studying this text will have shown you that it is rare for an organization to move directly from a domestic base to become an international business. The majority go through a transformation period of indirect exporting, direct exporting to internationalization, i.e. the process is evolutionary via a series of steps. The answer requires you to examine the following steps:

- Experimental or passive involvement
- Active involvement or exporting
- Internationalization

Your answer must describe the process of what is involved from a marketing and a management perspective. In addition to the material in this unit you might consider factors dealt with in Unit 1.

December 1994 A good starting point might be a diagram to explain the range of market entry methods (see Figure 8.1). Your explanation of such a variety should include:

- Level of involvement
- Risk and control
- Size and resources of the company
- Scale of the market opportunity
- Cultural influences
- Corporate objectives

Selecting various markets/countries, see how the entry method 'fits' the needs of each circumstance. You should choose a range of countries of differing characteristics and apply the criteria to demonstrate your knowledge. Figure 8.2 illustrates the point.

Product policy

Product policy and product management are key to any successful international or domestic marketing strategy. International marketing, like domestic marketing, ultimately depends upon satisfying customer needs. In order to do this the customers have to be presented with the right product or service which is capable of meeting their needs as they perceive them. This unit will consider both physical products and intangible services and will extend understanding to areas of product tangibles and product intangibles including packaging and after-sales service as well as branding and imagery. In this unit you will:

- Review the forces at work which will enable the international marketer to standardize a product offering across foreign markets
- Understand the factors which inhibit or restrain standardization
- Consider the relationship between product and promotion in international marketing scenarios
- Review the application of portfolio analysis to international product management
- Consider the factors affecting international branding and product positioning
- Consider the factors affecting choice of packaging for products and/or services in foreign markets.

Having completed this unit you will be able to:

- Evaluate the factors which influence the implementation of product policy in foreign markets
- Identify the scope for standardization and globalization of product policy in international marketing
- Evaluate the optimum product range through international portfolio analysis.

Product policy and product management are key to successful development and implementation of international marketing strategy. Although product policy as a separate item takes up only a fairly small part of the syllabus in International Marketing Strategy, the correct selection of the product–market match is essential for the development of any strategy and resulting marketing mix.

This unit cannot be studied alone and needs to be reviewed in conjunction with other major sections of this work book including globalization (Unit 7), customer needs (Unit 4) and the other major elements of the international marketing mix (Units 11–14). As you work through this unit remember that product is far more than just the physical product, the technology or the functional features offered to the customer. You will see from Figure 9.2 that the product needs to be considered in deeper terms than just that. The packaging and support services component of physical products and of services are becoming much more important in the competitive environment of the 1990s.

In addition, it has been argued in many papers that the intangible aspects of physical products as well as services are crucial to competitive success. As technology becomes more widespread and cheaper for many organizations to harness, a certain degree of standardization becomes inevitable. If you consider for a moment the case of motor cars, computers, washing machines or bedroom furniture there is little nowadays to choose among the actual functuality of various products. However, the difference perceived by customers in areas such as status, brand, design and styling are key features which lead to the ultimate choice of product or service.

Developing the international product policy

During the discussions of product policy in this unit we will be considering both physical (manufactured) product as well as services. Services differ from physical products in a number of ways. Most importantly:

- Intangibility – we are unable to see, touch, smell or feel services.
- Perishability – services cannot be stored and these left unsold today cannot be sold tomorrow.
- Heterogeneity – services are very rarely identical from one delivery to the next.
- Inseparability – the consumption of the service normally takes place at the same point at which it is created, therefore being inseparable from the source of that service.

(For a more detailed explanation of the nature of services and services marketing consider page 282 of *International Marketing Strategy* by Phillips, Doole and Lowe or *The Marketing of Services* by Donald Cowell, Butterworth-Heinemann.)

There are five key areas of analysis in international product management. They include the question of standardization/adaptation – to what extent can or should the international product be standardized for overseas markets? Second is product–promotion mix – how do standardized or adapted products blend with standardized or adapted promotional practices? Third, we will consider the question of image, branding and positioning of products in foreign markets. Fourth, we will describe the special factors influencing packaging decisions in foreign markets. Finally, we will consider the application of portfolio analysis to international product range decisions.

Product standardization and adaptation

As we have also seen from our study of Unit 7 (Globalization) the advantages to be gained from a standardized product range marketed throughout the countries of the world are significant. In today's highly competitive environment, savings that can be made in areas of production, research and development and marketing could be a valuable source of competitive advantage to the international organization. On the other hand, there are a number of reasons why a standardized approach to all overseas markets is unlikely to be feasible for all organizations. From Table 9.1 we can see a resumé of the arguments made in Unit 7 which illustrate the various factors that can be identified as either driving or restraining the organization from a significant move towards a standardized approach to product policy.

In Figure 9.1 we attempt to identify the situation which faces most organizations operating internationally in the 1990s. Although conditions will vary from one organization to another and from industry to industry, generally the current situation for markets, supply and competition are as follows.

Markets

Most markets generally are between either the national level market or the regional level (i.e., EU, LAFTA, NAFTA, etc.). Driven by tastes, available distribution channel, prices and predominant trade barriers, the majority of markets (especially consumer) exist either on a national scale or a regional scale. There is also a marked tendency for polarization here.

Table 9.1 Product standardization

'Drivers'	'Restrainers'
• Economies of scale in production • Economies of scale in R&D • Economies of scale in marketing • Consumer mobility • The 'French'/'American' image • Spread of technology • Flow of technology • Flow in information • Cost of investment • Reducing trade barriers	• Differing use conditions • Government factors • Culture and language • Local market needs • Local tastes • Company history and operations

	Markets	Supply	Competition
National			
Regional			
Global			
Critical issues	Tastes Channels Prices Trade barriers	Trade costs Technology Scale Investment	Cash flows Cross-subsidies Brands Positioning

Figure 9.1 Factors influencing standardization adaptation

Some markets by their nature are becoming more national and even sub-national as people search for products and services which reinforce their own local identity. Other markets, meanwhile, are becoming more regional than national in their nature as consumers respond to the significant economies of scale that are available from a standardized product. Examples of these two forms of polarization would include motor cars tending towards the regional market size while snack foods are tending to polarize more towards the national and local market.

Supply
Supply conditions generally tend towards the regional. This is driven by technology, by economies of scale and by the increasing costs of investment. We see also from Figure 9.1 that the supply is being drawn both towards the global for reasons of scale and ever-increasing investment costs and towards the local in order to satisfy increasingly individualistic/nationalistic needs.

For your organization (or an organization of your choice) can you identify the major trends in markets, supply and competition? What implications does this have for your marketing strategy?

ACTIVITY 9.1

Competition
Competition faced by most organizations is predominantly regional in nature. The larger international and transnational organizations operating globally or in regions such as Europe, North America or the Pacific Rim are the driving force behind most competition in the 1990s. However, there are also signs here of polarization towards competition of a much more local nature as markets driven by a sense of fierce individualism as well as global

competition in those industries and industry sectors which are driven by scale and investment decisions.

We can see from Figure 9.1 that the world appears to be facing a polarization of most economic variables. This should not necessarily surprise us and if we consider the international trading environment we can see the two trends being equally successful. The global trend to production of standardized products for worldwide consumption at highly competitive prices is meeting a section of the market's needs. At the same time, organizations and consumers are feeling an increased need to demonstrate their own local or national identity and sense of individuality. As both these trends accelerate, often within the same individual or organization, purchase patterns will continue to polarize.

Product adaptation

Where globalization or standardization of product is not possible throughout the world's markets, knowing why to adapt products and how products need to be adapted to meet local market requirements is often the key to international marketing success. Before we consider the nature of product adaptation it is worth reminding ourselves of the constituent parts which go to make up the 'product'.

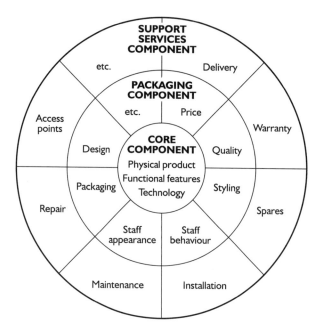

Figure 9.2   Product components

From Figure 9.2 we can see the classical approach to product components. From the customer's point of view the product or service which they eventually decide to purchase is much more than simply the physical product or functional features which go to make up a product or service. Customer choice revolves around the packaging and support service elements of a product offer as much as (if not more than) the actual core component itself. For example, the ultimate choice between two competing brands of washing machine or machine tool can equally be made upon the question of guarantees and after-sales service as they can upon the actual product features inherent within the core product component.

EXAM QUESTION

?

Various studies have shown that products are more likely to be standardized in international marketing than most other elements of the marketing mix. Examine how organizational structure might influence the product standardization of the new product development process (June 1992).

(**See** Exam answers at the end of this unit.)

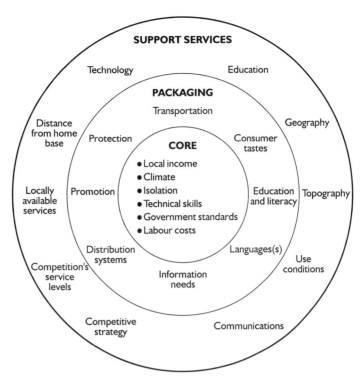

Figure 9.3 Product adaptation

The question of adapting products or services for overseas markets can logically be extended from this understanding of product components (see Figure 9.3). This diagram builds on the previous Figure (9.2) and attempts to identify a number of the characteristics in foreign markets which might possibly drive the producing organization to adapt or modify its total product offer in some way.

To explain the diagram in slightly more detail: a company considering marketing, for example bicycles in a foreign market, might look at the local pressures in the core component and consider that lower local income and isolation from points of service would drive it to 'de-engineer' the basic bicycle marketed in the home market in favour of one which had both less parts to go wrong and also was cheaper to produce. A cosmetics company might look at the packaging component and consider that transportation and distribution networks in the foreign market linked to differences in consumer tastes would drive it to a completely different form of packaging and presentation of the product than they would use to present the products in, for example, Selfridges perfume department. When considering questions such as adaptation within the context of the CIM examination this diagram produces a useful checklist which can highlight areas of market differences that demand changes or modifications in the basic (domestic) product or service offer.

The product–promotion mix

Having decided upon the optimum standardization/adaptation route for the product or service which the organization markets, the next most important, (and culturally sensitive) factor to be considered is that of international promotion. Product and promotion go hand in hand in foreign markets and together are able to create or destroy markets in very short order. We have considered above the factors which may drive an organization to standardize or adapt its product range for foreign markets. Equally important is the promotion or the performance promises which the organization makes for its product or service in the target market. As with product decisions, promotion can be either standardized or adapted for foreign markets. Figure 9.4 demonstrates the options available to the organization when it considers blending its product and promotional mix.

We can see from Figure 9.4 that there are four options open to the organization. The top left-hand position is that of standard product and standard promotion to overseas markets producing the global approach (Pepsi-Cola). The top right-hand box will be an appropriate strategy for organizations which find they need to adapt or modify the product in order to deliver the same perceived benefits on a market, national or cultural basis. A good example of this approach would be Phileas Fogg snacks.

Product

	Standard	Adapt
Standard	Global	Product extension
Adapt	Promotion extension	Dual adaption

Promotion (row label between Standard and Adapt)

Figure 9.4 Product–promotion matrix

ACTIVITY 9.2

Choose a product or a product class that you know or use. Try and identify the particular product–promotion mix strategies that are used in various markets. (A good holiday hobby!)

The bottom left-hand box in Figure 9.4 demonstrates the strategy appropriate to an organization that will produce a standardized product for overseas markets but requires an adapted promotions approach, often to support a different position in different foreign markets. An example of this strategy would be that used by bicycle and four-wheel drive vehicle manufacturers. A broadly similar product may be perceived as a transportation or utility item in some markets and a leisure product in others. The final box is that of dual adaptation, where both the product and the promotional approaches are also varied on a market-by-market basis. Many food items fall into this category with products such as sausages, soup and confectionery items being both different physical products and occupying different positions in the customers' perception.

Product positioning

The question of image, branding and positioning is culturally a highly sensitive area and it is true to say that real global brands are still surprisingly rare. Product and company positioning, we should remember, is not something we do to a product – it is something we have to do to the prospect's mind.

EXTENDING KNOWLEDGE

For a more detailed explanation of product positioning and differentiation see the companion workbook: *Strategic Marketing Management* (Unit 4) by Fifield and Gilligan (Butterworth-Heinemann).

Product positioning is a key element to the successful marketing of any organization in any market. The product or company which does not have a clear position in the customer's mind consequently stands for nothing and is rarely able to command more than a simple commodity or utility price. Premium pricing and competitive advantage is largely dependent upon the customer's perception that the product or service on offer is markedly different in some way from competitive offers. How can we achieve a credible market position in international markets?

The standardization/adaptation argument raises it head yet again. Depending on the nature of the product it may be possible to achieve a standardized market position in all or most of the international markets in which the company operates. On the other hand, the market characteristics and, most importantly, customer needs and values may be so different as to make a standardized position impossible. Examples of reasonably standardized market positions do exist (for example, Nescafé instant coffee) where the organization attempts to create and maintain a standardized position in all the markets in which it operates. To do this does not necessarily mean that the product itself is standardized. (In fact Nescafé offers a range of blends and roasts in order to achieve a standardized market position.) In other markets this standardized position is just not available. For example, the leading Japanese car maker in the North American market is perceived as Honda. If they were able to achieve a standardized position in all markets then one would expect them also to hold the number-one car position in the Japanese market – where, in fact, they are number four. What is the reason for this difference? Quite simply if you ask an American what Honda means he or she will respond with the word 'automobile'. If you ask a Japanese the same question the reply will be 'motorbike'.

Of course, existing, and possibly different, positions in various international markets does not mean that the organization cannot reposition in one or more of its markets to achieve a standardized international position. If this is deemed to be a profitable route for the organization to take then classical strategies on repositioning are appropriate in all international markets.

Closely linked to market positioning is the question of brands and product image. Brands are the names and personas which we give to our products and services and anything which involves language is liable to cause problems for the international marketer. There are a number of branding strategies and the four most commonly used are:

1   Corporate umbrella branding
2   Family umbrella names
3   Range branding
4   Individual brand names

(See Phillips, Doole and Lowe, pp. 301–306.)

We meet the question of standardization/adaptation again in the area of international product and service branding. Should brand names be internationalized to the extent that they can be used everywhere that the company operates? To what extent is such standardization possible or even desirable? As with the discussion about products and the standardization approach, there are many benefits to be achieved from maintaining standard brands across a number of markets. On the other hand, there are a number of reasons why organizations have tried and found this a difficult route to follow. The principal reasons why international standardized branding is difficult resides in the area of cultural and linguistic differences between markets. Many brands, brand names, brand marks or brand concepts simply do not travel well and need to be modified in order to gain market acceptance.

Packaging

Packaging for international markets also creates a standardization debate and to what extent adaptation will be required. As well as the obvious communications and presentation/promotional aspect of packaging which may or may not be standardizable for foreign markets, packaging also needs to consider any transportation and logistics problems. The decisions relating to international packaging might be dependent upon aspects such as:

In what ways do the demands of international marketing influence packaging decisions? Use examples to illustrate your answer (December 1992).
    (**See** Exam answers at the end of this unit.)

EXAM QUESTION

- *Local distribution considerations* How are products or services distributed within the marketplace? Are there understood and well-configured channels of distribution? Are there middlemen or intermediaries in the channel and what are their requirements? If retail distribution is an important feature, are they served or self-service outlets?
- *Climate* Is the local market subject to extremes or climatic swings? Will there be extremes of heat, cold or humidity which the packaging must withstand?
- *Geographical* How far will products or services have to travel? What is the logistics pattern that must be followed?

ACTIVITY 9.3

Choose two imported products in your home market. Can you identify those elements of the packaging that have been driven by your local market requirements? What factors in your market have made the changes necessary?

- *Economic* What is the predominant economic structure of the target market? To what extent will packaging be used after the primary product has been consumed? (Metal and plastic containers may be put to other, secondary, uses after purchase.)

Portfolio analysis

Standard portfolio analysis has been used by a number of international and multinational organizations to help them to identify priorities in their international marketing operations. The four most commonly used methods are the Boston Consulting Group approach, the GEC/McKinsey approach, the Arthur D. Little approach and Product Life Cycle Analysis.

EXAM QUESTION

Examine the problems of using product portfolio analysis in international marketing (June 1994).

(**See** Exam answers at the end of this unit.)

Students will be aware of the current discussion surrounding the use of portfolio analysis and some of the limitations which relate to its application. The same arguments apply to portfolio analysis within the international context as within the domestic marketing situation. Portfolio analyses of various sorts have been used over the past 20 years to consider options for both products and for markets that the organization might address. In international marketing the problems associated with portfolio analysis are probably even greater than in domestic marketing due primarily to the complexity of the data and the analysis required to produce a sensible result. If the evaluation of a portfolio within a single market produces problems then comparing the potential of portfolios across a range of markets becomes even more difficult.

As in domestic marketing, portfolio analysis is a good way of dealing with the product market match in conceptual terms – its use as a numerical model must be viewed as suspect.

Summary

In this unit we have seen that the primary question in international product policy is that of product standardization. The argument over standardization–adaptation is a very important one because:

- The economies of scale which can be obtained through a standardized approach to international markets are considerable.
- The reasons for an organization to adapt or modify its product/service offering to each separate international market are also compelling. At the end of the day, the primary consideration must be for long-term profitability and the candidate will be required to assess this objective against any situations presented in the questions or the case study. Remember also that profitability is not the same thing as sales maximization, nor is it driven out by economies of scale on their own. A balance needs to be struck between the needs of the organization and those of the marketplace.

Product policy is a key area in international marketing and decisions here will affect the entire marketing mix which follows. Customer considerations must always be top of mind for the marketer – domestic or international, and the role of market research in uncovering market needs cannot be overestimated in the international market situation.

Questions

As a check on your understanding of what has been covered in this unit, consider the following questions:

- What are the basic 'components' of the product? How will this understanding help your development of international product policy?
- What are the special aspects of services?
- What are the five key aspects of international product policy?
- What are the observed trends in markets, supply and competition?
- What are the benefits arising from a standardized product approach to international markets?
- What are the factors which might drive the company to adapt its product offerings to different markets?
- Explain the meaning and importance of the 'product–promotion' mix.
- How are products 'positioned' in international markets?
- How are brands managed in international markets?
- Can a company develop and maintain a global brand?
- What affects a company's international packaging decisions?
- Can portfolio analysis be applied in international product policy? What are the limitations on its use?

For a more detailed analysis and explanation of international product policy, read:

International Marketing, S. Paliwoda, Butterworth-Heinemann, 1993, pp. 201–250.
International Marketing Strategy, C. Phillips, I. Doole and R. Lowe, Routledge, 1994, pp. 281–320.

June 1992 In the exam itself, this question was not answered well by many candidates. Your answer should not have restricted itself to a long discussion about new product development but should have addressed the question posed. How is organizational structure related to new product development? The way that an international company organizes itself should be related to the markets it serves and its history. Strongly centralized operations are likely to maintain central R&D and marketing functions, so will develop new products aimed at identified international opportunities. Decentralized organizations' new product development activity is more likely to be focused on local market opportunities with possible adaptations made to suit other markets after proven success.

December 1992   To pass on the day, your answer needs to start with an understanding of the role of packaging in general but then *extend* this to the special needs of international markets. You should have considered issues such as extra protection requirements and adjustments to package design needed to cater for differences in culture, legal and brand positioning.

Good answers would also examine the cost and profit implications of packaging decisions as well as the different competitive marketplaces. If you haven't used examples to illustrate the points you make you would be unlikely to pass!

June 1994   To succeed with this question the candidate really needs to know something about portfolio analysis! A good answer would explain the role of portfolio analysis *and* then relate it to product planning in international markets.

Portfolio analysis has been criticized over recent years in domestic usage for a number of reasons. These reasons also hold good in the international area. In addition, the international marketer has the problem of acquiring data to feed the models which are both accurate and comparable. Very difficult!

Financial implications of international marketing

The financial implications of international marketing are too often ignored or are placed in a less important role by modern marketers. Finance and marketing are inextricably linked. Marketing is the primary source of revenue to any organization (interfacing as it does with the customer). Whether revenue produces profits, the lifeblood of the organization, depends on the ability of marketing and finance to work together. In this unit you will:

- Review the role of capital in international marketing operations
- Understand and be able to assess the risk involved in international operations
- Consider how profits are repatriated to the home organization. Having completed this unit you will be able to:
- Understand the financial implications of different international marketing strategies
- Evaluate suitable marketing strategies from any financial viewpoint.

The role of finance in marketing and international marketing strategy are relatively recent additions to the syllabus but are nevertheless essential for marketing management. The ultimate success of any marketing strategy must be judged on the profitability of the organization following the proposed strategy.

It is not always guaranteed that a question on the paper will be directed exclusively at the role of finance and financial implications of international marketing, However, it is clear from recent examiners' reports that answers to the mini case study which do not offer a clear perspective on the financial implications of proposed strategy will now be considered incomplete.

Prudent financial management is essential to the profitability and success of any organization, domestic or international. The major unique difference of an international organization is that the fund flows occur in a variety of currencies and in a variety of nations having distinct legal, political, social and cultural characteristics. These currency and national differences, in turn, create risks unique to international business. Additionally, a number of specialized international institutions and arrangements have developed because of these currency and national differences.

There are three principal aspects to the question of financial and international marketing strategy. This unit will consider these elements in order.

International capital

The organization embarking on international marketing must deal with a number of issues about its need for capital. Strategically the organization's capital requirements will depend largely upon the preferred method of market entry. In simple terms there are two forms of capital that will be needed:

- *Start-up or investment capital* is required to set-up the production, marketing, distribution and access processes before the sales process itself has started.
- *Working capital* is that cash required to finance the working transactions on a day-to-day basis. Working capital typically includes stock held and financing the debtor period between delivery and payment of invoice.

The international marketing organization's need for capital will be directly linked to its chosen method of market entry and level of involvement in international markets. For example, the organization exporting through agents or distributors will have fairly low capital requirements since it often has to produce few variations in product and only has to finance one or two deliveries at a time. If dealing through distributors, they will often take title to the goods and pay before they themselves have sold the goods on to the final users.

If an organization, for its own strategic reasons, has decided to enter a market through its own sales and marketing subsidiary, or even local manufacturing, it will require more capital to set up and establish the venture as well as additional levels of working capital to finance local stocks and wider product or service distribution in the target market.

Obviously, financial requirements may prohibit smaller organizations from taking on levels of involvement that are beyond them. Larger organizations may consider that their capital may be more profitably employed in other markets and will evaluate different market opportunities accordingly.

According to Eitman and Stonehill the financial management of any organization, domestic or international, can be considered as having four separate tasks:

1 The acquisition of funds
2 The investing of funds in economically productive assets
3 The managing of those assets
4 The eventual reconversion of some (or all) of the productive assets into funds to return to the original investors, creditors, suppliers, employees and other interest groups.

International capital requirements will probably be higher (in relation to total business) than is normally acceptable in the home market. International business will likely involve the organization in travel costs, shipping costs, duties, start-up costs, higher inventories produced by delivery time lags and smaller fragmented markets, as well as trade and export credit facilities.

International financial risk

There are two types of financial risk unique to international business:

- Foreign exchange risk
- Political risk

Foreign exchange risk

Foreign exchange risks arise from the need to operate in more than one currency. When an organization has assets or liabilities denominated in a foreign currency, or is doing business in a foreign currency, profitability will be influenced by changes in the value of that currency relative to the home or reported currency.

Why should a UK supplier invoice export goods in a foreign currency? Examine the advantages and disadvantages of foreign currency invoicing (December 1992).

(**See** Exam answers at the end of this unit.)

The most important foreign exchange risk is 'transaction exposure' which refers to gains and losses that arise from the settlement of transactions whose terms are stated in a foreign currency. Transaction exposure can be avoided, at a cost, by entering into forward contracts (this is a contract to buy or sell a given currency at an agreed price at an agreed future date).

Take a market of your choice, or one that is particularly important to your organization.

- What is the history of currency movement over the past 12/24 months?
- What is the future prediction for movement?
- What are the prices of forward contracts being offered?

Political risk

Political risk is the term used to cover those risks arising from an array of legal, political, social and cultural differences in the target foreign market. Such risk normally produces losses where there is conflict between the goals of the organization and those of the host government.

The government controls the nation's financial rules and structure as well as a variety of non-financial instruments designed to help achieve society's economic, political, social, cultural and ideological goals. Also, since the relative importance of the foreign government's goals is likely to vary from time to time the organization may find itself unprepared and therefore paying extra taxes and able to repatriate fewer funds than previously. The organization may also find itself employing more local managers or paying higher wages to its labour force.

International financial risk is an integral part of carrying out business in the international arena. It therefore cannot be completely avoided but its effects can be lessened by careful planning and prediction of likely future events.

Explain why exporting companies need to take special steps to reduce financial risk (June 1992).

(**See** Exam answers at the end of this unit.)

Repatriation of profits

In financial terms any project, including the decision to move into an international market or not, can be financially assessed according to the amount of investment required and the estimated funds which flow from the project. Internationally, of course, the organization will only take into account the funds which can be successfully repatriated from the foreign market in its assessment of the project.

Although the same theoretical financial framework applies to international as well as domestic projects, the calculation of returns is made more complex due to the special factors which influence international marketing. These factors include differing tax systems and legislation which affect the repatriated flows as well as differential inflation rates which can change competitive positions and so cash flows over time. Nevertheless, in the long run the international investment project must be judged on repatriated cash flows.

The organizations employing discounted cash flow methods of analysis (DCF) can assess competing domestic and international projects by building an additional amount into the discount factor to allow for the increased level of uncertainty in dealing in foreign markets.

Do you understand DCF methodology? Does your organization use DCF? What discount factors does it use for:

* Domestic operations?
* International operations?

How are these discount factors made up?

Conclusions

An understanding of the financial implications of any proposed international marketing strategy is essential for the international marketer if he or she hopes to get their project into the organization's list of priorities. Any organization exists to make a profit through satisfying its customers. International operations also need to be net providers of profit to the organization (see Table 10.1).

Having said that, there may also be non-financial reasons for the organization approaching certain international markets. Such reasons might include competitive defence of a major market through involvement in a minor foreign market, use of a particular foreign market as a test-bed for new product development or image and positioning reasons on a broader international basis

Table 10.1 Financial implications of international marketing

1 Capital requirements
   • Investment capital
   • Working capital

2 Financial risk
   • Exchange risk
   • Political risk

3 Repatriation of profits
   • Taxation
   • Political factors

This unit on financial implications needs to be read and understood alongside Unit 13 – Pricing in international markets.

Summary

In this unit we have seen that every marketing strategy activity in foreign markets has financial implication for the organization. The international marketer must understand the financial implications of any proposed strategy and given a choice between alternative strategic choices the marketer should be able to bring an understanding of financial implications to bear on the eventual recommendations.

Financial implications of marketing to foreign markets comes under three separate headings:

• Capital requirement
• International financial risks
• The repatriation of profits

Remember, business upon which we make no profit or for which we cannot repatriate the funds to the home office is business we can easily find in the domestic market!

Questions

As a check on your understanding of what has been covered in this unit, consider the following questions:

• What is the role of financial management in international operations?
• What are the three principal financial aspects to international marketing strategy?
• What are the two types of international capital that may be required?
• What are the two types of international financial risk?
• How can transaction exposure be avoided?
• How can political risk be reduced?
• What are the key problems associated with profit repatriation?

For a more detailed analysis and explanation of the financial aspects of international marketing strategy, read:

International Marketing, S. Paliwoda, Butterworth-Heinemann, 1993, pp. 261–263.
International Marketing Strategy, C. Phillips, I. Doole and R. Lowe, Routledge, 1994, pp 189–190, 439–440, 477–479.

EXTENDING KNOWLEDGE

December 1992 For your answer to achieve a pass grade you will have shown how invoicing in the currency of the customer, or a third currency, would give benefits to the buyer and help to secure the business against competition. The certainty of the cost of imported goods, the ability to compare prices and the reduction of exchange risk for the buyer are all valuable benefits.

The question, however, asks you to examine (not just list) the advantages and disadvantages of foreign currency invoicing. The approach is more customer oriented although extra difficulties are placed on international marketing strategy. Risks can be contained (at a cost) by forward buying currency or offsetting. The marketer must balance the extra profits from improved customer satisfaction against the risks associated with foreign exchange exposure.

June 1992 In the examination in 1992 the main reason for failure was candidates not understanding that simple PEST/SLEPT factors alone was not enough to answer the question. Obviously financial risk is the key aspect.

In order to pass, your answer should deal with currency fluctuation, non-payment and slow payment. These problems also take place with a scenario of different legal systems, different currencies and bureaucratic and administrative situations. Good marks are gained by explaining how financial risk can be reduced or avoided.

Marketing communications

Communicating in a multi-country setting is particularly difficult. The process involves dealing with language, culture, political and social constraints and local regulations. Customers differ, so how we address them needs careful consideration. Customers rarely buy features, they buy perceived benefits that reflect on their needs, motivations and behaviour. Applying a domestic SRC is of little use in international marketing. The subject of international marketing communication is a challenge. In this unit you will:

* Study the barriers to communication
* Appreciate the need to adapt the basic strategy to fit country/market needs
* Consider the implications of establishing a local sales force, mounting PR compaigns and using other Marcom tools
* See that sales promotion and advertising are particularly sensitive areas of communication
* Review briefly the problems of coordination and control in international communications.

Having completed the unit you will be able to:

* Understand that differences in macro and micro environments (markets and customers) affect how and why companies need to adapt their communication strategies
* Appreciate how marketing communications is driven by local needs
* Apply the tools of marketing communication to a given set of circumstances.
* Discuss the global versus local debate on branding and marketing
* Address issues concerning the international organization of marketing communication.

STUDY GUIDE

At the outset it is worth noting that students of this subject should also be familiar with the unit on international marketing communication in the *Marketing Communications Strategy* workbook.

The global versus local issue is one that is in constant debate. Here we set out the mechanics of marketing communications in dealing with the central issue of creating awareness, persuading and motivating customers from a rich, varied and diverse background to buy. This unit should therefore be considered alongside Unit 4 of this book, as it deals with customers and the international environment.

The management of international marketing communications (Marcom)

Marketing communications (Marcom) is the most culturally sensitive area of international marketing. Cultural barriers abound and the SRC must be avoided.

In Unit 4 we discussed in depth the issues of culture. Perhaps we can redefine it in simple terms: 'It's the way we do things round here.' Failure to recognize the difference and plan to take account of this will invite disaster. Remember, customers do not buy products but the benefits that accrue from them. These benefits are often mostly intangible. Marcom must ensure that all aspects of communication is compatible with the expectation and desires of the customer. Figure 11.1 indicates the potential 'break' in the flow of communication that can occur due to the cultural environment being different.

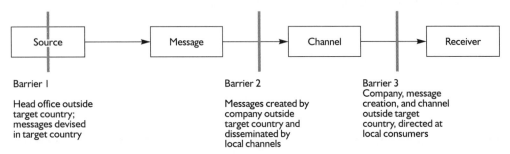

Figure 11.1 Barriers in the multicountry communications process (Jeannet and Hennessey, 1994)

The danger, of course, when faced with cultural barriers is to fall back on one's own SRC not just at the tactical level but at the strategic and management decision level. The textbooks abound with examples and case studies of companies who have failed to accommodate cultural differences in their Marcom planning and execution.

It is quoted that convergence and modernity is minimizing cultural differences and as such fosters the spread of globalization. But even such global giants as Marlborough, Coca-Cola, McDonald's, Sony and others take great care and fine tune their Marcom to meet local requirements. In purist terminology there is no such thing as a global brand, i.e. one that communicates with 'one sight, one sound, one sell'. All companies have some adaptation in their mix.

The international promotional mix

It is assumed that the reader is familiar with the tools of Marcom and their roles in persuading customers to buy. As markets differ, so must strategies. The first strategic consideration is whether to adapt a push versus a pull strategy. Figure 11.2 indicates how the tools of Marcom relate to their strategic decision.

Push strategy is less familiar in Westernized countries and is usually employed when:

1 The consumer culture is less Westernized
2 Wages are low and it is cheaper to employ sales-people than advertise

Figure 11.2 International and global promotion strategies (Jeannet and Hennessey, 1994)

3 A variety of languages, ethnic and racial groupings are present
4 Limited media availability
5 Channels are short and direct
6 The culture dictates its use (e.g. business etiquette)
7 The market is varied, i.e. split between urban and rural.

Pull strategy is familiar to the UK audience and is used when:

1 Advertising has great leverage in the consumer culture
2 Wide media choice together with the wide availability of other Marcom tools
3 Marcom budgets are high
4 Self-service predominates, i.e. supermarket culture
5 The trade is influenced by advertising.

Having decided the appropriate Marcom strategy, push or pull, the next decision is which Marcom tools are appropriate to the task and what difficulties arise in the international sphere.

Personal selling

This generally forms the major thrust in international Marcom when:

- *Wages are low*   Mitsubishi's Thailand subsidiary selling mainly air-conditioning units has 80 sales people in Bangkok. Philip Morris in Venezuela employs 300 sales people and assistants.
- *Linguistic pluralism exists* (multi-language)   There are two points to be made, contradictory in essence. The first is that there is a trend to spoken English in business-to-business markets. The second and more important point is that knowledge and understanding of the local language is essential. Never forget, it is the buyer who chooses the language, not the seller. In situations where linguistic pluralization exists (e.g. India) it is essential that personal selling plays a major role in Marcom – particularly when it is also the case that literacy is low and alternative Marcom tools are not relevant in the situation.
- *Business etiquette*   Success in selling can only be achieved if there is a relationship between buyer and seller. Few products are so unique that there are no alternatives or substitutes. Understanding and relating to the buyer's culture is a prerequisite of making the sale. Consider some examples. Lateness is inexcusable in Hong Kong – but expected in India; the performance of business introductions in Japan with the elaborate ritual of exchanging business cards; the banquets and frequent toasts in China; the lengthy process of familiarization between buyer and seller in Japan. These and many other examples make it clear that Western etiquette is at odds with many cultures. Even in Europe business etiquette varies considerably, e.g. meetings start early morning in northern Europe, not so in southern Europe. Incidentally, whoever invented breakfast meetings?

Negotiations strategies

Following on, it is apparent that negotiations and bargaining varies by culture. The Americans prefer confrontation with short exchanges and early decisions on the big issues leaving the details to later or to less senior management. The Japanese and the Chinese take the opposite view: great attention to detail, consensus within the group, long protracted negotiations. Before entering negotiations it is essential to understand the mindset of the other party. Being unprepared is a guarantee of failure. Other considerations are also important. For example:

- Location and space – where are the negotiations being held, how big is the room/office, seating arrangements (too close or not close enough)?
- Friendship – is it important to know your customer in terms of their family details?
- Agreements – are these rigid or flexible? (The Americans prefer rigid agreements, the Greek ones that are open to some interpretation and flexibility.)

Staffing the sales force

Increasingly, the trend is towards using local employees as opposed to expatriates. They are closer to the customers in culture and behaviour. They allow the company to position itself as an 'insider', reducing the risk of conveying a feeling of cultural imperialism. They subvert local restrictions on employing non-nationals. However, there are occasions when 'the person from HQ' syndrome still has a value.

Training or deployment of expatriates

Besides basic training in the PEST factors relating to a particular country it is sensible for the individual to acquire at least a basic understanding of the language. Having done that, an 'immersion' in the local culture prior to taking up a post is equally important. Toyne and Walters (1993) outline a programme shown in Table 11.1.

Table 11.1 Approaches to implementation

Initial training	
Length of training	Less than one week
Main objectives	Knowledge of key country facts and key cultural differences. Some words of the (main) country language
Training activities	Area briefings. Cultural briefings, Distance-learning kits of books, video and audio tapes. Survival language training
Location and timing	Before departure to assigned country
Follow-up training	
Length of training	One to four weeks
Main objectives	Development of a more sophisticated knowledge of culture and language. Attitudes and beliefs need to be considered and perhaps adjusted
Training activities	Cultural assimilation training. Role playing. Handling critical incidents. Case studies. Stress-reduction training. Moderate language training
Location and timing	Preferably before departure to the assigned country
Immersion training	
Length of training	More than one month
Main objectives	To develop appropriate competencies to manage in a culturally sensitive way and be functionally efficient and effective
Training activities	Assessment centre Field experiences Simulations Sensitivity training Extensive language training
Location and timing	In the assigned country during the work assignment, preferably front-load the activities

Source: Toyne and Walters (1993)

There is often the knock-on effect of how to deploy the expatriate sales person after the period of overseas activity and re-integrating him or her back into the company. Additionally, the cost of sending an expatriate overseas is increasingly expensive. Dependent on the 'attractiveness' of the location and the 'local' cost of living, it costs upwards of three times domestic salary to deploy someone overseas. The 'total' cost of employing a salesperson within the UK is currently put at around £60,000. Transferring the person overseas could easily exceed £150 000 p.a.

Recruitment, training, motivation – control of local sales force

The employment of a local sales force implies a single country and maybe even a single culture sales force. Briefly, the critical issues are:

- *Recruitment* Finding suitable sales representatives may be problematical, e.g. where qualified candidates are in short supply or because of the low status associated with selling. Selling may conflict with the culture. Local requirements may favour certain ethnic groups (not suited to selling characteristics). Tribal differences may forbid cross-cultural selling.

- *Training* Once trained loyalty may diminish if the culture is entrepreneurial or, alternatively staff may be 'head-hunted'. Who does the training? Are the trainers acculturalized with both company culture and local culture? Training of this nature is expensive in time and money.
- *Motivation* This may be more of a challenge than in the domestic market where money is the appropriate method. Titles, overseas trips, the size of office, entertainment allowances may all improve self-image which may be more important than monetary rewards, especially where selling is not held in high esteem.
- Control and evaluation Utilizing the commission method of reward control is easier than using straight salary. But the conventional rules of sales territory, call frequencies, quotas and strict reporting procedures may have little effect in some situations. Freedom to negotiate (failure means loss of face) may be paramount. Comparison among the sales team may also be culturally negative. So the conventional methods may well require modification although those basic principles should apply.

EXAM QUESTIONS

Analyse the appropriateness of using head office home-based, expatriates and nationals to develop an international sales force to cover a wide variety of country markets. (December 1994, Question 2).

What training and familiarization procedures would you propose for sales people, experienced and successful in the UK, to enable them to be effective in sales negotiations in a foreign country with a different culture and language. (June 1993, Question 6).

(**See** Exam answers at the end of this unit.)

Personal selling through intermediaries

Many companies sell indirect, via their distributors or licensees. Success increases if they think of the distributor's sales force as their own, keeping them motivated, abreast of domestic/global developments within the organization, mailing them regularly with information, involving them in the company, making them feel part of a far bigger organization, rewarding them as part of the organization. Run a sales conference for them. Invite successful sales persons to a pan-distributors conference. Make them feel important – they *are* important!

International trade fairs

These can be generalized or industry-specific and over 1500 international trade fairs occur annually. They play an important role in bringing buyers and sellers together in a way that would normally not be feasible – particularly for the 'missionary' firm wishing to enter a sub-continent or a region. The Hanover Fair, held annually, attracts 5000 exhibitors from around the world. Its origins were to make the link between East and West Europe but its scope and attractiveness is now global.

Trade fairs have many advantages:

- There is the interface between buyers and sellers
- Potential licensees or joint-venture partners may be discovered
- Products can be tested for interest
- Competitors' activities can be assessed
- They may be the only point of contact between buyers and sellers especially with former Communist bloc countries
- They are ideal for business-to-business organizations who often concentrate their Marcom budget around trade fairs
- Sometimes government assistance is available to fund the exercise. Contact the DTI for advice
- As such, trade fairs require careful planning, specialist advice and involvement, especially in language interpretation.

Contact the trade association for a major industry. Get some information on the scale of an international trade fair – they often are very much bigger than anything on the domestic front.

Consortium selling

This is usually associated with large-scale projects (airports, hospitals, hydroelectric plants, etc.). Partner selection is the crucial point here as is good to excellent relations with the host government.

Sales promotion

This is more common ground and most of us have familiarity with this area of Marcom. But beware, it is very culturally loaded. Sales promotions have a local focus both in terms of the offer and also from a legal perspective:

- *The offer* Airmiles are a great success in the UK but may have no relevance in most of Africa. Prosperity statuettes are popular in Chinese culture but would they work in the UK?
- *Cooperation from intermediaries* Retailers may be adept at processing coupons, handling oddly shaped premiums, creating displays, etc. – or they may not. Assuming that a French pharmacist is the same as a UK chemist would be a mistake. A country with small retailers may be difficult to contact (no phone, poor or non-existent postal service) and difficult to control.
- *Regulations* Laws relating to sales promotion differ virtually everywhere. The UK and the USA, for example, have few restrictions, other countries (e.g. Germany, Sweden, Japan) have many. What you can offer, where, when, how depends on the laws of each country. As of this moment there is no agreement within the 15 members of the EU. Table 11.2 shows current practice in Europe.

Table 11.2 Does you does or does you don't . . . ?

	UK	IRL	Spa	Ger	F	Den	Bel	NL	POL	Ita	Gre	Lux	Aus	Fin	Nor	Swe	Swi	Rus	Hun	Cz
On-pack price cut	Y	Y	Y	Y	Y	Y	Y	Y	Y	Y	Y	Y	Y	Y	Y	Y	Y	Y	Y	Y
Branded offers	Y	Y	Y	?	Y	?	N	Y	Y	Y	Y	Y	N	?	?	?	?	N	Y	Y
In-pack premiums	Y	Y	Y	?	?	?	Y	?	Y	Y	Y	N	?	Y	N	?	N	Y	Y	Y
Multi-by offers	Y	Y	Y	?	Y	?	?	Y	Y	Y	Y	N	?	?	Y	?	N	?	Y	Y
Extra product	Y	Y	Y	?	Y	Y	?	?	Y	Y	Y	Y	?	Y	?	?	?	Y	Y	Y
Free product	Y	Y	Y	Y	Y	Y	?	Y	Y	Y	Y	Y	Y	Y	Y	Y	Y	Y	Y	Y
Re-use product	Y	Y	Y	Y	Y	Y	Y	Y	Y	Y	Y	Y	?	Y	Y	Y	Y	Y	Y	Y
Free mail-ins	Y	Y	Y	N	Y	?	Y	Y	Y	Y	Y	?	N	Y	Y	N	N	Y	Y	Y
With-purchase	Y	Y	Y	?	Y	?	?	?	Y	Y	Y	N	?	Y	?	?	N	Y	Y	Y
X-product offers	Y	Y	Y	?	Y	?	N	?	Y	Y	Y	N	?	?	N	?	N	Y	Y	Y
Collector devices	Y	Y	Y	?	?	?	?	?	Y	Y	Y	N	N	?	N	N	N	Y	Y	Y
Competitions	Y	Y	Y	?	?	?	Y	?	Y	Y	Y	?	?	Y	?	Y	Y	Y	Y	Y
Self-liquidators	Y	Y	Y	Y	Y	Y	Y	?	Y	Y	Y	N	Y	Y	Y	Y	N	Y	Y	Y
Free draws	Y	Y	Y	N	Y	N	N	N	Y	Y	Y	N	N	Y	N	N	N	Y	?	Y
Share-outs	Y	Y	Y	N	?	N	N	N	Y	?	Y	N	N	?	?	N	N	Y	Y	Y
Sweep/lottery	Y	?	?	?	?	N	?	?	?	?	?	N	?	Y	N	N	N	Y	?	?
Cash-off vouchers	Y	Y	Y	N	Y	?	Y	Y	Y	?	Y	?	?	?	N	?	N	Y	Y	Y
Cash-off purchase	Y	Y	Y	N	Y	N	Y	Y	Y	?	Y	N	N	?	N	N	N	Y	Y	Y
Cash back	Y	Y	Y	?	Y	Y	Y	Y	Y	N	Y	N	?	?	?	Y	N	Y	Y	Y
In-store demos	Y	Y	Y	Y	Y	Y	Y	Y	Y	Y	Y	Y	Y	Y	Y	Y	Y	Y	?	Y

Y permitted, N not permitted, ? may be permitted with certain conditions
Source: Institute of Sales Promotion

- *Bribery*   Again a cultural reference – the way we do things round here! It is difficult and presumptuous to comment on practices in a specific country, simply to say corporate hospitality is an important customer motivator in the UK!

Sponsorship

This is growing in importance on the international front as global sports events proliferate. Coca-Cola, Mars, Gillette, Nike and other transnational organizations are busy building international awareness and identities via events such as the Olympic Games, World Cup Football, world tennis and golf, etc. Global media and communication will greatly expand and accelerate this trend – but it is only for the few companies that can create mass-market international customers.

Barter – counter-trade

Although, strictly speaking, outside the scope of Marcom, one of the biggest motivators in terms of purchase is counter-trade. Multinationals are extensively involved supported by and even initiating government involvement. Until recently it was the preferred method of exchange between East European countries and the West. Counter-trade and barter involves an exchange of goods or services. Its advantages are no currency risk, no trade barriers or taxes. In some cases the alternative to barter is no-deal. The disadvantages are numerous. To begin with, you might not want the counter-traded goods – having to dispose of them is wasteful of time and management resources. The quality of the goods you receive might well be variable, further handicapping your sale of them. However, it is thought that counter-trade and barter is on the increase, and as such, firms entering it must possess the required management expertise.

Track back through some quality press. Seek out examples of counter-trading – often with government support.

Direct marketing

This is well established in Western cultures and growing in importance. It is also expanding in countries like Hong Kong and Singapore – but has made, as yet, little impact in Eastern Europe and South America, most of Asia or Africa. It is culturally bound and limited by the dynamics of communication and distribution. Additionally, it is constrained by legislation playing a low key role in Germany, for example.

Telemarketing, like direct marketing is booming in the USA, growing in the UK but constrained for similar reasons elsewhere, particularly those of infrastructure. Having said that, 0800 marketing looks like being one of the major Marcom tools of the 1990s. Colleagues of mine regularly phone the USA to order computer equipment, pay by credit card and get delivery within 2 weeks. Dell computers have their pan-European help-line based in Ireland contacted by 0800 local rate calls and ICL's equivalent is in Delhi.

Door-to-door marketing is again dependent on the cultural reference. The concept is not well received everywhere and Amway, Tupper Ware and Anne Summers are hardly household names in every country. However, it is well received in Japan where even stocks and shares are sold door to door – and incidentally the technique has a place in the selling of motor cars. It was suggested that one of the reasons the Japanese stock market bounced back from a major fall in 1987 was the confidence gained from door-to-door sales persons exhorting customers to 'buy now, shares are cheap'!

Direct mail again is growing. It is increasingly sophisticated in its targeting and its creative delivery but again is limited in its development by cultural inhibitions and infrastructure. Recently Fiat had to apologize publicly in Spain for offence caused by a direct mail letter sent to females implying a romantic affair. It was to launch a new car but many were offended by its flirtatious tone.

Can you think of any instance of receiving any direct marketing communication from overseas? Will a fair proportion of the material you receive be postmarked Amsterdam? Can you explain why?

Public relations

Strictly speaking, the remit of PR extends beyond the scope of marketing to embrace corporate issues. Positioning the company within the host country is a corporate task. Being seen as an 'insider' is regarded as increasingly important – political links, employee relations and communicating with the wide spectrum of target markets such as the media, influencers, the general public, financial markets, local community, etc. The list is extensive. Foreign firms have a particularly sensitive role to consider in portraying themselves. We do not propose to cover the range of PR tactics but simply state the importance of PR in marketing the organization in overseas markets.

On a more tactical level (i.e. product level marketing) PR can be important where the market is both sophisticated or the opposite. In sophisticated Western markets PR agencies are employed in familiar terms of reference. In the case of developing markets PR is most important in spreading the message by word of mouth. Travelling exhibitions visiting small towns and villages, staging plays, sponsored by company X are frequently employed. In such an environment word-of-mouth communication has high believability.

Using an example of an organization opening internationally show how public relations could be used to address a variety of different specified audiences. (June 1994, Question 5).

(**See** Exam answers at the end of this unit.)

The development and management of international advertising

This is by far the most culturally sensitive of Marcom tools. Correspondingly no other aspect of international Marcom has been examined so critically. The textbooks abound with examples of international advertising misinterpreted and misused.

International advertising

Putting it simply, any advertisement is 'a message sent in code'. It is encoded by the sender and decoded by the receiver. Some messages are easy to decode (e.g. 'Harrod's Sale Starts Friday'!). Others are complex. But each message is designed to appeal to a targeted group and is invariably surrounded by its cultural reference. Since culture differs by country (and frequently within countries), decoding the message internationally becomes more difficult, is wrongly decoded or is irrelevant. Try explaining a Silk Cut cigarette advertisement to anyone who isn't British. So it is hardly surprising that sometimes controversy rages over international advertising. Perhaps Benetton is a good example here. It has variously offended cultural, ethnic and racial norms in several countries – occasionally its advertisements have been 'pulled' from a market. However, it is Benetton's aim to shock and to challenge accepted wisdom – and in this they have succeeded. Their message is probably 'if you're a non-traditionalist and a mould breaker by nature then Benetton reflects your mood'. Awareness of the campaign and the company is extremely high in all the countries it operates and, to date, sales appear to have benefited from the campaign. Other companies have not been so lucky.

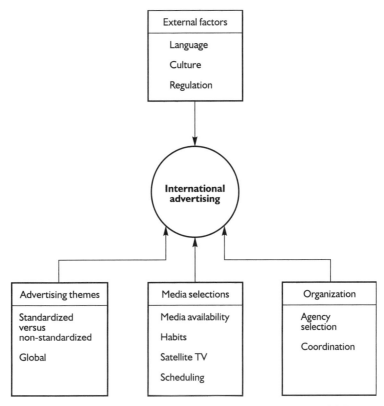

Figure 11.3 International and global advertising (Jeannet and Hennessey, 1994)

So the three central issues in developing international advertising are:

- *Message* What do we need to change in our advertising (from our domestic campaign) in order that foreign customers can decode the message? Alternatively, do we need to construct a totally different message?
- *Media* Having solved that specific question we have then to decide what is the appropriate medium to communicate the message.
- *Control* Finally, will we coordinate the various activities across countries?

Skim through some popular magazines and identify advertisements that you think are international (i.e. apart from language translation, they are used in a variety of markets).

Influence of external factors (culture, language and regulation)

Culture

It is apparent to all that culture is the most difficult aspect to master. Unit 4 addresses 'What is culture?' in depth and the pitfalls that surround it. Recently Moscow television screened some UK advertisements. Russian viewers understood the product-led features' dominant claims (but did not necessarily believe them). However, they seemed baffled by campaigns set in beautiful green countryside – the Timotei lady walking through Elysian fields. Only peasants live in the countryside was a typical reaction – what is she doing there? Similarly, although they liked the Andrex commercials with the lovable puppy they could make no connection between the advertisement and the product and thought it a waste of time.

Ronald McDonald's is not liked in Japan. His 'white' face is synonymous with death – white being the funereal colour in most of the Far East.

International advertising is full of anecdotal examples. Collect as many as you can and use them on the day!

Language

Pepsi-Cola's campaign of 'Come alive with Pepsi' translated into 'Pepsi will bring your relatives back from the grave' is only one of many *faux-pas*. The critical factor here is to transpose the language, not simply translate it. The textbooks abound with examples. The slogan 'Hertz puts you in the driving seat' can mean you are a chauffeur rather than a go-ahead business person.

Regulation

Each country has its own rules, laws and codes of practice. The Marlboro cowboy cannot run in the UK. There is a ban on cigarette advertising in France. What you can say, when you can say it, where you can say it and how you can say it varies across national boundaries. Muslim countries forbid campaigns showing scantily clad females or consumption of alcohol (although this varies by country). Advertising to children is another culturally sensitive area. Some countries do not allow commercials concerned with 'violent' toys and Power Rangers have been banished from Swedish television. Others forbid the use of children in commercials; others permit their employment but restrict them to certain categories of products. The list is formidable. Even now the EU has no harmonization proposals in place.

The role of advertising in society

Although a sub-sector of culture, governments occasionally take a standpoint on this issue. Recently Singapore and Malaysia have declared their opposition to advertising campaigns that are not consistent with the culture of the country – banning campaigns they consider excessively detrimental to the development of 'good behaviour characteristics' particularly among the young and adolescent. Good behaviour is defined as respectful to parents, religious values and authority.

Frequently the tone of voice of advertising reflects the culture of the society. German advertising is far more matter of fact and informative than its UK equivalent which relies more on humour. For the record, the most 'subtle' campaigns come from Japan, where talking about the product is considered bad taste. (For further elaboration on this point you should refer to textbooks commenting on low-context and high-context cultures.)

Advertising themes (standard versus non-standard)

The advantage of a standardized theme is obvious. It gives economies of scale and allows the creation of pan-regional or even global brands. But such campaigns are rare. The first requirement is a standardized product (or virtually standardized) with a standardized name. Such do exist (Kodak, Fuji, BMW). But the facts are that these are exceptions, not the rule, and there are few examples of successful standardized themes on the contextual content of the advertisement. The actors, their clothes, the situation in which the advertisement is set are all culturally loaded and open to different decoding. One successful campaign is for 7-Up, a soft drink which utilizes a certain character Fido-Dido. The product is always pronounced in English and the character remains unchanged – appealing to the 'one-world youth culture'. Campaigns for major international brands invariably differ by country/region (e.g. Levi have adjusted its 'Launderette' and 'Refrigerator' advertisement to meet the cultural requirement). However, what is important is that the theme of youth remains constant – it is the interpretation of it that varies (i.e. decoding of the message is unchanged). The danger of going down the route of a standardized campaign, creating advertising that has 'some' meaning in every country, is that it motivates no-one anywhere. Euro advertising campaigns occasionally appear on UK television mainly to the annoyance of all. At the very least, they appear irrelevant. See if you can identify some.

There is very little global advertising, although global positioning is on the increase. Coca-Cola's approach is to make a 'batch' of commercials which portray a similar positioning of the brand image and then discuss with country managers which commercials are most appropriate to their culture and environment. McDonald's adopt a broadly similar approach, taking a global position. Within Europe, Nescafé is positioned as the premier instant coffee with 'best beans, best blend, best taste' and uses as its icon the red mug. The transposition of 'best, best, best' is left to local marketers as coffee and instant coffee specifically has vastly different perceptions across the European marketplace.

Summarizing, standardized advertising requires similar consumers, with similar lifestyles and aspirations seeking similar rewards. Such clusters exist e.g. business travellers, senior business executives etc. and it often seems that the inhabitants of Upper East Side, Manhattan have more in common with their counterparts in Kensington, London than they do with their neighbours a block away. How else would you explain the success of Hugo Boss suits, Rolex watches and other designer type products, Armani, Versace, etc?

Media selection (media availability, satellite TV, scheduling)

Media availability

Setting aside regulations on advertising themes the choice of media to carry messages varies enormously. The UK has abundant choice in newsprint with six or seven national newspapers. Nowhere else has this breadth of choice. Newsprint in most European countries is largely regional, although Germany has the Continent's biggest circulation paper with *Bild Zeitung*, selling about 5 million copies per day. Circulation for the No. 2 newspaper *FAZ* is little more than 500 000. France is dominated by a regional press, with *Ouest France*'s circulation being double that of *Le Figaro* or *Le Monde*.

It is impossible to cover the subject of media availability in depth: it is sufficient to acknowledge its wide variability in terms of type of media – and the degree of penetration and influence in the marketplace.

For the record, media consists of television, newspapers and magazines, outdoor, cinema and radio.

Satellite TV

This is a recent development but one that will grow into enormous proportions by the end of the decade. Europe and the Far East are in the forefront of its current development phase with the creation of Sky Channel and CNN. Satellite, with its multi-country footprints, is becoming more prominent. Besides the language difficulties (i.e. transmitting in multi-languages) the beneficiaries of satellite are likely to be the major pan-regional advertisers. Satellite transmissions are being focused on by national governments as they frequently breach country regulations. Singapore and Malaysia have recently banned Star TV to protect their population from 'foreign values'. In the Far East, Star TV, a Hong Kong-based satellite company, owned by Richard Murdoch's corporation, overtook CNN as India's favourite foreign programme. It and others' growth potential in the Far East is colossal. Satellite will be a huge communication medium in the next century as technology advances.

Scheduling media

The timing of the delivery of the message is decided by the demand of the audience. Most products have a cyclical sales demand peaking seasonally or in line with religious festivals and national holidays. Obviously, these differ by country/region (the Southern Hemisphere's Christmas is in their Summer). But holidays are also key purchasing moments and since holidays vary, media must be scheduled accordingly. In France most of the country closes down in July–August. The Germans stagger their summer holidays by *landes* (their equivalent of counties). In some Muslim countries advertising is restricted, or banned, during Ramadan. Winters and summers vary in duration and intensity across the globe. Thus seasonal products such as de-icing equipment or air-conditioning units will be advertised at different times. The international marketing company needs to take account of differences in scheduling (and budgets).

What implications does the variability of media in different countries have for the strategy, implementation and control of advertising for the international manager. (June 1994, Question 9).

Examine the implications of variations in media availability, media cost and audience coverage on a company wishing to develop a standardized media approach to its many international markets. (June 1993, Question 5).

(**See** Exam answers at the end of this unit.)

Give serious thought to collecting examples of companies who utilize all the tools of marketing communications internationally. It might be useful to select a major multinational (not a UK company) and examine its Marcom plans in the UK. IBM is just such an organization. American, yet deeply entrenched in the UK. What are its advertising, PR, sales promotion, direct marketing and sales programmes?

Organizing and co-ordinating the advertising effort

Time and effort spent organizing and coordinating the advertizing effort is at least as important as time spent crafting the message and the media. The basic choices facing the multi-country international advertiser are:

1   *Domestic agency*   It is most common that advertisers use their domestic agencies when first expanding overseas, for reasons of familiarity, relationship, trust and knowledge of their business (all the normal reasons for choosing an agency in the first place). But

many smaller domestic agencies have no international experience themselves but form a liaison and association with similar-sized agencies overseas and service the advertiser's account by proxy. This generally is a stage-one operation.

2   *Appointing local agencies*   This is generally a step taken by advertisers who recognize the need for a differentiated campaign. Local agencies understand local cultures, have the relevant contacts among the media and can create or adopt campaigns to meet the local requirements. Jaguar found, to its cost, when advertising in the Middle East that Arab headwear differed in detail from country to country. Locals easily spotted the difference and ridiculed the campaign, which was attempting to appeal to all suitably wealthy males. Nestlé adopt a roster approach, appointing from an approved shortlist of advertising agencies, thus getting benefits of acculturalization by market and minimizing the degree of control to a few agencies.

3   *Centralizing the effort*   The 1980s in particular saw the spread of major agencies into the global arena. Many of the US majors were already established servicing global clients such as Esso, Coca-Cola, etc. But it was Saatchi & Saatchi who really began the trend towards global advertising, exploiting the theories of Levitt regarding globalization and persuaded major multinational corporations to develop world advertising (e.g. British Airways and Mars). It was Saatchi who coined, or at least popularized, the phrase 'one sight, one sound, one sell' – global communication. The advantages of such a campaign are apparent and have been discussed extensively in the textbooks. Similarly, the advantages of central creativity and global servicing through a single agency are equally obvious. However, although global agencies are still a growing trend they have been shown to have limitations in that the global advertisement has been elusive. To many it is seen as a shimmering oasis that appears wonderful but impossibly difficult to grasp or achieve. Having said that, IBM in 1994 has placed all its Marcom through Ogilvy & Master in an attempt to speak to all its customers with one corporate voice. It remains to be seen whether customers will respond to this positively. For decades McCann-Erickson played the role of guardian of the universal brand values for Esso ensuring consistency of corporate logo and brand communication. Until recently another inter-public group agency fulfilled the same task for Coca-Cola.

Who are the major advertising agencies in the UK? How many of them are international? Get a feel for what the structure of the advertising industry is like. How many international agencies have international clients?

ACTIVITY 11.4

Coordination

Whatever the strategic choice, domestic, local or central, international advertising has to be controlled both in terms of the message and in budgetary terms. This requires management expertise at the marketing headquarters (usually at the domestic base). While decentralization has its distinct advantages – the locals are closer to the customers – the danger is fragmentation, with country managers pursuing their own agendas frequently to the overall detriment to international brand values – imperceptibly at first but, over time, shifting consumer recognition and understanding away from the corporate goals. Decentralization requires very careful handling and control in terms of guidelines relating to advertising claims, tone of voice, logo, colours, etc. and in terms of scale of the budget and scheduling of the campaign. Conversely, heavy-handed centralized control can be equally destructive, stifling creativity if overprescribed. Creative personnel – with the talent for differentiating your product offer from competition – dislike working within rigid guidelines. Essentially, the way (the style) through which international advertising is administered is at least as important as the company procedures employed.

Summary

Marketing communication is probably the most discussed area of international marketing. Not only is it rarely out of the news (it invites controversy) but the majority of us have exposure to it. What makes it so interesting is that it is culturally loaded. Everyone has a view. The challenge for the future is increasingly to internationalize the communicative mix. World consumers, world competitors, world advertising agencies lead to a consolidation in strategic terms of the marketing effort. Yet the paradox exists. Consumers though seeking global benefits remain doggedly local in their outlook. While strategy can take the global view, marketing must balance the benefits of 'one sight, one sound, one sell' with local needs. Issues such as cost, coordination and control also require careful consideration before any decisions are taken.

Questions

- Explain the greater importance often attached to personal selling in overseas markets.
- What are the problems and difficulties in establishing a local sales force?
- Specify some of the issues involved with sales promotions overseas. How might the deployment of a local rather than a domestic sales promotions agency assist in overcoming problems?
- What factors influence the development of push or pull strategies in international marketing communications?
- Specify the conditions under which a company might employ a local versus a home-based sales effort.
- What patterns do you reserve in the use of sales promotion across Europe?
- What type of companies sponsor Formula 1 motor racing (apart from the oil giants)? What benefits do you think they gain?
- Is global advertising for the few, or do you see it developing as a major force?
- How should the advertising industry respond to the new technological trends in mass media communication (e.g. cable, satellite, Internet etc.)?
- Why are some global advertising campaigns successful while others fail?
  Illustrate your answer by examples.

Global Marketing Strategies, J.-P. Jeannet and H. D. Hennessey, Houghton Mifflin, 1994, Chapters 14 and 15.

International Marketing, S. Paliwoda, Butterworth-Heinemann, 1994, Chapter 12.

International Marketing Strategy, C. Phillips, I. Doole and R. Lowe, Routledge, 1994, Chapter 9.

International Marketing, V. Terpstra and R. Sarathy, The Dryden Press, 1994, Chapters 12 and 13.

CIM Workbook: Marketing Communication Strategy, T. Yeshin, Butterworth-Heinemann, 1995.

December 1994, Question 2   The answer needs to be set in the context of an international sales force and should be sub-divided into three constituent parts with each analysed separately:

HQ (home based)   – suitable for large capital projects
      – high profits to cover high costs
      – detailed knowledge required at highest level (e.g. installing turbines in hydroelectric schemes, development and sale of aero engines

Expatriates	–	where knowledge of the company and its systems is important plus ability to adapt locally
Nationals	–	linguistic and cultural compatibility
	–	lower cost
	–	understanding of company, its culture and system

The conclusion should be one of balancing advantages versus disadvantages and should include references to cost, efficiency and control.

June 1993, Question 6   The question might be divided into two parts – training and familiarization:

Training	–	Teaching of practical skills, language and cultural references, pricing, distribution and documentation. Language training covering social skills and the language of the particular industry. Language training will vary – some countries (cultures) will insist on fluency, others settle for less.
Familiarization	–	Role play in home country, preferably with person native to country concerned, followed by overseas visit (perhaps several) to gain experience. Shadowing local managers is another technique.

The important point is that to be an effective salesperson, skilled in negotiation, takes time and a full understanding of the local culture.

December 1994, Question 5   The starting point is to define 'operating internationally' and restrict your answer to a multinational enterprise. It is unlikely that an export-driven firm would employ PR internationallly, addressing a variety of different specific audiences. Then choose your organization – select one that you can write about with some confidence (e.g. IBM). Next, specify some audiences, as requested in the question.

The audiences are very varied, ranging from the government down to private individuals. You should identify five or six discrete publics. For each, show how PR can influence their varied concerns. For example, at government level, lobbying ministers, influencing MPs, factory visits, etc. ensure that IBM is positional as an 'insider' in the UK and is a major contributor to the UK economy. Do the same for each audience and don't forget the vital role of communicating with the company's internal audience.

December 1993, Question 7   There are relatively few global brandings, though their number is increasing fast (Kodak, Coca-Cola, Niké, Fuji, Porsche, Ferrari, BMW). In 10 years' time there will be many more. Your answer to global branding should include a clear definition in addition to naming them. Refer to Unit 2 and Unit 3 for more guidance.

Global marketing is more varied. Global names exist but the marketing may have a localized focus. Specify by examples where international brand names are adapted to meet local conditions. Nescafé is a good case in point where the brand name is constant worldwide but the product, its packaging and its marketing communication varies considerably to meet cultural requirements. Are they the same? Clearly not. Under what conditions might each succeed.

Global branding requires the existence (or creation) of global customers – a unique set of circumstances but one that is becoming more common as technology is creating convergence. Refer to Unit 2 and Unit 3 for more depth.

Global marketing is strategic adaptation. Your answer again needs elaboration by examples of customer, competition, market, and country differences.

June 1994, Question 9   Define 'media'. It is above-the-line (ATL) communication. Therefore do not write about PR, sales promotion, brochures or anything else!

Start by mentioning the depth and breadth of availability in the UK and go on to say no other country has a similar network with which to reach customers. Quote by examples.

Having comprehensively addressed availability (or lack of it) you should continue to specify, by example, other restrictions or constraints, legal, religious and social conventions, voluntary codes of practice, etc. Then under separate headings apply what you have said to (a) strategy, (b) implementation and (c) control. Dealing solely with (c) the starting point would be:

- Availability of data on audience, coverage, reach, in order to plan and set standards
- The context and image of the publication
- Ability to measure performance – who read what, for example
- What research facilities are there to track effectiveness (e.g. pre- and post-advertising research of a quantitative and a qualitative nature).

You should end with a conclusion. You would briefly say that it is extremely difficult to plan, coordinate and control international advertising.

June 1993, Question 5   This question overlaps with the previous one and gives you some insight into the frequency of examination questions dealing with the topic of international marketing communications and advertising in particular. Diploma candidates will note there is frequently a question on international marketing communications in the marketing communications strategy examination.

Your approach should centre around why advertising should be standardized and what are the benefits of this strategy, and note that it is a growing trend as the world becomes more of a global village and technology creates global consumers. The advantage of standardization is really of greatest benefit to new products/companies.

Your answers then should cover the following points.

- Media availability (see comment on previous question)
- Lack of 'international' media (but it is growing, e.g. satellites)
- Media cost
- Audience coverage
- Conclusion. It's difficult to implement, but more companies will seek to do it in the future.

Distribution and logistics

Distribution and logistics are fast becoming critical factors in international marketing. Speed or time is increasingly the critical differential linked to costs. Getting the product or service delivered to the customer when it is needed and responding flexibly to marketplace demands has now assumed paramount importance. Federal Express is the world's sixth largest airline, succeeding by fast delivery worldwide. Customerization and groupage are again logistic advances. In the field of distribution things are equally dynamic with technology and modernity changing old-established routes to the customer (e.g. garage forecourts have become a major competitor in grocery retailing terms in the past 5 years). In this unit you will:

- Study the factors important in developing distribution strategies
- Recognize the *cost* implications of logistics
- Be aware that service levels are a very important marketing tool
- Consider the management aspects of distribution
- Study new trends for the future.

On completing the unit you will be able to:

- Explain the basis of a distribution strategy
- Identify the step-by-step approach and the impact each step might have on the overall delivery
- Review the impact of cost versus service and the management implication emanating from service-level decisions
- Evaluate the changing patterns in distribution and predict trends in what is happening (or likely to happen) in the future.

This unit sets out to guide the reader through the balance of satisfying customers and making profits. Both are essential to commercial success. No business succeeds by totally putting one at the forefront.

International distribution and logistics is fast becoming the difference between success and failure. Customers will no longer wait on your terms. Your organization has to match their requirements or face the consequences.

The management of distribution and logistics

Getting the goods ready and available for purchase by foreign customers is an integral part of the marketing mix. Both the business environment and the cultural frame of reference vary by country – so therefore must the distribution and logistics underpinning it. The number of retail outlets per population varies enormously, as do the range and variety of intermediaries. The degree of government control over them also varies. What they sell, how they sell it and everything that goes along with effective 'delivery' of the offer is ultimately dependent upon one thing – the consumer. What we offer has to be available on terms that are compatible with the customers' needs and wants.

If this is so, then the company's distribution strategy is one part of the marketing mix and it needs to be consistent with other aspects of the marketing strategy namely product, price and communications. Furthermore, Stern and El-Ansary (1982) make the point that the marketing channel (distribution) is a continuation of interdependent organizations in the process of making the product available for use or consumption. As such, the distribution channel is different in that it is largely managed rather than controlled. The management of channel within the chosen market is a combination of:

1 The culture, business environment and customer expectation
2 The objectives of the company, its resources, the availability of suitable channels and the ability of the company to service the channel appropriately.

Factors in developing the distribution strategy

Jeannet and Hennessey highlight four distribution decisions within the marketing mix, making the connection that distribution must be consistent with the rest of the mix (Figure 12.1).

The four decision points are:

1 *Distribution density* What is the ideal number of sales outlets required in order to service the customer? Remember, to be successful we need to be available where the customer expects it, so the critical factor is the consumer's shopping/buying behaviour. In general, fast-moving consumer goods are expected to be in extensive distribution and if that means every 'Mom and Pop' store then so be it. If the culture is to sell the product in single units (e.g. one cigarette or one sweet via street hawkers) then the company has to respond. The opposite is true in selling speciality and up-market branded goods where exclusive distribution may be required. Similarly, the purchase of industrial or business-to-business goods varies by country, from selling direct to end users, on the one hand, to recognized government suppliers/intermediaries, on the other. But throughout it is the buyer/customer who decides.

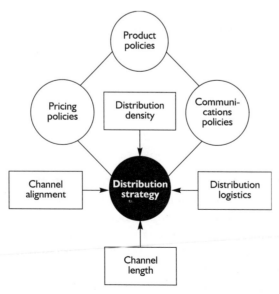

Figure 12.1   Distribution policies

2   *Channel length*   Put simply, this is the number of intermediaries involved in connecting the company, its product and the end buyer/user. Again, this is mainly determined culturally and varies by country. Japan, the leading high-tech country, has an exceedingly low-tech distribution system with many intermediaries connected via *Keiretsu* agreements. This makes distribution slow, wearisome and very expensive as each intermediary takes their 'cut'. Few Western companies have broken this internal mechanism and sell direct to customers. Toys'R'Us is such an exception but it took US government pressure to succeed – opening in direct competition with over 600 small traditional toy-sellers. *Note*: the successful innovations in creating different routes have been exclusively the major international brands/retailers who have had the financial muscle and government corporation (Coca-Cola, Nestlé, Niké, etc.).

Increasingly, in Western societies channel length is shrinking, making it at once easier and more difficult to break into a market. The UK grocery is dominated by five major multiples and, at a glance, it is easy to see how national distribution can be achieved. But failure to gain 'listing' means failure in the marketplace. France is undergoing remarkable change, leaping from a nation of village storekeepers to supermarket giants. For example, Mammouth, Leclerc and Casino have achieved national prominence in less than a decade, so don't assume a linear programme from small to large – it happens overnight, driven by technology and satisfied customers.

3   *Channel alignment*   This concerns the effective management of the various intermediaries in its distribution chain. For a company with no direct involvement in a foreign market this is a most difficult task. Distance seriously hampers coordination. Generally, one of the participants in the distribution chain stands out as the dominant member – major retailers in the UK; wholesalers in the USA; distributors (often the only importers) in emerging countries. The company has to recognize the dominant channel member country by country and align itself accordingly. Relationships are crucial, for the channel intermediaries are not and never will be in the control of the company. The skill is in managing the relationship.

4   *Distribution logistics*   Physical distribution management (PDM) is described by Kotler as concerning the planning, implementation and control of physical flows of materials and final goods from points of origin to points of use in order to meet customers' requirements. However, in this context we will limit ourselves to the logistical aspect, i.e. to view the process from the perspective of the customer and to work our way backwards towards the factory. We recognize, in passing, the very important point of cost, for it is the balancing between customer needs and costs that is the basis for profit. Drucker, some while ago, dwelt on the balance between efficiency (doing things right) and effectiveness (doing the right things). A combination of the two is the ideal – but the realities of international distribution logistics mean there is always a trade-off.

Select any industry in your domestic market. Specify the separate stages in the distribution process dealing with each outlet type separately (e.g. food/grocery retailing). Then try to second-guess some of the additional factors that might affect servicing the same industry/market overseas.

ACTIVITY 12.1

High costs in international logistics

Moving goods from country to country is expensive. Up to 35 per cent of the cost of goods can be accounted for by distribution (varying by distance and other visible/invisible barriers). Additional impediments include:

- Delivery scheduling
- Just-in-Time (JIT)
- Inventory holding levels
- Zero defect delivery
- Emergency need systems.

Intermediaries

Customers the world over are becoming increasingly demanding – the field of distribution logistics increasingly competitive, internationalised and dominated by major players. As mentioned earlier Federal Express has the sixth largest fleet of aircraft in the world, yet flies no passengers – dealing only with the shipment of goods.

ACTIVITY 12.2

Taking the same industry, determine what are the changes taking place that affect logistics (e.g. windows of delivery, development of new outlet types such as Garages). See if you can plot the dynamics of distribution and logistics.

The total distribution cost approach

Phillips, Doole and Lowe (1994) explain how and why international logistics not only incurs additional costs but is more complicated. The formula they propose is:

$$D = T + W + I + O + P + S$$

D = total distribution costs, T = transport cost, W = warehousing, I = inventory costs, O = order processing and documentation, P = packaging, and S = total cost of lost sales resulting in failure to meet customers' performance standards.

The extra costs in international logistics

1 Distance from customers means increased:
   - Transport time
   - Inventory
   - Cashflow
   - Insurance.
2 Additional variables include:
   - transport – sea
                  – air
                  – land
   - Documentation
   - Robust packaging (resistant to damage/pilfering)
3 Greater complexity
   - The dimension of culture
   - Language
   - More documentation
   - The management of additional transport modes.

ACTIVITY 12.3

In Unit 3 we identified macro factors influencing world trade. Can you relate some of these to the micro environment of distribution (e.g. the impact of urbanization)? Furthermore, examine the material towards the end of the unit dealing with global trends. Try bringing it all together.

Service levels

A few years ago successful businesses would have identified Information Technology (IT) as being the competitive differential. Today having IT means you can 'take part in the game', i.e. it is an essential prerequisite. The focus of competitive advantage has shifted to service.

Costs accelerate rapidly in response to increase in customer demands for availability and delivery. Near-perfect service (customer defined not company defined) is becoming the critical differentiator in the world marketplace as products become increasingly similar and it is difficult to distinguish one from another. Christopher (1987) identified the key discrimination as:

- Delivery response time to order
- Consistency and reliability of delivery
- Inventory availability
- Flexibility
- Ordering convenience
- Simplification of documentation
- Claims procedures
- Condition of goods on arrival
- Order status updates
- After-sales support.

These factors are difficult enough to deal with effectively on home territory. Problems magnify with physical and cultural differences. But remember, service standards will not be the same everywhere and the company, in order to succeed (profitably), must adjust its logistic to the needs of the customer and the marketplace. For example, in the UK, The Body Shop dictates a 2-hour delivery window on a designated date. Failure to comply means that its trucking company gets paid only certifiable costs and therefore delivers for free. Such demanding service levels are not universal, therefore why attempt to meet them? Deliver when the customer demands.

The subject of logistics is extremely complex. The international manager needs to be fully abreast of development in this field. However, the remit of this text is to remain strategic.

> Under market entry strategies we highlighted the importance of making the right choice. Can you make the important linkage between entry strategy (see Unit 8) and implementation activities in the market? There is a direct relationship. In other words, follow through your thinking to make the link with the customer – getting close to customers is one of the basic rules of marketing.

EXAM. HINT

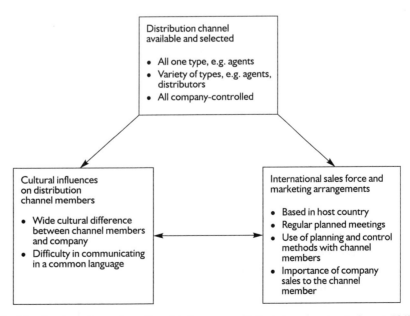

Figure 12.2 Distribution channels, cultural influences and their management. *Source:* Phillips, Doole and Lowe (1994)

Table 12.1 Different C methods for selecting distribution channels

Cateora	Czinkota and Ronkainen	Usunier	
Cost	Cost	Cost	
Capital	Capital	Capital	
Control	Control	Control	Efficiency
Coverage	Coverage	Coverage	
Character	Character	Character	
Continuity	Continuity	Continuity	
	PLUS	PLUS	
	Customer characteristics*	Customers and	
	Culture*	their characteristics*	
	Competition*	Culture*	Effectiveness
	Company objectives	Competition	
	Communication		

* External factors

Managing, selecting and controlling the distribution channel

Outside of setting up the firm's own distribution channel the organization is in part, or wholly, in the hands of intermediaries. Managing rather than controlling the channel(s) is critical to success in the marketplace. Here the dangers of SRC become apparent. Phillips, Doole and Lowe express this diagrammatically in Figure 12.2.

The management and control aspect of distribution will inevitably be influenced by the channels selected and the number of intermediaries employed. The methods of selection have been distilled by various authors to a number of 'Cs' (Table 12.1). The factors that combine to deliver the critical balance between efficiency and effectiveness become immediately apparent. The first six in both lists are essentially concerned with Efficiency, the remainder Effectiveness. If there is to be a trade-off then Effectiveness must dominate and Efficiency is judged subjectively by the Customer, Culture and Competition in the marketplace.

ACTIVITY 12.4

Study your own organization, even if it is a domestic-only one. Examine the balance between the efficiency factor versus the effective ones. Be critical. My guess is that 80 per cent of your company's effort is not behind being effective (from the customer's viewpoint). If you can't do it in your domestic base, what chance overseas?

Selecting the intermediaries

These may be self-selecting where there is little alternative on offer. Where choice is available selection might be based on:

- Compatibility with customer requirements
- Sales potential
- Geographic coverage
- Breadth of coverage – present and future (always think ahead)
- Financial strength
- Managerial competence
- Service-mindedness, self-motivation
- Synergy with company goals and management.

Occasionally quite different intermediaries might be necessary within a single country – dependent upon ethnic and racial differences, and the urban–rural split.

Motivation of intermediaries

Cateora (1993) identifies five key categories:

- Financial rewards
- Psychological rewards
- Communications
- Company support
- Corporate rapport

Money is not always the right reward mechanism, although it is a powerful motivator everywhere. In the USA individual rewards work best, likewise in south-east Asia. In many countries, e.g. India, the ethics of non-confrontation clearly clashes with performance-led reviews. An additional point worth remembering is a product with poor sales potential is hardly likely to enthuse intermediaries.

A feeling of belonging, participating in success, partnership bonding all go a long way to bring the company and its intermediaries closer. Relationship building through communication, support and feeling a part of the company add the value that brings success, especially if the product is only a small part of the intermediary's wider portfolio.

Control

This is generally reduced or limited when dealing with intermediaries and sometimes objective performance cannot be implemented. However, a contractual agreement may be arrived at although this may not be binding, more a statement of intent. The Western practice is to create written legal agreements – the Eastern practice often takes the form of obligation and working together. Care needs to be employed in introducing the Western SRC of formalizing control via mechanistic methodology.

Finally, the termination of an agreement may not be simple or straightforward. Exit distribution strategies can be extremely costly in some parts of the world where agents can demand up to five times the annual gross profit, plus other penalties to account for goodwill, the cost of laying off employees, etc.

How do the differences in distribution channel arrangements adversely influence international logistics? Examine how customer service levels can be managed to reduce the impact of these differences (December 1994).

(**See** Exam answers at the end of this unit.)

Global trends in distribution

Jeannet and Hennessey identify six major shifts in world distribution patterns:

1 *The internationalization of retailing*   IKEA, Pizza Hut, Marks & Spencer, KFC, Toys'R'Us, McDonald's, The Body Shop, Benetton and others have all migrated around the world. They bring with them world standards and systems, suppliers and financing and in doing so simplify the marketing environment.

2 *Large-scale retailing*   This is a corollary of the above – the inevitable trend is towards large-scale retailers. The small retailer is in decline everywhere – even in developing countries as consumer mobility increases. There are serious implications for employment and dislocation to traditional cultural patterns of shopping.

3 *Direct marketing*   This is restricted to countries with sophisticated infrastructure, nonetheless this field of distribution is expected to grow rapidly. Changing life-styles, the growth of women in employment, mobile phones and home PCs will fuel this growth.

4 *Discounting*   Lower distribution costs bring suppliers, distributors and customers closer, forcing down prices worldwide; just about everybody now lives in a 'deal culture' with few wanting to pay top price. A direct result of points 1–3 has generated

international competition with a driving down of prices. A further factor is the growth of regionalism, the removal of barriers, the ease and speed of distribution within the region – all serving to direct customers to bargain deals.

5 *Information technology* Suppliers source the world and so do distribution chains. The development of Just-in-Time inventory management means that products are delivered from all over the world, in a matter of days in some cases, broadening customer choice. In doing so they will simultaneously impair local customs and culture yet at the same time create world niche markets for products that otherwise might be restricted to a tiny corner of the world. An interesting paradox.

6 *Growth of own-label brands and development of retailer Eurobrands* Everywhere in the developed world manufactured brands are under challenge. The growth of major retailers has limited the power of the manufacturers to both develop and maintain their brands (e.g. Coca-Cola is under threat from Sainsbury's Classic Cola in the UK). As Sainsbury's and others internationalize (by acquisition or natural growth) so will the retailers' power place increasing pressure on manufacturers' brands. Whether this will be of long-term benefit to customers remains an open question. That it will happen is not in doubt. Eventually there may be greater overlap and vertical integration between manufacturers and retailers globally.

ACTIVITY 12.5

See what linkage you can establish between the points made concerning the changing dynamics of distribution and the main factors underpinning world trade in Unit 2 and Unit 3. There is a direct relationship.

Summary

Distribution and logistics is the fastest-changing area in international marketing. It is essential that companies monitor trends in international trade. Yesterday's methods can and are being outdated virtually overnight. Think how companies such as Direct Line have revolutionized the marketing of motor insurance in the UK and are now moving on to household insurance and mortgages.

Ideally, firms would like to deal direct with customers. It may happen in the UK but in overseas markets it may not be feasible. Political and other numerous factors prevent this. The firm would also like to use a similar distribution chain to its home market. Again it is extremely rare that distribution and logistical systems in one country is replicated elsewhere. There are too many variables. Whatever route(s) is chosen, care must be taken to plan and control the effort. Inefficiencies have to be minimized in order to succeed.

Questions

• Outline the key factors in developing distribution strategy.

• Put in charge of exporting JCB constructional equipment, what issues do you need to consider in entering the Kuwait market following the termination of the Gulf War?

• Having considered the dynamics of fashion retailing, what distribution strategies would you recommend for a worldwide manufacture of designer footwear (e.g. the Timberland range of shoes)?

• In what way might the element of an international logistics system be different from a domestic one?

• As the marketing manager of a range of car polishes and equipment sold to car owners you have been asked to consider an appropriate distribution system. As an export organization what steps might you take before implementing any distribution system? What logistical concern do you have and what control mechanisms might you apply?

International Marketing Strategy, C. Phillips, I. Doole and R. Lowe, Routledge, 1994, Chapter 10.

International Marketing, S. Paliwoda, Butterworth-Heinemann, 1994, Chapter 11.

International Marketing, V. Terpstra and R. Sarathy, The Dryden Press, 1994, Chapter 11.

Global Marketing Strategies, J.-P. Jeannet and H. D. Hennessey, Houghton Mifflin, 1994, Chapter 12.

Because of the complex detail involved in fully comprehending distribution and logistics the following reference text is included as recommended reading:

Elements of Export Marketing & Management, Branch, Chapman & Hall, 1990.

EXAM ANSWER

With the introduction of Syllabus '94 the emphasis of the examination paper has shifted away from the tactical aspects of marketing (e.g. export documentation) to a wider appreciation of distribution and logistics. There has only been one question set on this specific topic to date. Expect more in the future.

December 1994 In approaching the question it is simplest to begin with some definitions, setting out your credentials to the examiner and establishing points of reference. So begin with definitions of distribution channels and international logistics. Then specify the differences between domestic and international logistics demonstrating the development of a more complex chain. Candidates should also make clear the importance of the 'total distribution concept', i.e. the linkages between the various elements. Regarding the second part of the question (i.e. customer service levels) here you have an opportunity to show that delivering what customers want is only part of the marketing process – the manner of how it is delivered, appropiate to their needs, is increasingly the key factor for success. The managing of this process internationally is crucial, balanced alongside costs, inventory, etc. The text of this unit covers this point in more depth.

International pricing policy

Pricing policy generally is one of the most important yet often least recognized of all the elements of the marketing mix. If we stop to think about it, all the other elements of the marketing mix (both domestic and international) are costs. The only source of profit to the organization comes from revenue, which is in turn dictated by pricing policy. Internationally as well, the way in which an organization fixes and regulates prices in its foreign markets will have a direct affect on profits and profitability. In this unit you will:

- Evaluate the factors which influence the implementation of pricing policy in international markets
- Review the objectives behind pricing policy
- Understand how prices are set
- Consider how export prices are set
- Consider internal transfer pricing and methods of non-cash payment
- Review alternative pricing strategies for international markets.

Having completed this unit you will be able to:

- Appreciate the factors which affect pricing policy
- Understand how to respond to these factors and set market-based pricing strategies
- Integrate pricing policy into the other elements of the international marketing mix.

As already stated, the appreciation of pricing policy is essential to the long-term profitability and growth of any organization. Although often integrated into other aspects and questions such as marketing mix analyses, pricing forms a major plank between the organization and its customer base. Consequently, this unit on pricing policy needs to be studied in conjunction with many of the other units in this book, specifically Unit 9 (Product policy), Unit 10 (Financial implications) and Unit 14 (Evaluation and control systems).

As you proceed through this unit you should also bear in mind that international markets, like domestic markets, are driven not by cost but by value. While very few customers, both industrial and consumer, will automatically buy the cheapest product or service on offer they will constantly search for the offer which they believe offers them greatest value for money given their needs and aspirations.

Figure 13.1 Setting the right price

International pricing policy

Establishing the right price for international markets is no easy matter. There are a number of factors involved in the decision process and a number of stages which it may be worth reviewing before the organization sets its price or establishes any precedents in a foreign marketplace. Figure 13.1 shows a logical flow process through the eight major questions which confront the international marketer considering pricing policy. The rest of this unit will consider these steps one by one and the major issues involved in setting the right price.

How are prices determined in your organization:

- For the domestic market?
- For international markets?

Are they the same or different methods? Why?

Pricing objectives

Before we can decide what price or prices the organization should be charging for its products and services in an overseas market or markets we need to understand clearly the objectives behind the pricing policy that will meet the organization's needs. Some of the objectives which may be relevant to the organization are as follows:

- *Rate of return* Often useful for setting minimum price levels. What is the required internal rate of return that the organization needs to justify the investment in the overseas market in the first instance?
- *Market stabilisation* Keeping prices relatively constant and secure over the long term against competition so as not to provoke retaliation.
- *Demand-led pricing* Where prices are adjusted to meet changes in customer demand. These may be caused by seasonality or other market changes.

- *Competition-led pricing* Where prices are kept closely tagged to the competition and thereby maximising profit and profitability for all players.
- *Product differentiation* Pricing the product or service on offer to add to the sense and imagery surrounding the differentiated nature of the product.
- *Market skimming* Pricing to attract the very top end of any market at premium price levels, thereby also controlling distribution and sales and stocking levels.
- *Market penetration* The opposite of the approach above whereby the organization prices to maximize sales and normally operates at relatively low margins.

EXAM QUESTION

? Explain under what conditions a penetration pricing policy might be appropriate in international marketing. (June 1992).
(**See** Exam answers at the end of this unit.)

- *Early cash recovery* If the organization, for whatever reasons, requires fast recovery and cash in its balances to price the product or service accordingly to stimulate such a response from the marketplace.
- *To prevent competitive entry* Often a lower price is used as a barrier to prevent other organizations from entering into a market by making it unprofitable to do so.

Factors affecting prices

The second stage in the pricing process is to identify all those factors that are likely to affect the price that the organization sets. Factors affecting pricing can be broken down into three broad areas as follows:

- *Company and product factors* Would include corporate and marketing objectives as well as the market position held by the organization and the product. The product or service being priced also has a position in the product range and on the life-cycle and faces certain types of competition from the market in which it is to be placed. Cost structures within the organization as well as inventory and transportation costs will be major factors which will influence the final price level.

ACTIVITY 13.2

What is the relative importance of company/market/environment factors in the pricing policy in your organization? Do you think this is the right balance?

- *Market factors* Primarily centred around customers and their expectations and perceptions of the product or service which the organization is offering, exactly what price level is the market willing to pay? The local market situation in terms of distribution channels and accepted practice in discounting procedures as well as market growth and elasticity of demand will also affect the price potential. The extent to which the organization has had to adapt or modify the product or service and the level to which the market requires service around the core product will also affect cost and thereby will have some influence on pricing.
- *Environmental factors* Factors beyond the customer that will affect the prices charged will include competition (their objectives, strategies and relative strengths) as well as government and legislative influences (currency fluctuations, recession, business cycle stage, inflation, etc.).

All these factors will need to be analysed and assessed on a market-by-market basis to produce a pricing policy that is both profitable and acceptable to the local marketplace. At the same time, the international marketer must balance the local requirements and interests against the organization's aspirations on a broader international/global basis. While factors may push price levels in one direction for a given market, a close or neighbouring market may be influenced differently. Although, as we will see later, standardization of prices is not necessarily an objective that the organization should follow, neither should prices in neighbouring or comparative markets be too far out of line.

Examine the factors influencing the pricing of fast-moving consumer goods (fmcg) in international markets (June 1993).
   (**See** Exam answers at the end of this unit.)

Setting prices

There are a number of ways in which the organization might decide to fix its prices in its international markets. These are briefly described as follows:

- *Cost based*   The process by which prices are based on costs of production (and may include costs of distribution too) and then are normally marked up by a predetermined margin level. The cost-based approach to pricing is likely to produce price levels that appear inconsistent from a customer or market point of view. At the same time, this approach can be useful in order to stimulate a fast return of cash from the marketplace and/or inhibit the entry of the competition into that marketplace.
- *Market based pricing*   The customers' willingness to pay. This approach needs to be based on market research or a good understanding of the competition's pricing approach and can be a useful method of extracting the maximum profitability from the marketplace.
- *Competition based pricing*   Involves using the competition as a benchmark for fixing prices. Competition either in direct or substitutional form allows the organization to position its product or service relative to the competition in the customers' eyes and to establish a differentiated offer in the competitive range. This method can also be used as a way of creating barriers to entry with low prices preventing competitive entry to particular international markets.

Export pricing

When international marketing through exports (from domestic production) there is the question of what price to set relative to the domestic price. Generally, costs are slightly higher for export than for domestic operations because markets are often smaller and transportation costs tend to be higher. Prices could be higher to cover these additional costs but, at the same time, if they are too high they are likely to encourage parallel importing. Another question to consider in export pricing is the currency of quotation. Some organizations quote export prices in domestic currency and some in foreign currency. One of the two parties, the buyer or the seller, will eventually need to carry the transaction risk associated with currency fluctuations in international markets. The longer the period between quotation and invoice payment, the greater that transaction risk will be.

A final point in terms of export pricing, typically of interest to smaller organizations, is the possibility for export credit or payment guarantees offered by many governments throughout the world. Under this method (which in the UK is run by the ECGD), subject to certain conditions, the governments, in order to promote export sales, offers insurance against non-payment of export orders.

What is dumping? Identify three different types of dumping. Taking one type of dumping, explain why evidence of dumping might be difficult to establish (December 1992).

(**See** Exam answers at the end of this unit.)

Transfer pricing (internal)

Another pricing question which affects many international and multinational organizations is how to arrange the pricing between two subsidiaries of the same organization in different foreign markets. The three approaches open to the organization in this instance are as follows:

- *At cost*   The producing subsidiary supplies to the marketing subsidiary at cost. In this event the producing subsidiary is treated as a cost base and the profits are accumulated at the point-of-sale (the marketing subsidiary).
- *At cost plus*   Through this approach the profits are either shared between the two subsidiaries or, at the extreme, superprofits can be made at the producing subsidiary while losses can be incurred at the marketing subsidiary.
- *At arms length*   Under this approach the producing subsidiary treats the marketing subsidiary as it would any other customer and deals on a straight and strict commercial basis with the other part of the organization.

With transfer pricing international and multinational organizations have some degree of control about where profits are created in the organization as well as how funds might be moved among the various subsidiaries of the business. However, where profits are made is also where taxes are payable, and tax authorities on a worldwide basis are increasingly interested in how multinational organizations arrange pricing between subsidiaries. Penalties for misuse of the transfer pricing system are extremely high in many countries and the multinational organizations have only limited power to manipulate margins and the accumulation of profits on a global scale.

Questions on pricing and pricing strategy are regular in the examinations. Experience, however, has shown that candidates' grasp of the factors which influence pricing is shaky. Make sure you understand:

- The role of pricing in marketing strategy
- The special challenges in pricing for international markets.

Pricing strategies

When considering international pricing strategy international marketers have two broad extremes open to them. The organization can attempt to standardize its prices throughout all the markets in which it operates or it can opt to adapt them to local conditions on a market-by-market basis.

The arguments for standardization and for adaptation were well outlined in Unit 9 where we considered product policy. The same arguments apply in terms of pricing policy for international markets.

The optimum approach, as ever, will depend upon the market and the organization's characteristics. Generally, a balance between the two extremes will be the most profitable and most logical route for the organization to follow. Some degree of standardization or conformity on pricing is required, certainly among markets or groups of markets which are geographically close. On the other hand, the number of factors that drive prices are likely to vary to such an extent as to make standardized pricing an impractical proposition for most organizations.

Non-cash payment

In some international marketing situations the case may arise where payment is offered but not in normal cash terms. This is often the case with business from less developed countries (LDCs) and former Eastern bloc markets which may not have access to foreign currency or whose own local currency is not acceptable to the marketing organization. In these instances it is often wiser not simply to discard the transaction out of hand but to look at other still profitable ways of concluding the business. There are two broad areas in which such non-cash payments can be acceptable. These are:

- *Leasing* This can be used as an alternative to straight purchase in markets where currency or capital is simply not available to the purchasing organization. Leasing can be attractive to both the buyer since it enables use of a product or service which otherwise would not be available to them and to the seller since a sale is made and purchase price is staggered (possibly including full service and maintenance) over a longer period of time.
- *Counter-trade* This is a term used to cover a range of arrangements where some or all of the payment for the products or service is in the form of other products or services rather than in cash. Estimates vary as to the proportion of world trade which is covered by counter-trade measures but the proportion is significant. Arrangements included under the heading of counter-trade include items such as barter (a straight swap or transfer of goods) through to switch deals often including a third party which disposes of the bartered goods in exchange for currency through to buy-back arrangements whereby some or all of the cost of purchase is paid for through the production generated by the purchase items.

In your organization (or one that you know well), how important is non-cash payment? Have offers of non-cash payment been refused in the past? How might a western company be made aware of the potential for deals of this type?

ACTIVITY 13.3

Although Western marketers have a natural inclination to concentrate on arrangements which involve the transfer of cash, counter-trade should not be ignored. Not only does it open up markets which otherwise would remain closed for many years, it also, surprisingly enough, offers the opportunity for even greater profits than might be achievable through a straightforward cash transaction.

Have you heard of the 'Big Mac Index' as a method of assessing and comparing markets? Find out what it is and who might use it.

ACTIVITY 13.4

Summary

In this unit we have considered the array of factors which influence and should help the international marketer to determine international pricing policy. Pricing is probably one of the most complicated areas of international marketing strategy but has major impact upon the financial performance of the organization. Pricing also plays a major role in supporting product strategy (differentiation and positioning) as well as communication strategy where it has a major impact on perceived quality.

We have seen that in order to arrive at sensible prices the international marketer needs to understand the objectives behind the pricing approach as well as the factors which are often different from market to market. Standardized pricing approaches for international markets are not always necessary although some degree of coordination between markets may be desirable if only to stop the possibility of parallel importing.

Pricing is treated by many marketers as a tactical activity. In this unit you should have understood that pricing policy has a major strategic influence on the organization and should not be relegated to purely tactical decision making at a lower level.

Questions

As a check on your understanding of what has been covered in this unit, consider the following questions:

- How does pricing policy interact with other elements of the marketing mix?
- What might affect an organization's pricing objectives?
- What factors affect a final price?
- How might an organization go about setting the price for its product/service in an international market?
- How are the domestic and export prices linked?
- What are the three methods of transfer pricing?
- What is meant by 'non-cash payment'?
- Give examples of 'countertrade'.

For a more detailed analysis and explanation of international pricing policy read:

International Marketing, S. Paliwoda, Butterworth-Heinemann, 1993, pp. 251–284.
International Marketing Strategy, C. Phillips, I. Doole and R. Lowe, Routledge, 1994, pp. 419–456.

June 1992 In order to pass this question your answer should begin with an explanation of what is meant by 'penetration pricing'. You must then go on to consider this pricing method in an international context. Examiners will be looking for discussion about the nature of the economy of the target market as well as the development of an international competitive strategy. In June 1992 some candidates failed by confusing 'cost' and 'price'!

June 1993 Reading and understanding the question is essential. To pass this question well, your answer should deal with the issue of costs, competition, show specific international aspects of pricing and the answer must be set in the context of fmcg markets.

The answer requires company factors, market and specific factors to be taken into account. good answers might examine the impacts of variations in length of distribution channels in different markets and take account of differences in retail concentration and the way that this might reduce the manufacturers' scope to establish retail prices.

December 1992   In December 1992 some candidates who answered this question did not know what dumping was – they failed. Dumping occurs when products are sold in one country at a price lower than those in the country of origin. Dumping is a highly emotive issue. It is, in practice, difficult to establish an accurate cost position (e.g. marginal costs, marginal costs plus some contribution to overheads, all costs fully recovered, etc.).

The three types of dumping are 'sporadic', 'predatory' and 'persistent. To obtain a good pass, your answer needed to take one of these types of dumping and explain why evidence is difficult to establish. Other factors which make it difficult are: variability of negotiated prices, changes in exchange rates, changes in product specification and real differences in costs of production.

Evaluation and control methods

Evaluation and control methods are key issues in international marketing strategy. Nothing the international marketing manager can do can remove risk completely from business decisions that are made, but careful and proper evaluation of strategy before implementation, coupled with rigorous control methods during implementation itself, can reduce these risks to levels more acceptable in highly competitive situations. In this unit you will learn how to evaluate international marketing strategy and control strategic implementation. More specifically, you will:

- Review the objectives set for international marketing strategy
- Evaluate strategy against the set objectives
- Review the planning processes appropriate with the international business strategy
- Understand the control systems necessary to ensure proper implementations of international marketing plans.

Having completed this unit you will be able to:

- Evaluate the suitability of specific international marketing strategies
- Develop control systems for the implementation of international marketing strategy.

It is an important fact in today's markets that no matter how elegant, sophisticated or quantified an international marketing plan might be, unless it is executed in an equally sophisticated manner it will remain simply a document on a manager's shelf. Implementation and control systems are now key features on all Diploma examination papers and you are urged to prepare this section fully and be able to explain various measures open to the organization in your examination answer.

In this section you should be able to work carefully to apply the knowledge you have acquired in domestic marketing strategy into the international marketing arena. The Planning and Control paper and the Analysis and Decision paper now cover this element of the syllabus in great detail.

After you have completed this unit you should also spend some time talking to managers in your organization as well as looking beyond your organization to other industries to discover the different criteria used and control systems which are employed in practice.

This unit should be studied in relation to other units in this workbook, notably Introduction, Unit 1 (Identifying international opportunities) and Unit 6 (International marketing planning).

Evaluating strategies

How do we evaluate international marketing strategy? Here the answer is relatively simple and straightforward. It is the extent to which the strategy is expected to or is seen to achieve the objectives set for the activity.

When looking at organizations' objectives for international marketing strategy we should refer back to the introduction section of this workbook and specifically Figure I.4. This diagram, which outlines the international business process, starts, quite properly, with two key inputs. These are: information on foreign market potential and the organization's objectives. A clear, concise and understandable definition of the organization's objectives is crucial to the development of any robust and practical international marketing strategy.

Examination questions on evaluation and control are rare. However, a number of questions contain an evaluation or control element. The mini-case study is an area where control systems are important. The major case study (Analysis and Decision) paper has taken to making evaluation and control of international operations a major element to the questions!

Set against the background of a clear, concise and understandable objective for the organization, the evaluation of the marketing strategy becomes a relatively straightforward operation. As we can see from Figure 14.1, the strategic process as followed by all papers in the Diploma set of examinations essentially follows four steps. Stage 1 involves an audit of the organization's current situation, Stage 2 involves setting clear, concise objectives for the future development of the organization, Stage 3 involves strategic options and Stage 4 involves choice and control systems. For the international organization, having proceeded from Stage 1 through to 2 the next question is what are the various routes by which the organization might achieve its international objectives. Stage 4 (the section with which we are concerned in this unit) is about how we choose among the alternative strategic options and how we control implementation.

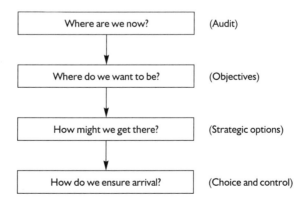

Figure 14.1

Evaluation of strategic options is never simple since nothing in the commercial world is guaranteed. We are never sure which strategic options are likely to work within the competitive environment and which ones, although looking very good, will not produce the results required.

How is international marketing strategy evaluated in your organization? Comparing the method to the ideas contained in this workbook, what changes, if any, would you recommend?

Typically, evaluation of strategic options falls under a number of concise categories. These are as follows:

Financial measures

The typical financial measures used in the evaluation of international marketing strategy will include:

- Profit
- Profitability
- Shareholder return
- Cash flow/liquidity
- Share price
- Earnings per share
- Return on net assets
- Return on sales

These are measures which will apply to any strategy for an organization in any situation, including international. The special aspect of international is that the strategy will normally be evaluated on repatriated cash flows in home rather than foreign currencies.

How are financial and non-financial measures of evaluation and control balanced in your organization? Do non-financial measures add an extra dimension to your organization's ability to control its international activity?

Non-financial measures

The non-financial measures of performance tend to measure external rather than internal performance of an organization and such measures may include:

- Market share
- Growth
- Competitive advantage
- Competitive position
- Sales volume
- Market penetration levels
- New product development
- Customer satisfaction
- Customer brand franchise
- Market image and awareness levels

These measures, naturally, will vary from market to market in the international area and will need to be measured on a market and a global/international basis for the organization's international activities.

It is important that the student of international marketing strategy be aware, first and foremost, of the primary measures of marketing strategy in a domestic situation. For further understanding of the measures of performance and evaluating strategies, the student is directed towards the readings on the area within domestic marketing strategy such as:

Strategic Marketing Management, R. M. S. Wilson and C. Gilligan with D. Pearson, Butterworth-Heinemann.
Strategic Marketing Management Workbook, P. Fifield and C. Gilligan, Butterworth-Heinemann.

Evaluating international business planning

In international marketing, as with domestic marketing, the use of models in planning is a way of evaluating strategic options. A number of models have been used in international marketing that were developed primarily for domestic marketing purposes. These include the Boston Consulting Group matrix, the GEC/McKinsey approach and the Arthur D. Little method.

Although there has been much in the recent literature criticizing the use of models such as these, they are still a valid mechanism to test the *conceptual approach* to international marketing strategy. These models have been described in detail elsewhere so they will not be repeated here. The use of models such as these and others can be a helpful way of discriminating between likely strategic options and the results that they will bring in the marketplace.

Control systems

If planning is defined as 'deciding what to do' then control can be defined as 'ensuring that the desired results are obtained'. Planning without control is a purely intellectual exercise. Control systems are essential to make sure that an organization drives through the content of its international marketing plans and achieves its organization's objectives in the marketplace. Control systems are varied and selecting the right method of control will depend upon the nature of the international markets that the organization is addressing, the particular goals and objectives which the organization has set itself as well as the environments within which the organization has to operate internationally. In simple terms, a control process can be described as in Figure 14.2.

Control systems, then, are a matter of balancing four primary issues:

1 Standard setting
2 Performance measurement
3 Reporting results
4 Taking corrective action (if required)

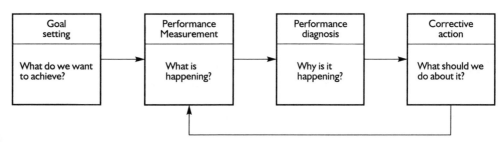

Figure 14.2 The control process

What control mechanisms are used in your organization? How, if at all, would you improve on your organization's control systems?

Setting standards is the role of the planning element of the process and the goals and objectives to which the organization's international marketing activity is directed. These activities are then translated into standards which, if met, will produce successful implementation of the international marketing strategy.

Performance standards tend to be measured in simple terms such as:

- *Quantity* How much was achieved? How much should have been achieved?
- *Quality* How good was that which was achieved? How good was it meant to be?
- *Cost* How much did the achievement cost? How much was it planned to cost?

Typically, divergence from pre-set standards is normally picked up in the organization through a process of:

- *Regular auditing* of the organization's finance and marketing activities or
- *Budgets* – developing and identifying divergence from budgeted inflows and outflows or
- *Variance analysis* – falling out of the budgeting process, the detailed analysis of the variance (difference between actual and expected results) that arises from the organization's activities.

Once the control system has been established and during the implementation phase of the international marketing plan, differences or deviations from the estimated (targeted) results can be highlighted. The international marketer's role is then to decide whether corrective action is required in one or more of the foreign markets and, if so, how to implement this action to bring the plan back on to target. The selection of corrective action depends to a large extent on the reasons behind the divergence from the planned results, and it is essential that the international marketer understands the reason for variances before simply setting off pre-planned contingency activities.

In the role of the director responsible for international marketing of a major blue-chip company, explain how you would identify and justify the resource requirements for a global marketing plan (June 1993).
(**See** Exam answers at the end of this unit.)

Factors affecting international controls

There are a number of factors which affect the degree and effectiveness of a control system for international marketing strategy. Some of the most important are:

For an organization other than your own can you:

- Identify an occasion where problems in the international control system caused inappropriate marketing action to be taken

- Identify an occasion where control systems resulted in proper action being taken in an international market.

- *Communications* Control systems rely on effective communications (two-way) for their accuracy. The opportunities for breakdown of communication systems in the international organization are varied and the problems of both timely and accurate communications between head office and subsidiaries and/or agents and distributors have been well documented. Before any corrective action is taken it is important that the marketer understands the reasons for discrepancies against planned outcomes and the role that communications or miscommunications may have played in the process.
- *Data* The accuracy and flow of international data has always been a problem in international marketing situations. As international activity moves beyond the developed Western markets the availability and accuracy of international market/product/industry data becomes increasingly less reliable. It is important to understand that control systems start off with data that may not be as reliable as in domestic marketing situations. In these instances greater degrees of latitude should be allowed in the control process before contingency plans are activated.
- *Environmental change* The diversity of environments within which the organization must operate internationally will undoubtedly affect control systems and the data used for their calculation. Currency values, legal structures, political systems, public holidays and the inevitable cultural factors will all influence the development and control of marketing strategy. The issue of diversity of local environments must be reflected in the control system.
- *Organizational culture* The organization's culture and management philosophy about issues such as centralization or decentralization, internationalization or globalization will affect development of any control system. A highly centralized/global organization will likely require a control system that is detailed and all encompassing. Organizations where authority and decision making is devolved to the local unit level are likely to require a much less mechanistic approach to control systems.

What steps would you take to ensure that agents are operating both effectively and efficiently as the distribution part of the export marketing mix of a company relying totally on agents as its export distribution channel (December 1991)?

(**See** Exam answers at the end of this unit.)

- *Size of international operations* Depending on the nature of the international operation, the organization and the relative importance that international earnings play on the organization's balance sheet, the control system may be fundamental to the organization's reported profit levels. In the organization where international business is a very small part of its day-to-day operations, control systems will be less rigorously applied and divergences from plan will be less closely scrutinized.
- *Faulty estimating* It may also be apparent from an analysis of the variances that the problem does not lie in the market nor in the organization's ability to deliver to a market's need but the original estimates set against which the plan was going to be judged. In this case the organization and the international marketer needs to re-estimate the rate at which the organization will achieve its strategic objectives.

Faulty estimating is rarely cited as a problem in control systems – managers tend to believe figures. The mini-cases and the major case (analysis and decision) may contain suspect data – use your intuitive skills to assess whether the given targets are right in the first place.

Summary

In this unit we have looked at the important stages of strategic evaluation and the control of implementation. First, we considered the problem of evaluating alternative strategies for international operations and deciding which strategic option offered the best chance of achieving the organization's objectives. Evaluation will be driven largely by the organization's objectives but can be measured both internally (financial measures), externally (non-financial measures) or, ideally, a combination of the two.

Second, we considered the control mechanisms that are necessary to ensure that the strategic plan is implemented in the foreign markets and the organization's objectives are achieved. We considered the range of analysis and control mechanisms which are used in different organizations including auditing, budgeting and variance analysis.

Finally, we considered the nature of the corrective action that can be taken by the marketer and the variables which affect the control mechanisms and the results that these give.

Questions

As a check on your understanding of what has been covered in this unit, consider the following questions:

- What is the role of the control system in international marketing strategy?
- What are the two categories by which strategy can be evaluated?
- What are the types of measure that are included under the heading of 'financial measures'?
- What are the types of measure that are included under the heading of 'non-financial measures'?
- How can strategic models be used in evaluating international strategy?
- What is a 'control system'? Give examples.
- What are the four key issues in any control system?
- By what methods can divergence from standards be picked up?
- What are the special factors that affect the efficiency and effectiveness of control systems in international operations?

For a more detailed analysis and explanation of evaluation and control methods for international marketing strategy, read:

International Marketing', S. Paliwoda, Butterworth-Heinemann, 1993, pp. 377–395.
International Marketing Strategy', C. Phillips, I. Doole and R. Lowe, Routledge, 1994, pp. 457–461.

June 1993 Your answer would be unlikely to pass if you have simply placed complete faith in a general list of the planning processes, perhaps augmented by a list of PEST/SLEPT factors. To reach a good pass standard your answer needs to show how marketing would justify its claim against competing claims within the organization. Opportunities, priority ranked, would be substantiated from the MIS. Amounts of resources would need to be viewed on a country/market and on an interrelated world market perspective. The justification would revolve around all the measures that comprise a control system: profit potential, return on capital employed, market share projections and competitive positions, linked to time scales and company objectives, as well as the ability of the control system to produce results.

December 1991   To gain a good pass mark it is important to be able to separate the 'strategic' from the 'tactical'. 'Effectiveness' measures should include questioning whether the company was using agents in the correct strategic way. Should we be using agents as a distribution channel in this market? Are our existing agents the most appropriate given our future plans? Do they give the appropriate market and buyer coverage? Are they capable of providing the appropriate level of information and persuasiveness? 'Efficiency' measures would be covered by steps taken to compare sales levels with agreed targets; frequency of call rate and success in selling to various types of buyers, etc.

The key to this question is achieving a correct balance between motivation of agents and an adequate control system to gather information and assess the agents' activity.

The mini-case study

OBJECTIVES

A mini-case is a compulsory part of the examination and designed to provide you with an opportunity to apply your knowledge to a particular situation. The purpose of this unit is therefore:

- To help you understand how best to approach the mini-case study
- To highlight the sorts of mistakes that are commonly made
- To give you an opportunity to prepare a number of practice solutions

By the end of this unit, you will:

- Be familiar with the sorts of mini-case studies that have been used over the past few years
- Have an understanding of the issues that they raise
- Have gained some practice at approaching these cases.

STUDY GUIDE

Although with each of the previous units it has been a relatively straightforward exercise to identify how long you should spend working on the unit, it is far harder to do this with the mini-case. Instead, you should recognize that the more practice you get with the mini-case, the more likely it is that you will approach it in your examination with a degree of confidence and an understanding of what is required from you. You should, therefore, spend as much time as you can familiarizing yourself with the format of the mini-cases and the sorts of questions that are asked. Practise preparing solutions to the questions and then compare your answers with the solutions that we have included at the end of the unit.

It needs to be recognized that the type of short case (popularly called the mini-case) set in the examinations cannot be treated in exactly the same way as the extremely long case set for the subject of *Strategic Marketing: Analysis and Decision.*

However, far too many students adopt a maxi-case approach, using a detailed marketing audit outline which is largely inappropriate to a case consisting of just two or three pages. Others use SWOT analysis and simply rewrite the case under the four headings of strengths, weaknesses, opportunities and threats.

Some students even go so far as to ignore the specific questions set and present a standard maxi-case analysis, including environmental reviews and contingency plans. Others adopt a vague and far too superficial approach. In each case, students are penalized. You should recognize therefore that the mini-case is simply an *outline* of a given situation whose purpose is to test whether candidates can apply their knowledge of marketing operations to the environment described in the scenario. For example, answers advocating retail audits as part of the marketing information system for a small industrial goods manufacturer confirm that the examinee has learned a given MIS outline by rote and simply regurgitated this with complete disregard of the scenario. Such an approach cannot be passed. A more appropriate approach to the scenario involves a mental review of the areas covered by the question and the selection by the candidate of those particular parts of knowledge or techniques which apply to the case. This implies a rejection of those parts of the student's knowledge which clearly do not apply to the scenario.

All scenarios are based upon real-world companies and situations and are written with a full knowledge of how that organization operates in its planning environments. Often, the organization described in the scenario will not be a giant fast-moving consumer goods manufacturing and marketing company but is instead an innovative, small or medium-sized firm faced with a particular problem or challenge. The cases are often, but not invariably, written from the viewpoint of a consultant and include an extract from a consultant's report.

The examination as a whole lasts for three hours. Including your reading time, you therefore have one-and-a-half hours for the mini-case.

EXAM HINT

On opening the examination paper, read the mini-case at your normal reading speed, highlighting any issues that appear to you to be particularly significant. Having done this, read the questions in Section 1 and then read the mini-case again, identifying and highlighting those issues which are particularly relevant to the questions posed. Remember that both questions in the section need to be answered and that the examination paper will indicate the split of marks. Allocate your time accordingly and do not make the mistake of spending much more than ninety minutes on the mini-case (Section 1).

The mistakes that candidates make

We have already touched upon some of the mistakes that candidates make in approaching the mini-case. We can, however, take these futher with the list of the ten most common errors that candidates make.

The ten most common mini-case errors

1   Ignoring the specific questions posed and providing instead a general treatment of the case.
2   Thinking that every mini-case study demands a SWOT analysis; it doesn't.
3   Not answering in the format asked for. You will normally be asked for a report, a memorandum or a marketing plan and should answer using one of these frameworks.
4   Making unrealistic assumptions about the extent to which organizations can change their working practices.
5   Assuming that unlimited financial resources will be available to you.
6   Failing to recognize the difficulties of implementation.
7   Introducing hypothetical data on costs.
8   Rewriting the case and ignoring the questions.
9   Failing to give full recognition to the implications of what is recommended.
10 Not spending sufficient time on the second of the two questions.

In order to assist students in their studies and to give an indication of what is expected of them, four past examination mini-cases have been included, together with indicative answers. The answers are not the only answers to the questions set but give clear guidance on the breadth and depth that candidates should aspire to.

World Freight Services (December 1994)

World Freight Services (WFS) was established in the 1920s to transport export business from the UK to a variety of destinations. Over the years WFS expanded to achieve a turnover of £76 million in 1993, employing well over 1000 people, mainly in the UK. WFS is one of a small number of large freight services companies in the UK. It has an important share of the European market but is not significant in other world markets.

The basis of WFS's business is a strong UK collection and delivery service; a worldwide freight-forwarding capability that includes all documentation and customs clearance requirements; a fast scheduled groupage service for both exports and imports to 51 locations in 15 different countries in the European Economic Area. WFS also runs a fast and direct scheduled groupage service to the Gulf (Saudi Arabia, Oman, United Arab Emirates, Bahrain, Kuwait and Iran) and to Japan.

In 1988 WFS carried out a thorough audit of their activities. Several issues emerged as significant threats. The start of the Single Market in the European Community would reduce customs and documentation requirements. The anticipated growth in intra European Community trade would help to offset some of the considerable loss (about 25 per cent of WFS revenue and profits) of customs clearance and documentation work. The opening of the undersea tunnel between the UK and France would again reduce demand for the freight services specialist. In addition, the more general developments in the integration of ownership among the buyers of freight services and among the providers of freight services would change the whole nature of customer service.

The difficulties forecast in 1988 had occurred by 1994. Unfortunately, the impact of the recession during the early 1990s compounded these difficulties, resulting in less demand for freight services. At the same time, competitors were putting pressure on WFS's margins by dropping prices and putting in low price quotations.

The marketing team at WFS was planning to use the country attractiveness/competitive strength matrix to aid its international marketing planning. They were unsure about which elements were appropriate to measure attractiveness and competitiveness in their market. In the countries in which scheduled and groupage services were offered, WFS had a considerable investment in storage and equipment, although its overseas risk exposure was minimized by the careful selection of agents and joint venture partners. The other parts of WFS's business: freight service provision through deep-sea, air-freight, complete documentation services and freight management and consultancy services could include almost any country or client in the world. In practice, however, most of WFS's business related to UK clients.

Question 1

(a) What are the main strategic options available to WFS in international markets? Examine how you could use country attractiveness/competitive strength and other analytical techniques toimprove WFS's international marketing strategy. **(25 marks)**

(b) Examine the particular difficulties that WFS would be likely to experience in implementing its international marketing plans. **(25 marks)**

Question 1(a)

What are the main strategic options available to WFS in international markets? Examine how you could use country attractiveness/competitive strength and other analytical techniques to improve WFS's international strategy. **(25 marks)**

Note: Read both questions carefully. Question 1 is multi-dimensional and breaks into three sub-parts:

- What are the main strategic options?
- Demonstrate country attractiveness/competitive strength
- Show your knowledge of other analytical techniques.

The final line in Question 1 establishes that the question is strategic and not tactical. Candidates should write a balanced answer.

Question 1(b) asks you to examine particular difficulties in implementation. Your effort should be specific to the case and not a general overview of implementation of international marketing plans.

Question 1(a): answer

General observations

WFS is a mainly UK-based organization of considerable size. It has strong European representation but is weak elsewhere. Its current position is that the environment in which it operates is fast changing; in particular, events in Europe have created serious erosion in sales (−25 per cent) *and profit*. So the central issue is clear and unambiguous: WFS must change or die (albeit slowly):

1. WFS must replace lost business
2. WFS must expand into new areas of business.

Main strategic options

Before answering the question it is perhaps worth outlining briefly the nature of the business. WFS is a service organization serving the needs of a diverse customer base. In fact it is the interface between two groups of customers. As such, WFS must be flexible in what it offers so that both parties are satisfied.

The next stage is to set some clearer objectives before establishing the strategic directions. The information in the mini-case suggests the following.

Objectives

1. Improve efficiencies in existing markets to protect margins and enhance profitability
2. Develop new markets broadening the business base, particularly in markets where margins might be generous
3. Develop new products in line with the changing customer dynamics, i.e. finding out what it is customers need and want in a fast-changing world.

The proposed model for exploring strategic options in line with the declared objectives is Ansoff (modified) (Figure 15.1). Dealing with each:

- *Penetration* (1)   As an urgent priority WFS must consolidate and strengthen its position in Europe (EU). It is the core business. Failure to address changes and challenges here will result in further accelerating decline.
- *New market/countries* (2)   WFS is good at what it does. It is efficient and is successful with a range of products/service offers. It is a big player currently restricted in geographic coverage. It should expand into new markets. This is priority No. 2 in terms of strategic options.

| | Service | |
	Existing	New
Existing	Penetration 1	NPD 3
Country/ market		
New	Market development 2	Diversity 4

Figure 15.1

- *New product development (NPD)* (3)   This always takes time to develop. Customers would need considerable researching. However, this is an important area as the freight service market is one that is undergoing rapid change as technology drives the business and customers are requiring faster and higher service levels. NPD is seen as a priority No. 3 – one for the medium term. The medium term in this context means 2–3 years, as in this business you are either 'up with the game' or you are not a player!
- *Diversification* (4)   Acquisition could and perhaps should be considered. WFS is a major player – it has assets and if it needed to move quickly to counter a change in the business environment it could do so. But for the moment it is not considered a top priority.

Country attractiveness/competitive strength

The approach taken is to consider the implications of strategic Option 2, i.e. market development. What is important is that WFS matches its strength with that of market/country needs – or rather with that of the customers in a given market. With much of the world to choose from it is vital that WFS develop a systematic approach in order to narrow its options from many to few. Having identified and prioritized key market opportunities, further in-depth analysis and research into customer needs would be implemented.

WFS strengths

In the first place we might consider (briefly) WFS strengths, which are considerable:

- Strong UK collection and delivery
- Worldwide forwarding including documentation and customs
- Fast scheduled groupage to 51 locations and 15 European countries
- Fast groupage to the Gulf and Japan
- Managed risk exposure overseas.

Further detail would be given by WFS to prioritize those strengths and match them to countries/markets to create the best possible 'fit'. Again research would be required initially via secondary research to establish this.

The basis for establishing the criteria of country attractiveness would be an analysis of SLEPT factors, e.g.

- Social: culture, language, religion
- Legal: country specific such as foreign ownership
- Economic: rate of growth, business sophistication, size, etc.
- Political: tariffs, other barriers, etc.
- Technology: infrastructure, speed of entry.

A recently developed model that would aid identification of 'best opportunities' is Harrell and Kiefer (1993) (Figure 15.2):

- *Primary* opportunities represent the best fit strategically, i.e. the best opportunity to develop long-term business. Having identified these WFS would then embark on a thorough research programme.
- *Secondary* markets that have either a higher risk factor, or obstacles to entry would require considerable costs in time, personnel and money. These markets would be handled pragmatically with WFS responding to and being proactive but from a distance. They would be markets earmarked for greater future involvement as WFS gained experience in dealing with them.
- *Tertiary* – high risk and/or low return. There is absolutely no reason not to do business in these markets but each contains situations that would be considered on an individual basis. Short-term profit would be the business driver not long-term investment. No serious investment would be considered and no research of any scale considered.

Other analytical techniques

There is no one way that is absolutely correct in assessing potential markets. Briefly, other models might be considered appropriate, e.g. the General Electric/McKinsey approach

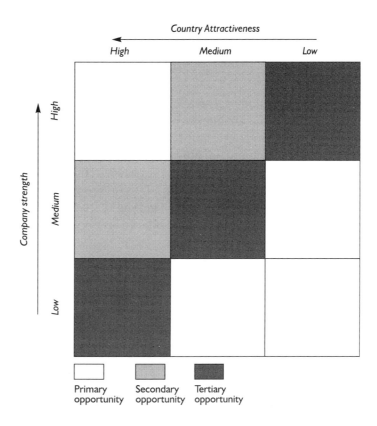

Figure 15.2

which is similar to the method described in Question 1(b). Alternatively, the model created by Gilligan and Hird (1985) could be applied in which markets/countries are screened in terms of existing, latent and incipient demand and the firm's products graded on their competitiveness. Finally, it is worth mentioning that other methodologies might include:

- Demand pattern analysis
- Accessibility/profitability/market size analysis
- Analogy estimation (more suitable for Third World countries than to WFS's core customers)
- BERI – Business Environment Risk Index.

Michael Porter's work on generic strategies and his five forces could also be applied. Time precludes addressing the mechanics of the above; they are simply mentioned as alternatives.

Question 1(b)
Examine the potential difficulties that WFS would be likely to experience in implementing its international marketing plans. **(25 marks)**

Question 1(b): answer
The question is broad based. In the absence of a specific marketing plan it is difficult to be objective or indeed be overspecific in terms of addressing the question. However, it is possible to identify a number of individual particular difficulties that WFS might encounter.

Identification of difficulties
- Identification of the appropriate (specific) key product/service offers that international customers might want, i.e. the service ↔ customer match
- Adapting to the changing business environment impacting on the freight industry, i.e. adaptation to meet the SLEPT factors
- Speed of implementation. This is a fast-response industry
- The ethnocentric orientation of WFS
- The creation and development of a balanced international organization
- The need to find and keep non-UK clients

- Financing the change in company orientation
- Issues of monitoring and control.

Dealing with each in turn (briefly):

1 *Identification of service ↔ customer match* WFS acts as a service facilitator. There is no physical product. The company interfaces between two customers. Success is about responding to their needs, quickly and efficiently. It is truly a business where being 'close to customers' is paramount. Identifying precisely what customer service levels are appropriate and what customers are prepared to pay is vital in expanding this business. (Unprofitable business can be got anywhere.) Careful research among customers and a critical review of competitors is essential in getting the service offer right. Flexibility is keynote as customers want/demand a customized service. WFS will need to invest in market research and information technology.

2 *Adapting to the environment* Following on from above, it is essential that WFS monitor the SLEPT factors via an MIS/MKIS. Without specifying details it is apparent that the freight industry is highly competitive and, increasingly, customers succeed or fail on the basis of delivering on time. In a marketplace where products are often similar the cutting edge in determining success is service response. WFS in its marketing plan must take full account of this, e.g. technology is driving the marketplace. Next-day delivery anywhere in the world is commonplace. The manner in which a product is delivered becomes critical.

3 *Speed of implementation* This is a further endorsement of the previous point. Just-in-Time (JIT), bulk break, cutbacks in inventory levels all affect profitability. A firm that can enhance customers' profitability by fast response will win the battle. WFS will need to accelerate its already successful activities. To do so will require investment in Information Technology.

4 *Ethnocentricity* WFS is basically a UK operation. To be successful long term on the international front requires establishing a network around the world. This requires a change of orientation from ethnocentric to polycentric operations with responsibilities devolved. There is no other way that WFS can overcome the difficulties mentioned in points 1–3. Furthermore, to speed up international development WFS will need to find suitable partner organizations and establish either a series of joint ventures or strategic alliances.

5 *Balanced organization* Again following on, WFS will need to establish a balanced organization. This will require a careful re-examination of its management structure with leadership and control implications. On the marketing front WFS will need to create an international marketing structure with clear lines of communication, responsibilities and control.

6 *Finding and keeping non-UK clients* To succeed in its ambitions WFS must set in place a process of identifying potential customers. Again careful research and investigation is the key. A polycentric staff would have greater knowledge, insight and contacts in overseas markets. Market research would also be usefully employed as would international marketing communications. How else would potential customers know of the existence of WFS? Establishing overseas market research operations and overseas marketing communications expertise is another difficulty to be considered.

7 *Finance* Establishing a wider international organization would have an impact on the short-medium-term profitability. But WFS has no option other than to commit resources. Entering new markets and creating international networks is expensive.

8 *Control* This is a major issue. Consideration of the previous seven points makes it obvious that WFS is addressing major difficulties. Establishing benchmarks, objectives and performance standards of all kinds is essential. Measuring them, establishing feedback channels and the development of control mechanisms is a prerequisite for the success of WFS.

Examiner's comments

No answer to questions of this nature is complete. Candidates may well add to this list of difficulties. However, it is important to recognize that in international marketing, issues other than ones dealing with the marketing mix are very relevant.

Leisureworld Bicycles (June 1994)

Leisureworld is a company that specializes in marketing consumer goods products through appropriate retail and other distribution channels. Eighty-eight per cent of sales are to West European countries with 10 per cent to the USA and 2 per cent to Canada. The company is not a manufacturer: it buys (or sources) its products from around the world. If assembly is required, as it is for bicycles, this is arranged with an appropriate manufacturer. The finished bicycle is always branded with the Leisureworld name.

The strong upsurge in demand in the bicycle market during the 1980s and the early 1990s was an attraction for Leisureworld. With the company mission centred on leisure, bicycles provide a clear and close fit in many country markets.

The bicycle market is influenced by fashion and fitness trends, the weather, the quality and safeness of the road and other cycle track infrastructure, and by the lack of hills. Regions in flat areas – for example, the northern Italian plain, the Netherlands and Beijing in China – all have very large cycle-owning and using populations.

Over the past 15 years different forms of bicycle have become popular. In the early 1980s adult small-wheel bikes were in vogue; later, children's all-purpose tough BMX were introduced and achieved substantial sales in most advanced industrial countries. Mountain bikes, introduced via California in the late 1980s, made a dramatic impact.

Bicycles are aimed at many different market segments. In the more affluent markets in the world, leisure, fitness and cycle racing take the majority of the market. In addition, bicycles specifically made for children are an important part of sales, accounting for up to half of the total market by volume in most industrially advanced countries. While in all countries there is a market for bicycles as a means of basic transport, it is in the lesser developed and the developing countries around the world that this segment is highly significant.

Mike Bowen, international marketing manager of Leisureworld, is currently trying to resolve a particular problem. In 1992 bicycles accounted for 27 per cent of Leisureworld's £146 million turnover. Unfortunately, the impact of the recession in many markets and the considerable penetration achieved in many country markets for mountain bikes resulted in a saturated and overstocked market during 1992 and 1993.

A new craze in bicycles might start at any time. However, at the moment there is no evidence of what form that might take. Product modification and price cutting are the main approaches being taken at present.

Production of bicycles in low-cost countries – for example, China and Taiwan – is a threat to the established manufacturers such as Raleigh in the UK and Peugeot in France. Leisureworld, by sourcing from whatever they regard as the best source at the time, are able to keep their costs low. Another important factor in this market is the substantial success of Shimano, a Japanese manufacturer of a wide range of component parts. Shimano are a highly innovative company and have succeeded in making their parts – for example, gears and pedals – to be in strong demand by customers for cycles. In effect, it is now difficult to sell bicycles in many markets without Shimano components. The points of difference between many bicycles are often related to company and brand name, colour and graphics, distribution outlet and price.

To add to Mike Bowen's workload, Leisureworld have been offered a share in a top cycle-racing team. The team will compete in the major road-racing events around the world, including the high-prestige, month-long Tour de France. If Leisureworld accept this opportunity the major part of their bicycle marketing communications budget of £0.9 million would be devoted to the costs of the cycle team and the related publicity surrounding each cycle race.

As an adviser on international marketing retained by Leisureworld:

1　Propose and justify the ways in which the company should carry out market segmentation on the world bicycle market. **(30 marks)**

2　Examine the advantages and disadvantages of using most of the bicycle marketing communications budget on the cycle racing team. On the assumption that Leisureworld go ahead with the cycle racing team, explain how the racing team could be used by Leisureworld Bicycles in its international marketing communications.

(20 marks)

Question 1

Propose and justify the ways in which the company should carry out market segmentation on the world bicycle market. **(30 marks)**

Note. It is important that candidates:

1   Adopt a structural approach
2   Subdivide their answers into proposals and justification
3   Express knowledge of the basis of segmentation

Question 1: answer

Overview

Leisureworld is facing more difficult market conditions in the mid-1990s than it has over the past 15 years. The recent recession and the resultant oversupply of bicycles in the developed Western economies has made it more difficult to increase the current demand of about £40 million (1992).

Market segmentation

Based on the information supplied and our discussions with you, we propose a more focused approach to the diverse markets for bicycles, through the use of market segmentation. The use of market segmentation will enable a more customer-oriented approach to each market and its needs, and supply a competitive edge to Leisureworld offers. We should thus be able to increase the efficiency of our marketing efforts when they are more precisely aimed and tailored to specific segments of (potential) customers who share certain characteristics that are significant in marketing terms.

There are many approaches to market segmentation. The one we propose below clearly identifies a group of substantial and accessible markets which exhibit a need that Leisureworld can satisfy. By focusing your marketing effort on these countries you should improve substantially sales to these markets, subject to economic factors (such as possible continued recession in some countries). In exploiting such markets, the opportunity to market other Leisureworld products through similar distribution systems or to similar customers should be taken, thus avoiding a too high reliance on the bicycle market.

Segmentation proposal

We propose to start the segmentation exercise by drawing a matrix which links the two main parameters of demand – the ability to purchase as measured by level of economic development and the need satisfied as measured by the use for which the purchase is made. This results in the matrix shown in Table 15.1. The final 'use situation' in the table includes children's bicycles.

We can now place countries in one or more cells in the matrix according to the degree of substantial demand based on a particular type of usage and the level of economic development. Where actual data are available through your own or trade sources, the actual percentage of the market for each category should be stipulated, together with the estimated market size.

Table 15.1

	Use situation				
	Transport	Leisure	Fitness	Racing	Play
Level of economic development					
Less developed					
Early developed					
Semi-developed					
Fully developed					

We can now proceed to filter out those countries which, for various reasons, may be unattractive. Thus, in a particular segment, those countries whose market size is too small can be eliminated. Similarly, segments that are not leisure oriented (the company mission) can be ignored.

Justification

Leisureworld's mission is based on leisure and your main competitive advantage is that of keen pricing based on global flexible sourcing. You can build on this strength by focusing your market efforts on those countrues that are sufficiently developed to have a substantial leisure segment. Given the set-up and running costs in a particular market, it should be possible to calculate a minimum market size for a country to be viable in profit terms to Leisureworld.

Besides the infrastructure for bicycling and the wealth to pay for leisure bicycles, it follows that such markets will also be viable for other leisure products. Similarly, the level of economic development almost certainly ensures a well-developed distributive and retail infrastructure, allowing Leisureworld access to the customers.

The one assumption we have made is that such customers will be receptive to low-cost leisure bicycles. As a market develops and matures, the major purchasers are the 'late majority' who, while desiring the product, are more cost conscious than the fanatical early adopters. It is therefore likely that the markets identified will be in the early stages of maturity and thus likely to be more receptive to low-cost alternatives.

Question 2

Examine the advantages and disadvantages of using most of the bicycle marketing communications budget on the cycle racing team. On the assumption that Leisureworld go ahead with the cycle racing team, explain how the racing team could be used by Leisureworld Bicycles in its international marketing communications. **(20 marks)**

Note: Again the correct technique is to examine advantages and disadvantages separately (sub-divide the page of your workbook vertically if you wish). Then under a distinct heading deal with issues relating to international marketing communication. So again this is a three-part question.

Question 2: answer

Given the international nature of Leisureworld Bicycles, an important consideration of any sponsorship must be the international appeal and application of any communication expenditure. Any promotional vehicle used by the company needs to be adaptable and capable of being 'rolled-out' in the form of a fully integrated communications package that will make a fundamental contribution to company objectives of:

1 Building a positive brand image based on the Leisureworld name
2 Adding significantly to market share by producing significant sales growth.

In particular, it is essential that Leisureworld Bicycles give careful attention to the advantages and disadvantages of heavy investment in the cycle team. A full cost-benefit analysis should be carried out taking the criteria below into account.

Advantages of sponsoring the cycle team

1 The Tour de France is an event of international significance. Its activities and media coverage are European-wide – a key market for Leisureworld. The intense media coverage – especially if the team were successful – would bring associated publicity benefits to the company and its products.
2 Sponsoring the team would allow the company to feature specific personalities in the team and add character endorsements to the product range and brand. Quality, professionalism, toughness and style would be the characteristics transmitted via appropriate media placements, visits, endorsements, competitions, etc.
3 Core viewers/audiences for cycle sports undoubtedly form a substantial part of Leisureworld's key markets – particularly in the sport and leisure segments. Moreover, even young children are influenced by successful sports persons (e.g. the recent Niké campaign).

4   Racing does lend itself to an integrated campaign. The events are both geographically dispersed and spread out over a wide time period. Key events like the 'Tour' tend both to concentrate on key markets for Leisureworld (Europe 88 per cent) and to be timed at peak purchase periods (early summer in Europe). The use of endorsement, sales promotion and advertising can enable the interest to be maintained well into the other key buying period of late autumn (for the Christmas/children's market).

5   From a defensive point of view, the absence of Leisureworld from such key events would place other competitive sponsors in a very strong position regarding image and brand awareness that could leave Leisureworld having to rely exclusively on price to market its bicycles.

Disadvantages of sponsoring the racing team

1   Concentration on one vehicle for promoting the brand constrains both the direction and flexibility of any communication strategy. In particular, the schedule of races would determine to a large extent the timing and location of any promotion. Careful research would be required to establish the degree of 'fit' between the team's activities and the purchasing decision patterns of Leisureworld's diverse markets.

2   There is also some doubt as to the degree of cross-market transferral of image that takes place, from the predominantly sports-centred racing team to other segments such as leisure and children's markets.

3   In some cases the images of speed and risk suggested by cycle racing may be counterproductive in markets where safety is a key buying criterion.

4   If the team should perform badly or get a bad image, this may reflect on Leisureworld – as in the Pepsi/Jackson fiasco last year. Nike encountered a set-back during the 1992 Olympics when several of its stars featured in an international advertising campaign failed to win medals.

Exploiting the team sponsorship

Assuming Leisureworld go ahead with the sponsorship, the following integrated communications plan is proposed:

1   Agency selection would be a critical first step. Such an agency should have European-wide resources to cover the Leisureworld key market. A thorough knowledge of the industry and its markets combined with a creative approach to bicycle marketing would be essential.

2   The initial campaign should cover the key periods from July to December and would most likely involve the following elements:

3   Sponsorship and public relations events centred around the team. Public appearances, product endorsements, and opportunities for team members to 'champion' the brand should be created.

4   The developments of a definite 'Leisureworld' logo and style should be carried through to the team clothing, equipment and bicycles, and act as a house style for advertisements and point-of-sale materials.

5   The use of brand extension to cover cycle clothing and equipment via team endorsement should be exploited both in the bicycle market and in the leisure clothing market in general.

6   The use of competitions and gifts based around the team can be utilized to continue to build brand awareness and interest.

Sunlands Holidays (December 1993)

The long wait to make a telephone call reminded Thomas Bochardt of Europe in the 1950s. The ancient Siemens manual telephone switchboard at Etosha Game Park in Namibia was in stark contrast to the modernity of some parts of the Namibian economy.

Bochardt was in Namibia to finalize a franchising deal based on Sunlands travel marketing expertise and financial muscle. Twenty-two farms had been selected on the basis of the quality of their location and the quality of the guest service provided at the farm. Sunlands have various motel, hotel and leisure complexes and franchise operations in Europe, run from company headquarters in Munich, Germany. This was their first venture into Africa.

Namibia is one of Africa's newwest countries. It has an estimated population of 1.3 million, with one of the lowest population densities in Africa at 1.5 persons per square kilometre. The country has had a chequered history. The earliest inhabitants of Namibia and adjoining Botswana were the San (Bushmen) people. The Portuguese were the first Europeans to show an interest in a country which is very dry and desert-like. In the nineteenth century, Britain and Germany became interested because of the mineral wealth (including diamonds), fishing and opportunities for cattle ranching. Germany took control of the country from the late 1890s until the First World War in 1915. South Africa, under a League of Nations mandate, administered the country until independence was achieved in 1990.

One of the legacies of history is the variety of languages spoken. English and Afrikaans (based on the Dutch language) are the official languages, but, in addition, German and the Bantu and the Khoisan groups of languages are spoken.

Namibia has an official government tourism policy based on low environmental impact. It wants to avoid some of the tourist development excesses in Europe and other parts of Africa. The policy is to attract low numbers of high-spending international tourists. Tourism is a vital part of the economic development of the country. Only mining and agriculture generate more wealth than tourism. The manufacturing base is comparatively weak and depends on South Africa. The country has over 30 per cent unemployment. Rural tourism is thus very attractive to the economic planners.

Namibia has a significant number of attractions for tourists. For example:

- *Etosha National Park* one of the best game parks in Africa. It has very good viewing possibilities for seeing lion, elephant and many other species of game
- *Fish River Canyon* second only to the Grand Canyon in the USA
- *Sossusvlei* reputed to have the highest sand dunes in the world
- *Rock paintings and engravings* reputed to be the oldest in the world
- *Skeleton Coast* a unique region shaped by the cold Benguela sea current meeting the hot desert coast. It is the graveyard of many ships blown onto its bleak shores.

Namibia is a favourite for film makers and photographers because of 300 + days a year of sunshine, clear skies and a low cost of living.

According to the marketing research information available to Bochardt, most tourists in Namibia come from South Africa. Unfortunately, most spend little money. They come for camping or fishing trips with their vehicles packed with food bought in South Africa. The 'interesting' tourists come from Europe. The main existing flow is from Germany, Italy, France and the UK. Some tourists come from the USA, but very few from Japan.

The various farms selling guest accommodation promote themselves both independently, and collectively through the Namibian Tourist Board. There are variations in the products and service offered by the farms. What they specialize in is a peaceful rural location, close to either spectacular scenery or to game parks with wild animals. Farms typically have five to ten self-contained rooms. Part of the attraction of the farms is the personal interest of the farmer and the family in the venture. Disadvantages of the farms are the limited ability to invest in facilities; for example, swimming pools and a rather fragmented promotional effort. The Sunlands Holiday franchise would make the difference. It would move the farms into the mainstream of tourism for the twenty-first century.

What concerned Bochardt was the costs of providing many facilities. How many customers would want to pay for the extra facilities? Would they stay longer than the typical one to two nights? Did different nationalities want different facilities and different service levels?

The franchise deal was for Sunlands Holidays to create a unified image, which would be promoted in suitable countries, and to finance the upgrading of accommodation and the provision of some recreational facilities. Each farm would set its own prices within prescribed limits. Each farm would pay a negotiated franchise fee based on the services provided by Sunlands. However, the important feature of the personalized service provided by the farm to its guests would remain.

Question 1

Identify and justify a marketing research plan to enable Thomas Bochardt to make objective marketing decisions with regard to the franchise deal and 22 farms.   **(25 marks)**

Question 2

Explain how promotional approaches and product service packages might be developed and how might they interrelate for Sunland's venture into franchising with the 22 farms in Namibia.

(25 marks)

Note. Candidates should read the instructions carefully and address all parts of the question. In doing so they should produce a balanced approach. The question asks for information leading to the development of objective marketing decisions. Therefore do not write everything you know about market research. Be specific to the issues in the mini-case. Take full account of the scale of the task, the resources and capability of the company.

Question 1: answer

Summary

1   Because this is Sunlands Holidays' (SH) first venture into Africa, desk research will be a key first step to establish more about the African travel market.
2   Using a profile of up-market, high spending tourists who presently visit Africa, marketing research will be carried out to assess likely demand.
3   The research will be carried out amongst people who have visited Africa from the main countries which are identified as the main markets from the initial desk research.

Data sources

At present SH do not have basic information about the travel market in Namibia. Secondary data should be used to establish numbers of people visiting, the length of time spent in the country and where the visitors come from. In addition, secondary data should be collected for African countries, and perhaps other competitor countries in other parts of the world. These data can be used to build a better picture of the opportunities for the proposed Namibian venture. Some countries in Africa – for example, Kenya – have well-developed travel industries linked to game parks. Zimbabwe with the Victoria Falls and Egypt with the ancient Egyptian civilizations are two other African countries with a history of tourism development.

The scale of the proposed franchise deal is not large and therefore SH will need to find low-cost sources of information; this means secondary data sources such as:

• The equivalent of ABTA (Association of British Travel Agents)
• Tourist boards for the various countries
• Travel companies and their holiday brochures
• The travel press
• Syndicated reports – for example, EIU or Mintel – plus the SLEPT factors in Namibia relevant to SH.

The scale of the proposed venture can be judged from 22 guest farms with five to ten rooms. This would give a maximum number of tourists at any one time of 400–500.

Secondary data will indicate the extent of the potential market and whether the tourist market in Africa is growing. This might show that the proposed franchise operation is not viable.

The secondary data will also indicate the main countries from which tourists come to enjoy African holidays. This information would add to the existing information on the main existing flows of tourists. It might, in addition, shed some light on why few visitors come from Japan and comparatively few come from the USA.

The marketing research agency or internal marketing research brief
Objectives

1   To identify the key markets for tourists
2   To establish the main characteristics of potential visitors.

The types of specific information required would include:

• How many people are likely to come on SH to Namibia?
• What is the probable pattern of seasonal demand?

- What facilities will tourists expect at the guest farms?
- What price are they prepared to pay?
- How long will they want to stay?
- What will be their key interests?

A marketing research budget will need to be set, dependent upon the number of countries that need to be investigated. It is possible that respondents could be accessed from the customer database built up by Sunlands Holidays in its European operations.

Likely means of research

The number of people who have visited Africa on similar holidays will probably be small in number and difficult to track down. The likely primary data research will be:

1 A small number of depth interviews or focus groups in each of the main country markets with potentially strong tourist flows to SH's Namibian holidays
2 A postal questionnaire, in the relevant languages, to assess the likely level of demand
3 Convenience sampling of existing guests at Namibian guest farms.

Conclusions

Initial desk research will be important to analyse the main demand patterns. The secondary data exercise can be carried out using SH's in-house marketing expertise. The secondary data will be used to identify the main key markets. Only in these key markets will primary data be collected.

Qualitative and quantitative research will be carried out in Namibia and key markets to assess are:

- The attractiveness of Namibia as a holiday destination
- The attractiveness of the appeal of the 'package' deal
- Some indications of preference for different types of farm facilities and tour balance between, for example, game parks and sand dunes
- Some indications of market segmentation possibilities; for example, for wild game viewers, film makers or photographers.

Senior examiner's comments

This answer covered the main elements required and reached a good pass standard. Typical errors in answering this question were to place too much research emphasis on a detailed analysis of the socio-cultural, legal, economic, political and technological (SLEPT) elements of Namibia. SH need to know about Namibia in detail. However, the marketing research plan needs to concentrate on potential customers to the 22 farms. These customers will come from other countries. SH could develop a number of approaches. It might concentrate on trying to identify market segments of high-spending tourists in neighbouring South Africa, or on its visiting customer base of Sunlands Holidays' customers in Europe. It is likely that SH will need to market these specialist interest holidays to customers from a number of countries to fill the capacity throughout the year, while for several peak holiday weeks it might be able to rely on its German customer base. Alternatively, it may be the case that in the short term SH should focus its marketing on one country – e.g. Germany – leaving the wider European challenge to later. What is important is that candidates must approach the problem with a sense of realism and proportion as SH is a small organization in reality and has only 22 farms at present.

Question 2

Explain how promotional approaches and product service packages might be developed and how they might interrelate for Sunlands' venture into franchising with the 22 farms in Namibia.   **(25 marks)**

Question 2: answer

Summary
1 The product and the marketing communications packages will be based upon the marketing research programme.
2 Marketing research will help to analyse the different packages and related market segments.
3 The franchisees will thus be split up to reflect the potential market. Perhaps split by:

- Quality
- Location
- Style – Western/Namibian
- Language abilities.

Marketing research and product packages

Initial marketing research will probably begin to identify different needs for different groups who will be interested in using the various SH packages:

- Relaxation seekers
- Sightseers
- Wild life/big game seekers
- Families/couples/singles.

Different Sunlands franchisees will be able to meet the needs of these different groups. Different groups might relate to different country and language groups.

The types of facilities will need to be adapted to the needs of different market segments. For example:

- Relaxation seekers would want facilities such as swimming pools, sauna, bar, etc.
- Sightseers will need farms that are located close to the main sights
- Wild life watchers will be located near game reserves
- Photographers would require extra services; for example, a dark room for processing or specialist advice on how to improve their photographic technique.

The franchisees are the SH product in Namibia. SH will need to train their franchisees in meeting the needs of the different market segments. This will require training courses, a programme to match farms with facilities with appropriate market segments, customer service training and marketing courses to ensure that the franchisee fully understands the marketing-led expectations of customers from a variety of different countries.

Sunlands will have to link closely with the franchisees because SH will want to sell the package and extra services and further travel to customers. Some customers will be on a SH-organized package and will be delivered in groups to the guest farm. Some customers will come independently on a SH-organized fly–drive arrangement. However, customers will regard the franchisees as part of the holiday experience. SH will need to ensure that the links are 'seamless'.

Promotional mix

The target market, defined by marketing research, will be defined as the equivalent of AB, high-travel spenders with previous experience of 'exotic' holidays. If databases of the target market are available in the key markets than a direct mail campaign should be carried out. Language adaptations will need to be made.

Certain societies and clubs might have profiles similar to the target market. Advertising and/or inserts in their publications should be considered. Alternatively, address lists may be available for direct mail use. However, it is most unlikely that SH will engage in the traditional use of advertising via 'mass market' media.

The main Sunlands Holidays brochure should include Namibian guest farms. It might be appropriate to develop a specialist interests brochure of specific existing SH holidays to which the Namibian holidays could be added.

The promotional messages will need to be adapted to the particular market segment. 'Relaxers' will be shown the pool and the consistent sunshine. Photographers will be exposed to the 'unique' photography experiences, the special light and the exotic photo opportunities. The wider, more general packages could be advertised in the specialist press following the approaches taken by the UK operator, Voyages Jules Verne.

Conclusion

Marketing research will be crucial to help identify target groups and then to monitor the match between product service packages and the promotion to target market segments. Sunlands Holidays will need to harmonize the match between different customer groups and the different franchisees. SH will need to establish whether they can repeat-sell to the same customers or whether they need to plan to find new customers each year to enjoy the Sunlands Namibian holiday experience.

Senior examiner's comments

The above answer, while to a very good standard, could be improved in a number of ways. Promotional approaches should consider how to make the best use of the promotional approaches of the individual guest farms and the Namibian Tourist Board. SH might wish to develop a consistent standardized approach and would therefore wish to prevent the individual and perhaps amateur efforts of the guest farms. On the other hand, SH might wish to build strong relationships with the Tourist Board and would welcome its support. The potential conflict between the Westernized corporate promotion and the individual African experience should be considered.

How can the best balance be reached? The extent to which the basic farm 'product' can be modified has important cost and profit indications. Some facilities will be expensive to install; for example, swimming pools. It could therefore be more appropriate to upgrade the accommodation to a high consistent standard but to restrict extra facilities to low-cost services which can be charged as extras; for example, four-wheel-drive rides to view sunrise at the sand dunes or at Fish River Canyon.

Star Engineering (June 1993)

The annual planning process was well under way at the London headquarters of Star Engineering. In two weeks' time the final international marketing plan must be presented to the board of directors.

Star Engineering was established in 1910. It had grown from a local to a regional and then a national company. In the 1970s the company became active in exporting. It had been particularly successful in the Middle East and in South-east Asia. Competition was particularly strong in the USA and in Germany. Because of this, Star had, in the past, made a policy decision to avoid entering these two markets. Star currently has 65 per cent of the UK market, in total worth £20 million. In the Middle East it has 20 per cent of a market worth approximately £10 million, in South-east Asia it has 25 per cent of a market worth £18 million.

The main strategic thrust of the planning process this year is an expressed corporate aim to move towards world leadership, or as the company chairman preferred to call it, to become the world Star, instead of a rather modest world player.

Company sales turnover for 1992 had grown by only 1 per cent to £21 million. The world recession impacted particularly severely on the civil engineering industry, Star's main customer group. In all the circumstances a 1 per cent increase was a very creditable performance. Net profits, on the other hand, were reduced by 11 per cent to £1.6 million.

During the 1980s Star Engineering began a process of becoming a more international company. Initially all non-UK sales came from exporting. However, sales offices were set up in Kuwait and Singapore. Later, a distribution depot was established in Singapore. This helped sales through improved customer services and the reassurance to customers created by Star's tangible presence.

In the future the company intends to manufacture in several other sites in addition to the UK. This would create some benefits for Star's international performance, but would also involve increased risks, particularly those created by political change.

The company needs to develop a more international marketing culture within the company. Currently, it is unsure how to proceed.

Question 1

Evaluate the organizational control and marketing implications of moving from a modest international marketing approach to the approach required to achieve the corporate aim of world leadership. **(25 marks)**

Question 2

What approach would you propose to Star Engineering to evaluate existing and new overseas markets given its existing level of expertise and involvement? **(25 marks)**

Note. This is a case where a company already involved in international marketing wishes to deepen its level of involvement and increase the internationalization of the organization. To do so requires more thought than just marketing issues.

Your answer should adopt this strategic viewpoint. It should also address the organizational control issue and the marketing implications separately.

Question 1: answer

1 Introduction

Star Engineering is currently a medium-sized manufacturing company that is actively seeking to increase both market share and market coverage in specific worldwide industrial markets. The company has developed steadily over a number of years, progressing from a traditional exporting sales approach to international sales offices and a distribution centre.

2 Future plans

Star Engineering has a corporate objective of worldwide leadership. This is a challenging objective. The time span for its achievement is long term, say 10 years. A number of different routes, including international manufacturing and perhaps joint ventures and alliances, might be required to enable the world Star status to be reached.

3 Strategy

Careful consideration must be given to the strategic issues of how Star will achieve world leadership. Both product development and market development will be needed. Expansion within Star's existing markets needs to be considered. It is probable that the UK market share of 65 per cent will need to be defended vigorously. The important positions gained in the Middle East and South-east Asia should be considered for further growth.

Market development into new country markets will be a key strategic area for Star. The major markets in the world need to be identified and decisions made about the suitability of market entry. The significance of the world triad of the USA, Japan and Europe cannot be ignored. Past decisions to avoid the German and US markets needs to be challenged in the light of the new corporate objective.

Organizational control

4.1 The main issue facing the management of Star Engineering is whether to maintain full control of all company activities from the UK headquarters or whether control should be decentralized to various countries and regional and continental groupings.

Inevitably the organizational structure of Star will need to undergo significant change and development in order to meet its stated commitment to world leadership. The current organizational structure will need to change, perhaps in several stages, to strengthen the international/world focus and to increase the degree of expertise and involvement in the major markets for Star's products. For example, the organization could be separated between the UK market, a South-east Asia division, a Middle East division and a 'new countries' division (perhaps Germany or the USA). In the longer term, mechanisms to coordinate different markets will be needed. In the short term the UK head office will remain the central focus of the company, but each division will have delegated authority for business and marketing in its own area. An important point to note in such a structure is the coordination and cooperation of each division and the UK head office to ensure that corporate objectives are considered and met.

4.2 The cultural implications of organizational change   The changes proposed for Star in terms of its organizational structure represent a major cultural change for the company. The company will move to being committed and being heavily involved in international business and, as such, its employees will need to be prepared and developed to cope with and contribute towards the new focus on international business. The local, ethnocentric view, will be replaced by an international outlook. Each employee will be part of a 'worldwide' organization as opposed to a 'British' company.

5   Marketing implications

5.1   The marketing focus and operation will also change dramatically during the process of increased international involvement. Under the proposed organizational changes the marketing of Star Engineering will no longer be strongly centrally controlled. Rather each division (i.e. UK, South-east Asia, etc.) will carry out its own marketing programme with budgetary and strategic planning control exercised in the UK headquarters. This reflects the need for adaptation in each area of involvement and the need to assist the process of improving customer relationships. It was seen in Singapore that the establishment of the distribution outlet helped greatly in terms of Star's customer orientation. This will be emphasized further in the new international moves.

Further details of the increased international involvement will be examined through the four Ps of the marketing mix.

5.2 Distribution implications   A variety of options are open to Star Engineering in addition to its existing methods:

(a)   Licence
(b)   Contract manufacture
(c)   Joint venture or other forms of alliance
(d)   Wholly owned subsidiary

Star must evaluate the risks involved, particularly in the high-cost/high-risk foreign direct investment decisions. Successful companies need to achieve internationally competitive cost structures. To gain this position Star will need to look at the lower-cost countries for some of its manufacturing and product sourcing.

The distribution network must offer Star significant coverage of their potential market and give high levels of customer service. This will be particularly important in the US and German markets, if entered, because of the high levels of competition and because of the recognized high expectations that buyers have in these markets of their suppliers.

5.3 Product implications   Technical standards vary in different countries. Star must be aware of the main standards and be recognized in these standards in their major country markets. If the cost and operational implications of this are high, there will be major strategic choices to be made upon which standards to concentrate. Some standards and technical capability might need to be gained through acquisition and/or joint ventures and alliances.

The posture of the world leadership implies that Star will invest in R&D and will be developing innovative and relevant engineering solutions to customers around the world.

5.4 Price and promotion implications   Legal requirements relating to tariffs and technical standards will influence price as will competitors and Star's marketing objectives in different markets.

In achieving world leadership Star will need to develop a corporate personality that adds value to its products and services around the world. Decisions will need to be made on the suitability of the Star name and logo for extension to world markets. Progressively, the company will need to use trade exhibitions, public relations and targeted advertising to reach its specialized business markets in different countries.

As can be seen, Star Engineering has many aspects of change that it must encompass in order to fulfil its corporate aim of world leadership. A further example of this will be the need for internal communications among its growing numbers and diversity of employees, in different countries, from different cultural backgrounds and engaged in a variety of tasks. Without care Star could grow, but fail to achieve cohesion. It might thus fail to convince world customers of its major status because the 'Star' people are unaware of Star's importance.

Senior examiner's comments

This answer covered the main requirements of this question and reached a good pass standard. The answer could be developed further by using a more specific organizational approach and relating it to the progressive movement towards world leadership. Star could concentrate upon certain key markets and then develop major clusters of countries before achieving a substantial market coverage of the world.

The use of expatriate, national and international managers, used in various combinations, will give a multi-cultural input in decision making and implementation at Star. This will need to be reflected in organizational control and will impact on its international marketing programmes.

Question 2

What approach would you propose to Star Engineering to evaluate existing and new overseas markets given its existing levels of expertise and involvement?   **(25 marks)**

Note. There is frequently a tendency for candidates to write extensively on Question 1 leaving insufficient time to gain a pass in Question 2. Plan the time frame carefully to ensure you write a balanced paper. If the examiner is in doubt of your capabilities he or she will consider Questions 1 and 2 holistically, i.e. has this candidate exercised/demonstrated a breadth of knowledge of the marketing process applied in an international setting.

Question 2: answer

An approach that can take account of the current position of Star Engineering is to look at market attractiveness, given the corporate long-term objective of world leadership, and to take account of the existing and potential business position for Star. Market attractiveness can be evaluated by market size, market growth trends, market profitability, the vulnerability of the market to competition, barriers to market entry and economic, political influences on company assets and the repatriation of profits. The business position of Star can be assessed through estimates of obtainable market share, return on capital employed, company sales and company profits.

The current position for Star Engineering is that 62 per cent of its sales come from the UK, 21 per cent from South-east Asia, 10 per cent from the Middle East and, presumably, 7 per cent from the rest of the world. In the answer to Question 1 we have already identified that strategically it is probable that the UK position will have to be defended and the South-east Asia and Middle East position will have to be expanded.

In these existing markets Star could develop its marketing information system, especially in South-east Asia and the Middle East. In particular, Star needs to track competitors and to distinguish between those operating within one (or a few) country market(s) and those international companies selling in a number of countries. An attempt should be made to view whether each company is operating country by country or whether it has a more coordinated international marketing approach. Such competitors would challenge the emerging Star Engineering and its world Star aspirations.

Star would need to scan the external environment, but because it is already marketing within the country, it will be able to put the information into an appropriate economic and business setting. Star needs to identify the profit potential within its existing markets. If it is proposing to commence manufacturing in a country, the high levels of risk need to be minimized by a much more detailed country evaluation of political, economic and financial factors.

In approaching new markets Star Engineering needs to establish suitable countries to enter, those to avoid at all costs, and those to enter with caution. The company must carry out a comprehensive low-cost scan to identify market attractiveness and the probable Star Engineering position within those markets. Initially, the company is looking for published secondary data to give indications of size, trend and stability in country markets. However, it is likely to find that market statistics for Star's part of the engineering market are not readily available or are, perhaps, subject to considerable margins of error. It is difficult, therefore, in new markets to evolve marketing plans unless more detailed market assessments are carried out. The extent of the country market evaluation needs to take account of the importance of the market and the degree of financial risk to the company. In the more detailed country analysis, using methods to collect primary data, Star Engineering would need to use a marketing research agency with experise in business-to-business markets and are capable of operating in international markets.

The corporate aim of Star Engineering drives it to search for major new country markets, while needing to safeguard its existing markets. The type of engineering markets in which Star is operating means that secondary data sources are unlikely to be particularly specific. The evaluation of markets will, therefore, rely on secondary data sources to cover SLEPT factors and primary data sources for significant risk product markets. The evaluation approach used for the new markets should be based on the lessons learnt from the existing markets. The marketing information system for existing markets should be extended to give an increasingly complete world coverage.

Senior examiner's comments

There was a temptation for some candidates to answer this question by lising a series of SLEPT (socio-cultural, legal, economic, political and technological) factors and to fit this into a marketing research exercise. Good answers, as shown above, need to take account of internal and external factors and to use marketing research, but they must be set in the context of developing into a world leader position.

The answer could be improved by using a more developed market attractiveness/business position model or other similar approach as outlined on page 153. This would show the learning capabilities necessary for Star to develop from its existing position that challenging position of world leadership.

As an Additional Observation a good candidate might comment on the feasibility of Star Engineering's ambition to become a world leader.

Index